SOCIAL PHILOSOPHY TODAY

WAR AND TERRORISM

VOLUME 20

Edited by
John R. Rowan

Social Philosophy Today is published by the Philosophy Documentation Center.

For information regarding subscriptions or back issues, please contact:

Philosophy Documentation Center
P.O. Box 7147
Charlottesville, VA 22906-7147
800-444-2419 (U.S. & Canada); 804-220-3300
Fax: 804-220-3301
E-mail: order@pdcnet.org
Web: www.pdcnet.org

ISBN 1-889680-40-0
ISSN 1543-4044

© 2004 by the Philosophy Documentation Center.

All Rights Reserved.

Designed and produced by the Philosophy Documentation Center, Charlottesville, Virginia

All rights reserved. Copyright under Berne Copyright Convention, Universal Copyright Convention, and PanAmerican Copyright Convention. No part of this book may be reproduced, stored in a retrieval system, or transmitted in any form, or by any means, electronic, mechanical, photocopying, recording, or otherwise, without prior permission of the copyright holder.

Table of Contents

WAR AND TERRORISM

Volume 20

Table of Contents

Preface v

Introduction 1

Part I: Terrorism: Potential Justifications, Reasonable Responses

Terrorism for Humanity
  Ted Honderich 15

Terrorism, Self-Defense, and the Killing of the Innocent
  Whitley R. P. Kaufman 41

Evil, Ignorance, and the 9/11 Terrorists
  Todd Calder 53

Beyond Retribution: Reasonable Responses to Terrorism
  Richard M. Buck 67

Selective Disobedience on the Basis of Territory
  Ovadia Ezra 81

Part II: Terrorist Motivations, Democracy, and Human Rights

Terrorism and the Root Causes Argument
  Alistair M. Macleod 97

An Evaluation of the "No Purpose" and Some Other Theories (Such as Oil) For Explaining Al-Qaeda's Motives
  Doug Knapp 109

Weighing Evils: Political Violence and Democratic Deliberation
  Matthew R. Silliman 129

Rawls's Decent Peoples and the Democratic Peace Thesis
  Walter Riker 137

Terrorism and the Politics of Human Rights
  Sharon Anderson-Gold 155

Part III: Social Philosophy

Trotsky's Brilliant Flame and Broken Reed
  Nelson P. Lande 167

Transsexualism and "Transracialism"
  Christine Overall 183

Part IV: NASSP Book Award

Church and State: Comments and Questions
  Johann A. Klaassen 197

American Constitutionalism: A Formula for Religious Citizenship
  Sharon Anderson-Gold 201

Citizenship and Religion In Liberal Democracies
  John R. Rowan 207

Reply to Klaassen, Anderson-Gold, and Rowan
  Paul J. Weithman 215

Contributors 231

Preface

The North American Society for Social Philosophy brings together philosophers, legal theorists, political scientists, and social scientists to discuss important contemporary social issues. This is accomplished through its annual international conferences, its contributions to the programs of other learned societies, and its publication program, including The Journal of Social Philosophy and the Social Philosophy Today series. All of the essays in this volume, number 20 of Social Philosophy Today, were selected by peer referees from the best papers presented at the Twentieth International Social Philosophy Conference, held in July of 2003 at Northeastern University in Boston.

The editor would like to thank the many individuals whose efforts made this volume possible. In particular, Stephen Nathanson of Northeastern hosted the conference at which these papers appeared, and in this role he spent considerable time organizing the events and attending to an extraordinary number of details. Jeffrey Gauthier and Nancy Snow were the conference organizers, selecting papers for presentation and assembling the conference schedule accordingly. Appreciation is also expressed to Purdue University Calumet, which provided various resources that contributed to the completion of this volume.

Additionally, the society owes a tremendous debt of gratitude to Cheryl Hughes, the outgoing editor of Social Philosophy Today, who is responsible for bringing the publication schedule up to date, establishing revised guidelines for submission and acceptance of papers, overseeing the many aspects of changing publishers, and enthusiastically contributing her expertise and advice to the new editor during the process of completing this volume. The present high quality of this series is due largely to her efforts over the past several years. For her many contributions, the editor and the entire society are extremely grateful.

John Rowan, Purdue University Calumet

Introduction

The philosophical questions spawned by the events of September 11, 2001, are not new. Human rights, the killing of the innocent, just war, and other related issues have long been discussed by philosophers and political theorists. Indeed, it is the norm for academicians to ponder ideas, develop theoretical principles, and test those principles for coherence, consistency and moral justification. However, nothing seems to test theoretical principles more than real world events.

The terrorist and military actions that have occurred over the past few years have provided an opportunity for those engaged in social philosophy to revisit their ideas, as these events have allowed the basic questions to be posed in more specific ways. For example, the question concerning the justified killing of the innocent emerges in the context of terrorism, which most condemn precisely because the perpetrators intentionally target innocent civilians. In Western societies, an overwhelming majority views terrorism as absolutely wrong—as permissible under no circumstances—and the killing of innocents certainly plays a major role in the adoption of this view. However, what if the terrorist activity is carried out in an effort to *protect* innocents? What if it is carried out in self-defense? Would moral culpability be mitigated if the perpetrators were in relevant ways ignorant of the evil they were inflicting?

Again, few in Western societies would be willing to answer affirmatively to these kinds of questions. Among those who do, only a fraction would be prepared, for instance, to relieve al-Qaeda of any blame for its actions in bringing down the World Trade Center towers. Nonetheless, it seems clear that when a fundamental moral question (such as the killing of the innocent) is applied to the context of terrorism in this way, it paves the way for novel discussions of both the concepts in question and the different lenses through which the actual events may be viewed and analyzed.

Another effect of this sort of investigation is that it motivates the consideration of any number of related questions. For example, how are reasonable responses to terrorism to be determined? Is the military action in Iraq spearheaded by the United States "reasonable" in that sense? What role do human rights play? Though many would point to human rights as the basis for condemning terrorism, could they actually justify terrorism in certain circumstances? For that matter, what *is* terrorism, exactly? Are we required to consider its causes before we can condemn an instance of it as morally abominable?

In this volume, contributors have taken up these and related questions in papers selected from among the best presented at the Twentieth International Social Philosophy Conference, held at Northeastern University in July, 2003. While the title is *War and Terrorism* in keeping with the theme of the conference, most papers presented at that conference focused more on the nature of terrorism and brought elements of war into the discussion as needed. For this reason, the bulk of the entries in this volume pertain primarily to terrorism and are divided into two sections: the first addresses potential justifications and reasonable responses, while the second addresses terrorist motivations and connections to democracy and human rights. In keeping with the practice of including in *Social Philosophy Today* the very best papers from among those presented at the conference and submitted for publication, the third section of the volume carries the simple label Social Philosophy and includes papers not directly related to the theme. Finally, the fourth section is devoted to Paul W. Weithman's book *Religion and the Obligations of Citizenship*. Each year, the North American Society for Social Philosophy presents its annual Book Award to the book judged to have made the most significant contribution to social philosophy during the previous year. Commentaries from referees and a reply from Weithman are included in that fourth section.

I. Terrorism: Potential Justifications, Reasonable Responses

"Suicide-bombings by the Palestinians are right." This highly contentious claim is offered by Ted Honderich, who in the first paper defends the morality of terrorism in certain circumstances. He begins by pointing out that moral questions pertaining to terrorism do not, contrary to the beliefs of many, offer many clear answers. It is abhorred largely because it involves the killing of innocents, but further inspection reveals the existence of mixed intuitions on this count. Consideration of the atomic bomb dropped on Hiroshima at the end of World War II makes this clear; despite its deadly effects on thousands of innocents, a reasonable number of people take that action to be justified. "Impulse" reactions to terrorism are thus inappropriate.

Honderich also considers whether the existing widespread condemnation of terrorism supports the proposition that it really is wrong in all circumstances. Convention, he admits, does seem to have a pull on us. Nonetheless, widespread opinion can be misguided; ignorance, falsehoods and the like (which Honderich claims have been operative under the Bush and Blair administrations) can drive a wedge between majority views and morally-relevant truths of fact. So the conventional views of terrorism provide no necessary connection to any truth regarding its absolute wrongfulness. On this count, even appeal to democracy, with its majoritarian commitments, will not help to yield an alternative conclusion.

Introduction

Honderich's position is that terrorism, when carried out for humanity, may be justified. Terrorism for humanity is terrorism with the aim of the principle of humanity, a moral principle developed elsewhere by Honderich which speaks to six great goods of human existence. Thus, whether the prima facie wrongfulness of terrorism is overturned in a given case depends on whether it has a decent chance of gaining the end in question. Certainly, these are delicate issues, often complicated further by additional twists (such as whether the excepting condition is met by a terrorist who, despite not having a decent chance of gaining the end, fights because doing so will someday provide others with the requisite decent chance). Honderich claims that the actions of Palestinian suicide-bombers are justified in that they meet the conditions of terrorism for humanity. The Palestinians, he claims, have had their homeland violated, their way of life overturned, and—in conflict with the principle of humanity—have been denied the great goods of humanity, and as their terrorism is the only means of acquiring the things to which they have a right, it is justified.

In contrast, Whitley Kaufman suggests that an attempt to justify terrorism, if it has any hope of succeeding, must be grounded in a principle of self-defense. This is because terrorist activity, which deliberately targets innocent civilians as victims of violence, is clearly wrong as a means to a political end if there is no wrongful aggression being perpetrated in the other direction. His aim is therefore to examine whether self-defense can in principle justify at least some terrorist activities. In concluding that even self-defense cannot serve as the requisite justification, Kaufman indicates that terrorism is therefore always wrong.

The principle prohibiting the killing of the innocent is extremely powerful. After reviewing the relevant meaning of "innocent" in this context, Kaufman engages in an analysis of when killing the innocent can be justified as a form of self-defense. He argues that four conditions must be met: first, the force used to kill the innocent aggressor may only be used against an *unlawful* aggressor; second, the use of force must be *necessary*; third, the amount of force used must be *proportionate* to the harm being averted; and fourth, the attack must be *imminent*. While each of these is a bit vague and is certainly open to some interpretation, Kaufman provides a brief discussion suggesting how to use each one in the task of application to practical contexts.

The next step is in fact the application of these conditions to the context of terrorism. The first condition is not met, according to Kaufman, because victims of terrorism are not aggressors at all, let alone unlawful aggressors. The same reasoning speaks against the fourth condition; if the victims are not aggressors then they are not attacking, and so it follows that there is no attack being perpetrated by these victims that can rightly be labeled imminent. Attempts to stretch the meanings of the conditions fail; there is no reasonable description of innocent victims of terrorism that includes their being aggressors. The attempt to reconceive terrorist activities as acts of war, even if such a reconception could be made plausible, would also fail to generate a persuasive objection, since the wrongfulness of intentionally killing innocents applies to war as it does to other contexts. Finally, Kaufman considers a reformulated version of the doctrine of self-defense which seems to have the potential to provide for a different conclusion about the possibility of terrorists killing innocent civilians in self-defense. However, such a reformulation is overly consequentialist, failing to take adequate account of deontological constraints.

Thus, it seems that self-defense cannot be a justification for terrorism. A related question is whether ignorance of the fact that one is engaging in such evil can excuse (not justify) the terrorist from moral culpability. Todd Calder assesses the open question of when ignorance precludes genuine evildoing on the part of an agent, and from there he proceeds to the question of whether the 9/11 terrorists can be excused on this basis, the possibility being that they were ignorant of the evil nature of their actions because they genuinely believed they were engaged in rightful conduct.

Calder proceeds in an organized manner, first describing a theory of evil he labels the Desire Account of Evil, which entails two conditions. The first is the requirement of significant harm, and the second is that this harm must follow from an "effective desire" (or "e-desire" in Calder's theory). Unless these two conditions are met, any action cannot be described as an instance of evil, and Calder supports his case by providing further discussion of the nature of desire and situating his view in light of consequentialist and deontological considerations.

He then moves on to consider when, if ever, ignorance of particular facts provides a legitimate excuse for one who causes significant harm. Had the 9/11 terrorists been systemically indoctrinated into extremist Islamic culture with no exposure to contrary evidence or viewpoints, then it would not be unreasonable to suggest that their actions were not "evil" in the sense Calder describes. However, these were not the circumstances of the terrorists, who had all (to varying degrees) had time to interact with Americans and other Westerners. This interaction should have provided the evidence, contrary to the claims of Islamic extremists, that Americans are not universally evil and deserving of the wrath of Allah.

It follows that ignorance cannot serve as an excuse for these terrorists. Ignorance is defensible only when, according to Calder, "given the information readily available to us, it would seem to any unbiased person who had similar cognitive and deliberative powers that our false beliefs were true." The likelihood, Calder says, is that the 9/11 terrorists were instead engaged in self-deception.

In the next paper, Richard Buck investigates the ethical aspects of responses to terrorism. He suggests that a reasonable response must achieve an acceptable balance among three aims: protecting the lives of potential victims of terror; protecting the lives of noncombatants living among the terrorists; and preserving the possibility for secure and meaningful negotiations that will end the conflict. After describing

Introduction

the particular definition of terrorism he uses, Buck points to two significant challenges faced by any just government attempting a response to terrorist activity: the challenge of protecting the lives of noncombatants and the challenge of responding proportionally. The first is difficult to achieve given the common terrorist strategy of mixing in with the (noncombatant) civilian population. The second is the challenge that a response conform to a justifiable principle of proportionality. While Buck notes that a backward-looking principle of the sort defended by Michael Walzer has advantages, he questions its applicability to the context of terrorism. Instead, he suggests a Principle of Reasonable Response, which includes three additional conditions. Specifically, a response will conform to this principle only if: its aim is to apprehend or otherwise incapacitate those responsible for previous (terrorist) actions; due care is taken to avoid killing and to minimize the suffering of noncombatants; and the nature of the response is such that any harm that does occur does not erode the possibility of future good faith negotiations aimed at resolving the conflict.

Buck's Principle of Reasonable Response combines the backward-looking elements of Walzer's principle with forward-looking elements, in particular the consideration of pertaining to future good faith negotiations. Regarding the first challenge, concerning the issue of noncombatant deaths, his principle also has the implication that any deaths of noncombatants resulting from a response to terrorism do not automatically render the response morally problematic. Such a condition would be too demanding, he claims, and hence the condition of due care is added. This principle is then applied to the context of two responses to Palestinian terrorism. The responses—military actions carried out in 2002 by the Israeli Defense Forces—are found by Buck not to be justified.

In the final paper in this section, Ovadia Ezra discusses a particular form of civil disobedience, namely disobedience undertaken by Israelis refusing the order to perform their military service in the occupied territories. This response mirrors military civil disobedience during the Vietnam era, the basis for which was *jus ad bellum* (justice leading up to the war). Ezra describes a similar disobedience during the Israeli-Lebanese war of 1982, in which some Israeli soldiers refused to take part for reasons that were both internal and international. He then brings these considerations to bear on his principal concern, Israeli military presence in the occupied territories. Himself a dissenter of this occupation and one who has been imprisoned for refusing to perform military duties, Ezra points to human rights pertaining to freedom, autonomy and self-determination. In the case of the Palestinians, their rights are being violated by the occupation, and Ezra employs the Golden Rule in explaining the conscientious decision made by himself and others not to participate.

From there, he extrapolates to the absolute refusal to be drafted into Israeli military service, no matter the responsibility one would have. The reasoning is that any participation in the military, even with duties that appear to have no direct effect on the occupation, nonetheless contribute indirectly to that wrongful force. The harmful effects on the Palestinians are unjustifiable morally and in violation of just war theory, given the disproportionate nature of the Israeli actions and the indiscriminate disregard for innocent Palestinian civilians. Incorporated into this broader claim about refusal even to be drafted is a notion of responsibility. Ezra argues that one can be responsible for even indirect contributions to the immoral occupation, even when one's clear military duty has no direct bearing on the occupation.

II. Terrorist Motivations, Democracy, and Human Rights

In his paper, Alistair Macleod argues for the importance of investigating the "root causes" of terrorist activity. He cautions that such an investigation does not imply a forgiving attitude toward terrorism. The exercise is explanatory rather than normative, though the explanatory answers that are uncovered would likely have implications for normative questions down the road. Another caution is that the root causes of terrorism cannot be ascertained by confining one's analysis only to the reasons of the terrorists who perpetrated the violence of September 11, 2001. Indeed, a focus on the motives of any actual terrorist agents is unduly narrow. More information will be necessary if the broader aims are to understand the nature of terrorist threats and to use that understanding to devise effective and appropriate responses.

The notion of terrorism as utilized by Macleod is (admittedly) sketchy, but it does include at least four assumptions about terrorist acts. First, such acts are politically motivated. Second, terrorism results from a wide variety of political aims which are not themselves necessarily evil; after being subjected to scrutiny, some such aims may be found. Third, terrorist acts are assumed to be wrong without qualification, even where the political goal motivating the action is justified; the idea is that terrorism is never acceptable as a means of achieving even justified ends. Fourth, terrorist acts cause deliberate harm to innocent civilians.

With this broad understanding (if not definition) in mind, Macleod proceeds to suggest that an important root cause of terrorism is the existing attitudes and beliefs of the societies from which the terrorists themselves emerge. The societal attitudes, beliefs, sentiments and concerns cannot be ignored as an important causal factor, even though the terrorists themselves, at the time of their deeds, may not have these in mind as reasons for their actions. He concludes by suggesting two further directions in which investigation into the root causes argument might proceed, directions pertaining to the powerlessness and relative scarcity that tend to characterize societies from which terrorists emerge.

Discussions of the motivations underlying terrorist activity occasionally (though not frequently) include the possibility that there is no end that the terrorists are attempting to bring about. The idea is that terrorism is simply an expression of anger and has no actual purpose. In his article, Doug Knapp argues against this "No Purpose" argument. Among his claims is the contention that the sort of anger inherent in the no purpose argument is of a blind, uncontrolled, undirected nature, and that the meticulous planning involved in carrying out terrorist activity is inconsistent with such anger. While there may be an expressive component present, there is good reason to believe that an instrumental component is also present in the motivational picture. In the specific case of the 9/11 terrorists, Knapp provides reasons in support of this instrumental component, citing bin Laden's displeasure with continued U.S. troops in the middle east, continued economic sanctions against Iraq, and continued support for Israeli initiatives—considerations suggesting that he had at least some particular aims in mind.

Knapp goes further in suggesting that oil likely plays a significant role in this context. He outlines, historically, some U.S. actions that have been directly aimed at securing oil interests in the Middle East, actions that he suggests have the effect of engendering and increasing the hatred of the U.S. by certain constituencies in that region. This consideration is connected up with the three grievances of bin Laden noted above in ways that imply the relevance of oil to the purposes of the al-Qaeda terrorists. In turn, there is the implication that the "No Purpose" argument is implausible. This conclusion is strengthened, he claims, when it is noted that supporters of the No Purpose argument typically assume the aim of the terrorist action must be global in nature. It is entirely likely that any goals of al-Qaeda would be more local, including such things as uniting the Islamic community.

Knapp concludes by applying these considerations towards a critique of President Bush and other U.S. government officials in their assessment of al-Qaeda's motives.

Proceeding from the assumption that terrorism is wrong, Matthew Silliman points out that its degree of wrongfulness is still something to be addressed. We consider terrorism to occupy a special place among moral evils, but ascertaining a basis for this intuition is more difficult than one may initially think. Any answer will require the utilization of some mechanism or notion relevant to the special context of terrorism that will facilitate understanding of its particular harms. Silliman points to deliberative democracy as a notion worthy of consideration. While physical violence and harm come to mind immediately when thinking of terrorism, the underlying psychological violence done across the victimized community may have effects that are even more debilitating to a society. According to Silliman, although this psychological component often receives much less consideration, it stems from the political nature of the terrorist violence and has the effect (if not always the intent) of undermining political discourse, thereby threatening "the trust and safety necessary for safe, open communication."

While this consideration helps to frame the severity of terrorism's violence, it does not establish its uniqueness among other moral evils that might resist the label. Silliman welcomes this observation, pointing out that his analysis thereby serves to elevate the perception of the wrongfulness of moral transgressions that are in his view comparable, even if they are not always recognized as such. He concludes by discussing one possible consequence, which is that so-called "state violence," in which formal governments are the agents of "terror," may not enjoy privileged moral status with respect to "non-state" violence, despite intuitions to the contrary.

Questions of democracy arise in Walter Riker's paper, in which he examines the issue of liberal democracies engaging in the democratization of Rawls's "decent peoples." Riker discusses various aspects of Rawls's notions of peoples and decent peoples, and in reviewing some implications of these claims, he includes Rawls's example of Kazanistan, an idealized Islamic people. He also points out Rawls's view that liberal peoples are superior to decent peoples, even though both can affirm a set of principles that would contribute to global peace and justice.

This sets the stage for the Democratic Peace Thesis, which consists of the two related claims that democracies are not likely to fight wars against each other and that some feature (or features) of democratic society causes this peace. The causal connection is central here, and Riker discusses five different accounts of that connection: satisfaction (the idea that citizens of democracies are sufficiently satisfied as to not be motivated to go to war); constitutional constraints (according to which legal requirements prior to establishing full-fledged war entails the likelihood that alternative, peaceful solutions will be found in the process); reelection constraints (according to which the political costs of war to incumbent leaders serves as a negative motivation); shared norms (which cause democracies to perceive each other as relatively peaceful and nonthreatening); and interdependence (according to which the benefits of international trade deter democracies from engaging each other in war).

The conclusion is that the existence of decent peoples (rather than the preferred liberal peoples) is not a threat to the continued (democratic) peace, and according to Riker this shows that Rawls's allowance of them in his world order does not undermine the global stability of that order.

Sharon Anderson-Gold takes on the issue of humanitarian intervention into the activities of sovereign states. In discussing how the United Nations Charter has impacted the role of human rights insofar as they serve as constraints on the sovereignty of nations, Anderson-Gold points out that the Charter necessarily entailed the legal subordination of national interests to international law. This does not mean, however, that national sovereignty was diminished in any significant way. Indeed, some took the view that the prohibitions in the Charter, grounded in its language of human rights, were in actuality not enforceable by third parties.

Introduction

In response to the tensions for sovereignty created by international attempts to enforce human rights violations, the language of "humanitarian" interventions has arisen, spawning referents such as "peace keepers" to be used in place of "military troops" in the relevant situations. Anderson-Gold suggests that if the normative assumptions underlying such language are to be plausible, there must be a single global entity (to which all are equally subject) overseeing such interventions, an idea she finds in the writings of Jovan Babic. This requirement follows from the observation that humanitarian interventions, conceived as a kind of "police action," presupposes a global law and an authority overseeing it. Such an authority is not found in the United Nations, and given the current configurations of power in the world, it may not be found any time soon, since any such authority would likely be connected with the most powerful of nations and would thus be likely to have some self-interested reasons for acting. She also discusses relevant views of Jurgen Habermas, in particular the claim that human rights have the ultimate purpose of bringing into existence a successful cosmopolitan constitution that would serve the appropriate international function. In serving this function, however, human rights must become part of a global communicative structure that can provide the foundation for cosmopolitan law.

Drawing on these considerations, Anderson-Gold points to United States actions that seem to expand unreasonably the "justifications" for humanitarian intervention. The United States has been unwilling to submit to any international authority, acting instead on the basis of its perception that dangers to human rights exist. This basis, however, opens the door to intervention for a wide array of subsidiary reasons, including the possible possession of weapons of mass destruction, weak governments (perhaps unable to secure human rights protections for its citizens), undemocratic governments (unwilling to secure such protections), and so on. When terrorist actions are added to the mix, there seem to be few if any limits to actions the United States could take in a "war on terrorism." An indefinite policing of the entire globe by U.S. peacekeepers (i.e., troops) seems to be called for.

III. Social Philosophy

As noted previously, *Social Philosophy Today* includes the very best papers, as determined by a system of referees, from its international social philosophy conferences. Some papers delivered at each conference are, to varying degrees, outside the conference theme. Two such papers, recommended for inclusion in this volume despite their being somewhat outside the "War and Terrorism" theme, are included in this more open-ended section.

The first, by Nelson Lande, provides insights into the political views of Leon Trotsky. In his 1920 book *Terrorism and Communism*, Trotsky outlines his attack on democracy, support of revolutionary terrorism, and endorsement of repressive labor policies. Lande spells out the specifics of the arguments underlying each of these three. Regarding Trotsky's attack on democracy, for instance, Lande points to arguments that depend on Russia's "October Revolution," such as the rise of the Bolsheviks in the Congress of Soviets and the prospect of Petrograd falling into German occupation. There are also arguments for this position that are independent of the October Revolution, including various Marxist arguments about the dim prospects of liberating the working class through the peaceful means of parliamentary democracy. Regarding the defense of revolutionary terror, Lande points to several arguments forwarded by Trotsky, including the necessity of shooting hostages for victory, with the prospect of victory over capitalism providing further (moral) support for such action.

Regarding the endorsement of repressive labor policies, Lande focuses on Trotsky's handling of the dictatorship of the proletariat. In that era (thought to be commenced by the Bolshevik revolution), the state will have to use legal compulsion in order to carry out the crucial task of reconstructing the economy. The only alternative means of achieving this necessary end involve market incentives, which on Trotsky's view would work only on the (counterfactual) condition that the state is sufficiently wealthy to make these attractive. Thus, for the crucial time period in question, forced conscription of labor will be necessary for the survival of the Soviet state, and this provides the justification for such action.

On a very different and rather novel subject, Christine Overall's paper is devoted to the notion of transracialism. Modeled after the term transsexualism, pertaining to the crossing from one gender to the other, transracialism as discussed by Overall is the "voluntary crossing or attempted crossing from being a member of one race to being a member of another," and she notes that Michael Jackson may be a popular example of one to whom this concept likely applies. While some may hold to what they perceive as morally relevant differences between the acts of changing genders and changing race, Overall see the two processes as parallel; if some change genders on the basis of the belief that they feel they really are members of the other gender, then it seems reasonable to think that some might change their race on the basis of a similar belief relating to race.

The moral claim she makes is that if transsexualism and the provision of medical and social resources for that purpose is morally permissible, then it would follow that transracialism and provisions of medical and social resources for this purpose is permissible as well. As this claim is a conditional, she does not address in her paper those who deny the antecedent. Nor does she address those inclined to agree, though they may find in her discussion further support for their agreement. Rather, Overall is most directly concerned with objections likely to be forthcoming from those denying the conditional claim. To this end she considers eight distinct objections grounded in different ways, including naturalism and personal identity, the importance of group identity, racism and social oppression, harm to others, and lack of competence and autonomy. After reviewing carefully the merits of each, she finds none to be persuasive, and she concludes by offering some speculation about the relevance of this finding.

IV. 2003 NASSP Book Award

It has been the practice of Social Philosophy Today to devote the final section of the volume to the Book Award sponsored by the North American Society for Social Philosophy. In 2003, it was determined that the deserving book published during the preceding year was Paul W. Weithman's *Religion and the Obligations of Citizenship*.

In his book, Weithman challenges the so-called "standard approach" according to which citizens of liberal democracies are not permitted to base their votes or advocacy for an issue on the basis of their religious commitments alone. Rather, the standard approach requires that citizens provide, or at least be willing to provide to their fellow citizens, secular reasons for their votes or advocacy. Weithman rejects this position, arguing that citizens of liberal democracies are morally permitted to rely exclusively on their religious comprehensive moral views, including their religious views.

Crucial to his argument is empirical research suggesting that religious organizations play significant roles, on two levels, in the achievement of realized citizenship. The concept of realized citizenship consists of an objective condition (which is met when a citizen possesses the relevant opportunities and resources) and a subjective condition (which is met when a citizen effectively identifies with her citizenship). Weithman's claim, grounded on empirical considerations and in particular on the role of churches in the United States, is that religious organizations contribute significantly to these on individual and social levels. Individually, they promote certain civic skills (e.g., leading meetings, speaking in public, writing letters of advocacy) which are important to realized citizenship. Socially, religious organizations have tended to address issues that are vital to the interests of marginalized citizens, especially the poor and racial minorities. Without the contributions of these organizations to the public political debate, issues important to these segments of the population would likely never have been introduced on the national political agenda, thereby preventing a sizeable portion of the population from achieving realized citizenship.

The three members of the book award panel prepared critical commentaries on various aspects of Weithman's arguments. Johann A. Klassen poses questions pertaining to the nature of religious speech, religious reasons as "justifying" reasons, and liberal (as opposed to conservative) voices from the pulpit. Sharon Anderson-Gold explores the connection between Weithman's remarks and American Constitutionalism, especially the "separation" between church and state, and she also tests the waters of religious liberty as such. John Rowan, meanwhile, poses questions pertaining to the possibility of illberal and undemocratic religious inputs, the highly empirical nature of Weithman's arguments, and the notions of accessibility and surrogacy, concepts which play central roles in some attempts to maintain the "standard approach." The section concludes with a piece by Paul Weithman in which he replies to the points made in the three commentaries.

Part I:
Terrorism: Potential Justifications, Reasonable Responses

Terrorism for Humanity

TED HONDERICH

Abstract: This paper takes forward reflections begun in my book *After the Terror* and then continued in a paper, "After the Terror: A Book and Further Thoughts." Maybe this third offering on the terrible subjects in question will be the last from me for a while—despite my not having got as close as may be possible to proofs or the like of some principal propositions. It must be easier to deal with the terrible subjects if strong moral convictions about Palestine or whatever come together with great confidence about the very nature of moral philosophy and the possibility of proofs. Still, silence or hesitancy is not an option.

I. Some Particular Moral Propositions

Our failing to save the lives of Africans now living, twenty million in one sample, is wrong. Israel's taking more land from the Palestinians beyond its 1967 borders is wrong, as is our support of this neo-Zionism. Suicide-bombings by the Palestinians are right. 9/11 was wrong. The war on Iraq was wrong, unlike other wars that did not happen because we overlooked reasons for them. It is wrong for neo-Zionists in and around American government to conceal their divided loyalties, not to declare an interest that is other than American. African terrorism against our rich countries would be right if it had a reasonable hope of success. In our rich countries, those of us do a particular wrong who bring it about, by way of the media they own, that many people out of ignorance believe that what is wrong is right.[1]

These are some particular moral propositions that many people, possibly a majority of humans who are half-informed or better, agree with or find it difficult to deny. My purpose in what follows here is to look mainly at some philosophical issues that come up with the proposition about Palestinian suicide-bombing and also a more general proposition that has to do with what has the name of being *terrorism for humanity*.

You may ask, given my purpose, why propositions about more than terrorism have been mentioned.

It is the practice of courts of law not to let the jury know of the accused's previous offences, if any. His record, however, *is* read out if he is found guilty of the charge in hand. Among the good reasons is one that may be overlooked. It is that previous offences give confidence in the particular judgement of guilt that has been made on him by the jury. More obvious is the reason that previous offences give further basis and confidence with respect to the sentence to be passed by the judge.

No doubt the previous offences should be kept from the jury while they are deliberating on the present charge. They may give rise to mistake. But it is absurd to say that these past offences have nothing to do with the question of whether he has committed the offence with which he is now charged, and in particular his culpability in it, say his degree and kind of intentionality. Of course they do. A man previously convicted of five rapes is very much more likely to have committed the one now being considered.

It is not only terrorists who are accused in our world. We are held to be guilty too. You have only to get on an airplane to another sort of country to be reminded of it forcibly, in more ways than one. They may try to kill you. And the accusation, for the sort of reason just noticed with the court of law, has more that is relevant to it than just the charge in hand against us, say active complicity in the wrong done for decades and still being done to the Palestinians.

Do you allow that this different kind of guilt by association is part of the natural fact and practice of morality, but say that strictly speaking it is a mistake, a kind of human weakness or failure? How is that? Records about action X change probability-judgements about action Y, if X and Y are both instances of some Z. And probabilities about Y alter moral judgements about Y. The wrong of it can become clearer.

To ignore this is to lose touch with the reality of moral judgement. You can see that some complicity in a wrong, or a war, is an instance of a pattern of excessive self-interest and delusion. It is not something with special or unprecedented features, maybe historical, maybe a war on a monster, to which a lesser or excusing response is in order. It is also to forget our own practice. It is to forget that we ourselves do most certainly include the previous records of terrorists in judging their last wrongs. We do not stop there. We also include their whole cultures, and in particular their religion.

Do you still wonder if it is already a mistake, before we get around to this guilt by association, to attend to something other than terrorism, to attend to charges against us rather than charges against terrorists? You and I disagree there. Even if there were *no* connection between any of our guilt and any of theirs, it would be natural enough and no mistake to think about the two things together. Agendas are not let down from heaven, or decided in Harvard Yard. Asking a moral question about X can indeed get your thinking about the morality of Y, get you thinking about the whole of life rather than a part, particularly when X is taken as a kind of global event.

To disregard our own records, furthermore, even if there were *no* connection between them and terrorism, would actually be mistaken. A comparative viewpoint must enter into thinking about any such issue as terrorism, and terrorism for humanity in particular. Morality does indeed have what can be called *data* in it, and general truth, and certainly consistency. But it is a matter of more than reports and consistency-tests. It is a matter of judgement, and such judgement cannot be decently made in isolation or self-deception.

You will get a part wrong if you don't know about the whole. You will feel differently about the dirtiness of killings by others if you remember that you have had to wash your own hands regularly, and notice that there is a need to do so right now, maybe because of a lot of killings today. A proper reaction of the guilty to the guilty plays some part in morality.

That is not all. It is not just that we stand accused ourselves of particular offences to which more offences are relevant, and that pieces of moral and political philosophy do indeed have freely chosen subjects, sometimes with a natural unity, and that judgements need to keep the judges themselves in mind. That is not all. It is only persons of certain committed minorities who can pretend to suppose that there is no connection between any terrorism and charges against us. There must be the possibility, to say no more than this, that some of what we do, say with respect to Palestine, enters into a justification for some terrorism. Blair, the leading politician of my country, says otherwise. But that incidental proof of my proposition is not needed.

II. Killing Innocents, and the Problem of an Impulse About It

Contemplate two acts of killing. The first is by a young Palestinian suicide-bomber of an Israeli in Israel, a passer-by. The second killing, by a crew-member of an Israeli helicopter-gunship, is by rocket. Those who die, in Palestine, are a terrorist leader of the Islamic Resistance Movement—Hamas—and a Palestinian passer-by. You may recoil from such examples, maybe humanly. But you cannot simply recoil and also do well in thinking and feeling about our subject-matter. It plainly calls for more rather than less engagement. Also a wide human sensitivity rather than a narrow one.

The victim of the suicide-bomber and the second victim of the man in the gunship, the two passers-by, are non-combatants, civilians, and, as at least their own people say, innocents. If they are children they *are* innocents, even if they are or have been throwing stones. We might think about trying to improve on these categories a little, by replacing them with the categories of non-combatants, unengaged combatants, half-innocents, clear innocents, and civilians.

Non-combatants are not armed or otherwise personally life-threatening at the time of their deaths, and are not in the army or police or any other life-threatening organization, say a terrorist one. We could decide to add that they are not officers of state or certain organizations either.

Unengaged combatants are not armed or personally life-threatening at the time, but are in the army or other life-threatening organization. Maybe they make bombs or maintain helicopters. We could add that they may be officers of state, overwhelmingly more responsible for wrongs than are engaged combatants.

Half-Innocents are not armed or otherwise personally life-threatening at the time of their deaths, and not in the army or the like. These non-combatants and unengaged combatants, however, are by choice or consent benefiting or profiting from wrongful killings by their state or their people. They are as well-named as being *half-guilty*. They may be settlers on the land of those people they are not personally threatening.

Clear innocents are not life-threatening at the time, not in the army or the like, and are not by choice or consent benefiting or profiting from wrongful killings by their state or their people. They include almost all children.

Civilians, for what this fifth category is worth, may be non-combatants, half-innocents, or clear innocents. They may be none of these, but rather combatants and not half-innocents or clear innocents.

Very clearly these five categories need work in order to be made more determinate, particularly in connection with choice and consent. If they can be improved, they may still not be of great use, since we are likely to be unable to say who was or is in what category at the time of a conflict.

Since the beginning of the current *al-Aqsa* intifada in Palestine in September 2000, a total of about 2,100 Palestinians, of a population of about 3.4 million, have been killed. A total of about 700 Israelis, of a population of about 6 million, have been killed.

Of the 2,100 Palestinians killed, about 1,650 are said to have been "innocent civilians" by a good Palestinian source.[2] About 100 were children under the age of 12.[3]

Of the 700 Israelis killed, about 500 are said by a good Israeli source to have been "civilians."[4] How many of the 500 were also non-combatants, etc. is left open. An exact number for the very many fewer Israeli children killed is not readily available.

The figures are not merely dwarfed, but are made trivial or insignificant numerically, when compared to numbers of deaths, in the very many millions, owed to genocides and politicides carried out by states and governments.[5] In particular, the deaths owed to the Palestinians, these deaths owed to non-state or non-governmental action, are barely anything numerically to the numbers of deaths in state or governmental genocides and politicides. The deaths owed to Palestinians are yet fewer, relatively speaking, when compared to state or governmental killings in war generally as well as genocides and politicides.[6]

Do these comparisons matter? Well, they may wake somebody up, somebody who has been exactly half asleep, but that is all. They do not matter at all to the Israeli family whose daughter and sister is killed by a bomb. This brings into focus a reason why the comparisons cannot really matter to us in these reflections either. There is a fundamental moral or human sense in which a death by killing does not become of less consequence when it is one of few or many such deaths. With a death, a whole world goes out of existence. It also seems this must override what complicates it, what was said about the reaction of the guilty to the guilty being some part of morality.

One question that arises about kinds of innocents and so on is whether it is possible to judge Palestinian and Israeli killings by staying at the level of the five categories, however improved. One way of trying to do so is by announcing, as a properly-respected philosopher of peace of my acquaintance does, that killing innocent people is wrong.[7] In his view, as it seems, that is all there is to say. A human impulse, certainly.

Would he persist in this if asked for the rationale of killing non-innocents in his sense rather than innocents? Could he say that his announcement is of a moral truth that needs no rationale? Well, there is no avoiding the usual question about a terrible choice between killing one or a few innocents or killing many innocents. Does what we choose not matter? There is no avoiding a question, either, about the choice between killing a few innocents and allowing another horror, say the starving to death of many thousands of innocents, or a million of them. Do you say this proposition is in conflict with an implication above, about a single death and a whole world? I do not think so, and I am *sure* you are not going to succeed in making morality simpler.

If the questions to the philosopher of peace are distasteful and conceivably dangerous, they are necessary ones. To his credit, I doubt that he would say, in effect and obscurely, that he cannot be faced with such choices, and thus the need for a rationale, because he would not be responsible for the choice-situations—or just that his own life's inner purpose precludes his doing any killing with his own hand.[8]

The fact of the matter seems to be that we cannot seriously even try to stay only at the level gestured at. There must be a reason for embracing the simplicity of the equivalence of very diverse and differently consequential killings of innocents. There must be a reason for the supposed non-comparability of killings of innocents and the other horrors.

Some reason is necessary for going against the distinctions written into the whole course of civilization, including its religion. We ourselves have defended immense numbers of killings of innocents—in the naval blockade of Germany in World War I, in the terror bombing of Germany and the destruction of Hiroshima in World War II.[9]

Certainly, despite a common utterance to the contrary, *some* killing of innocents does not lead to more of it. Even if it does, to repeat the question, are there no circumstances, no human hells, that rightly call it up? Would a world without killing, no matter what else it contained, be better than any other world? No society has ever thought so. No society thinks so now. If societies are wrong about a lot, they can hardly be wrong about this.

So surely we cannot condemn Israel just on the ground of its killing of innocents. Nor can we condemn it efficiently on the ground that it is killing more innocents than the Palestinians. Further moral thinking is unavoidable.

III. The Morality of Humanity

It is no easy thing to see what ordinary morality comes to in all of its nature. It is easier to see what should be in an adequate morality—a philosophical morality or the like. Such a morality, a proposal or recommendation for a possible or an actual world, must contain a single principle or summation or idea, or can have one put on it, and also secondary proposals or recommendations of parts or sides of life, say politics or business. It very likely needs to have in it moral data or moral touchstones, and also a preferred clarification of our shared moral concepts and their relations, say those of right actions, moral responsibility, and decent persons. Such a morality must contain, too, particular moral propositions like the eight with which we began.

Separate from all these elements will be reasons for them. These will be propositions of fact, larger and smaller, general and particular, of various kinds. They are as essential to the enterprise as the single principle and so on. No adequate morality is unreasoned. There will be propositions of fact at every level of the enterprise.

It is not being assumed, of course, that the more particular parts of adequate moralities are *deductions* from the more general. The generalization or summary is a way of getting the whole thing in view, and a particular kind of check on other elements, as they are on it. This picture of adequate or reflective moralities, I take it, covers those of Aristotle, Aquinas, Kant, Bentham, Nietzsche, Marx, and Rawls.[10]

It also covers the morality of humanity. This rests on our human nature and mainly on our desires for the great goods, six according to my classification, variously interdependent. The goods, under one description, are a decent length of life, say 78 or 79 years rather than 37, bodily or physical well-being, freedom and power, respect and self-respect, goods of closer and wider relationship, and such goods of culture as knowledge. That brief list, however, is so unenlightening as to the human importance of the things in question as to be a parody. It is as unenlightening to gesture by implication at lives *deprived* of the great goods, lives very different from those of well-being and perhaps satiety, sufferings of great evils, lives of wretchedness and other distress.

Morality of humanity also rests on other truths. A second, more or less implicit in the first, is that humans, or wonderfully more than enough of them for the purposes of argument, are alike in another way.[11] Consider yourself, and a certain judgement you will make. Consider a conceivable conflict between (1) you or your family escaping from wretchedness and (2) a further improvement for me or my family in my or our existing well-being, perhaps my having more of the great goods to the point of satiety. You will certainly judge there is greater reason for (1) the help for you or your family. You know that right now.

There is reason for the help, you will judge, that is greater than any reason offered by me for my self-indulgence. Say my reason of private property, or a morality of relationship and non-relationship, or a supposed categorical imperative about treating people as ends as well as means, or some theory about the need to help the wretched *in general*, as distinct from you in particular, maybe the trickle-down theory in political economics.

You will not be moved either by an invocation of any political morality or moral politics, say liberalism in its obscurity, or of course conservatism, or indeed socialism if it can be made use of in this unlikely cause, or of course the amorality of national self-interest, what is called political realism. Nor will you take your or your family's wretchedness to be a lesser reason than any so-called *ethical* as against merely *moral* reason of mine for self-indulgence, say my integrity, or my life-project, or a kind of personal necessity, or an absence of responsibility for what I can in fact prevent, let alone my moral luck and yours.[12]

Nor is this truth of human nature about distress and indulgence only a matter of contemplated or imagined circumstances. There are almost certainly analogues of it in actual conflicts in your own lived life. Consider life-threatening situations. You do not give more weight to the ambulance-man's not really exerting himself because he is badly-paid than you give to your own need to get to the hospital. You do not put the understandable self-concern of unrespected teachers ahead of your child's being saved from ignorance.

A third truth, never successfully denied except in practice, is that reasons are general. There are no one-case reasons. For you to be committed to the rescue of yourself or your family, in a contemplated or an actual circumstance, is for you to be committed to actual rescues in actual circumstances around us, say African and Palestinian circumstances. This is a rationality that cannot be avoided, whatever attempt is made to pretend otherwise or to obfuscate it.

Finally, there is the relevant truth of human nature that we have some dispositions of character that support this latter rationality. We can act on it. To act on it is to do what is also sympathetic, human, generous, and comes out of fellow-feeling. Those are not terms that describe nothing in us. If there are also clear wants of humanity in our natures, so demonstrated by conventional morality, there *are* the facts of sympathy and the like. Philosophical moralities that recommend themselves as *undemanding*, as realistic in that way, overlook or understate these human facts. To my mind, they must be under suspicion, along with the political tradition of conservatism, of wanting to reduce these facts in the aid of personal comfortableness.[13]

The morality of humanity owed to these four truths, to state its summative principle quickly, is that we must take actually rational steps, which is to say effective and economical ones, to get people out of defined lives of wretchedness and other deprivation. This is what it comes to. It is different from all other moralities and utterances in which the given truths of argument can be taken to issue, including the passionless vacuity of the Golden Rule, as lacking in content as it usually is in determination.

The main rational steps can be put into a few policies. These have to do with rescuing people from bad lives by means that do not affect the well-being of the better-off, with rescuing them by means that do affect that well-being, with reducing inequality-demands, and with violence—the latter policy allowing for less exception than other policies against violence.

Of the rest of what might be remarked here about the morality of humanity, let me say only that it is more engaged in the world than alternative philosophical moralities, and by its nature not embarrassed to be so. For good reasons, it is more political. I take it to be more committed to factual truth than alternatives are. It thus speaks not only of the *violation* of Palestine by the Israelis, but also of Palestinian *terrorism*, of killing that rightly has that name. It does so despite this killing's also being *resistance, resistance to ethnic cleansing, self-defence,* a *liberation-struggle,* an *uprising of a people,* which certainly it also is. Quite as much.

As you will have anticipated, I take the morality of humanity to issue, of course by way of various additional propositions of fact, some of them historical, in the particular moral propositions about the 20 million Africans, Palestinian terrorism, and so on. Or rather, because moralities can differ fundamentally in more than what can be called bare propositional content, and can have their distinctive nature in their kind of commitment, affirmation, mildness, resignation or pretence, it is better to say something else. It is better to convey the principle of humanity's resistance to a *consensus of civility*. It is better to say this morality issues, for present purposes, in roughly the following group of particular moral propositions.

Letting 20 million fellow human beings die makes the American way of life, say, into an evil giving rise to an evil. The Israelis have violated not only principle and law but also another people and their homeland. The Palestinians do indeed have a moral right to their terrorism, and would have this right even if their terrorism was not a response to state-terrorism—to say they have a moral right is to say that their terrorism has the support of a moral principle of force, indeed the moral principle more capable than any other of justifying actions. As for 9/11, it was hideous and monstrous in its moral irrationality. Nothing else can be said of it. The invasion and occupation of Iraq, if conceivably rational in terms of a certain end, was another attack on humanity. Bush and Blair are moral criminals, whatever their capability of realizing it. They would be criminals in international law if that thing was what all victors and some lawyers pretend it to be. Blair has lied. Further, he is either a liar, a liar with ends about which he is confused himself and which he seeks to obscure, or he is in a way culpable in his persistent self-deception, in fact less honourable than a liar in his avoidance of evidence he does not want. Such information-providers as Murdoch and others who make for or add to the stupidity of a society have a guilt in at least their related self-deception.

IV. Whether Some Terrorism Is for Humanity

There are more things to be said of how the morality of humanity can issue in or contain, in particular, a support for the kind of terrorism of which the Palestinian is an instance.

Terrorism for humanity is terrorism with the aim of the principle of humanity. That is the aim of getting people, including whole peoples, out of lives of wretchedness and other deprivation, bad lives, lives of great evils. Do you think there is room for a certain question? Do you think there is room for the question of whether the killings by the Israeli in the helicopter-gunship, rather than the killing by the Palestinian suicide-bomber, is terrorism for humanity? Some will say that.

It would be reassuring if the question of whether some terrorism has the end of humanity were always open to a confident answer. That is not so. There is often difficulty about deciding if a line of action, terrorism or whatever else, has, as we can quickly say, the end of humanity.

The matter comes into view by way of the invasion of Iraq. It was not in my view terrorism, given its large scale, despite being against what there is of international law and therefore akin to terrorism reasonably defined.[14] Was this war aimed at saving people from bad lives owed to a dictator? Was it a war for humanity? Americans were told by their politicians that something like this was its justifying aim. The British, differently, being a people a little more affected by international law, had to be told by their principal politician that the justifying aim of the war was not bringing down Saddam but rather disarming Iraq of weapons of mass destruction that existed as an immediate threat against us. We could be killed by them in 45 minutes.

Did the war in fact have the end of humanity? The best sort of answer, perhaps, consists in pointing out that the war, like many such endeavours, plainly had a considerable number of aims.

One was trying to deter terrorism, including terrorism for humanity, by a demonstration of power against a suitable country. For this aim it was not essential that Iraq itself had carried out 9/11, or even contributed to it in any material way whatever—although that belief by half or even two-thirds of the American people was useful, and largely owed to its politicians and other leaders. It was not necessary to the anti-terrorist aim that Iraq had done anything more than half the world does with respect to terrorism for humanity—*understand* it, as some say.

The war aims also included control of oil supplies, certainly the removal of a possible defender of the Palestinians, the removal of an otherwise anti-American leader of great audacity, wider American interests and strategies, and the removal of one of the world's ruthless and anti-American dictators. These latter aims were not greatly less significant than the aim of deterring terrorism. There was also something less obvious. This was an ideological aim, the assertion of ideology as an end in itself, killing as assertion.

This needs to be distinguished from aims having to do with the satisfying effects of imposing an ideology, some of them just remarked on, including profits to American corporations. Killing as assertion is announcing what is right in such a way as to get attention, having the reassurance of being heard. It is also aimed at the comfort of having fewer moral critics in the world, fewer moral judges, or anyway quieter ones. It is related to what is known as the justification of punishment in terms of communication or expression, different from deterrence or other prevention.[15] Other forms of such self-expression, without the killing, are common enough.

The war on Iraq also had the aim of putting in place new international deferences and expectations, no doubt under the name of international law, and of course a significant aim having to do with American domestic politics. Not for the first time, people were killed in anticipation of an American president's election campaign. There was also, on the part of an English prime minister, a lawyer-politician's view of England's material self-interest in maintaining an alliance. Who avoids the opinion that his careerism was also in it, talked of by his cabinet colleagues in terms of his anticipation of a place in history?

If you now ask again what counts as terrorism for humanity, one short answer is that it is that it is terrorism whose aim is more clearly the rescue of people from bad lives than was our war against Iraq. The war against Iraq serves as an excellent ostensive definition of what terrorism for humanity is not.

We get a further answer to our question by returning to Palestine.

The state of Israel ought of course to have been constructed out of a part of Germany after the genocide of the Jews. But that it had to be established somewhere is a kind of moral datum, certainly in accord with the principle of humanity. So too, to my mind, given what seemed to be the necessity and the particular possibilities at the time, was it right that Israel was set up where it was, partly by way of Zionist terrorism for humanity, and despite its being an historic injustice to another people.

That is consistent with the fact of the violation of Palestine by the neo-Zionism of Israel since 1967. This is indeed an offence of moral viciousness. It is an offence of both neo-Zionists and also those who travel with them, in Israel and the United States above all. It has the disdain of all Jews who are within that current of compassion in Jewishness, so free from legalism and divine revelation, clear and strong in its intellectual and other contribution to the struggle for humanity. This is the current of compassion of the Jewish Left, singular and to be honoured without reservation.

That the great goods have been wrongly denied to the Palestinians is made clear not by political history, let alone casuistry about who did what when, but rather by the figures for Arab and Jewish populations in Palestine since about 1876.[16] There is only room for merely partisan dispute as to the proposition that one people took over the land of another. Any real dispute about particular numbers can only be trivial.

To speak more generally of the great good of a people that is their freedom and power in their homeland, its value has been better demonstrated historically than any other good. That it is one of few things that can be said to have formed our human history is a proof of this desire and the human worth of its satisfaction. It would be childish to try to disdain the worth of what our nature gives this proof.

The elucidation and explanation of the pain and suffering of its denial must include its being necessary to other great goods, respect and self-respect above all. It is no surprise that Palestinians can now be made the objects by some Jews of a racism of which Jews themselves have had unique experience. Things of the same sort can be said of the necessity of freedom and power to other great goods.

It is my own view, importantly as a result of these facts, that the terrorism of the Palestinians is a paradigm case of terrorism for humanity, terrorism with the aim of humanity. The most salient of these facts is the established necessity of this terrorism, the clear absence of *any* alternative policy whatever for dealing with rapacity. The terrorism of the Palestinians is their only effective and economical means of self-defence, of liberating themselves, of resisting degradation. It is to me ludicrous to contemplate Israeli state-terrorism, whatever else it may be called, having the end of humanity.

But that this or any other terrorism is terrorism for humanity is not enough to make it right. The thought that all terrorism with the aim in question is right would be as absurd as the thought, sometimes inexplicitly and viciously relied on, that more or less any policy or action of a democracy is right. The proposal, rather, is that the only terrorism with the *possibility* of justification is terrorism for humanity, as the only war with such a possibility is war for humanity.

V. Innocents, Our Fundamental Moral Concepts, Double Effect

It was maintained earlier about the two killings in Palestine and Israel that we cannot think about them only at a certain level, the level of a simple absolute about the kind of action in question, killing innocent people somehow defined. That is not to say that the only reflection that is needed is well above that level, at the level of such a general moral principle as that of humanity. Of course there is need for further thinking on killing the somehow innocent, and of how to approach it. To do so is of course not to join those spokesmen of democracy on television whose concern for the innocent is only for *their* innocent, not for the innocent killed by their democracy. This may actually be merely a concern for the innocent, their own innocent, in the enterprise of taking more land or keeping more land already taken.

Is it the case, in particular, that further thinking on terrorism for humanity in connection with innocents can establish that although terrorism for humanity has a unique possibility of being right, it nonetheless is not right, or that some instance of it, say Palestinian terrorism, is not right? That there is a disproof of its rightness?

Our fundamental moral concept is that of *the right thing* to do or bring about—the right action, policy, kind of life, institution, society. The right action or the like is a matter of rationally-anticipated consequences. It is at least in large part a matter of the six great goods—a decent time to live, bodily well-being rather than pain, freedom rather than subjection and impotence, respect in place of disdain and contempt, connection with others rather than isolation from them, knowledge and the preservation of the history of one's people.

To this concept of right action we add that of a person who gets *moral credit* for a particular action or the like, someone approved of for his or her moral responsibility for it. This is importantly a matter of his or her intentions. Thirdly, we tend to distinguish a person's *moral standing* over time, maybe a lifetime. Perhaps this is the result of both rightness in actions and moral credit for them.

That right actions are fundamental, these being a matter of certain consequences of actions, is in a way provable, in the following way. A certain world is conceivable. It has in it only persons who persistently or even consistently get moral credit, at bottom for good intentions and effort. As a result, their standing over time is high. But they are very ignorant and unlucky, and produce a world of misery. Another conceivable world has in it persons who get less moral credit and are of lesser standing—a matter, let us say, of their mixed intentions. For whatever reason, however, their world is not one of misery but of well-being. Maybe almost all people in it have all of the great goods.

Does anyone, save an occasional moral philosopher with another agenda, hesitate when asked which world it would be right to bring into existence? An intention, after all, is not a spiritual mystery, a funny reality that is a source of obscure rightness. It is a mental event including desire and belief that both represents or pictures and gives rise to an action then or later, which mental event gets the person credit or not. Does anyone say it would be right to bring into existence a world filled with the agony of torture as against the good things of which we know, in order to have the world with better intentions in it?

That is not to say that moral credit and moral standing are irrelevant or unimportant. We want persons of credit and standing because they are more likely than others to do the right thing. Very differently, it may be that we need the many conceptions of credit and standing in order to have an adequate view of precisely the rightness of actions—effects are typically characterized by likely causes, or indeed seen by way of them. But, as good as indisputably, these are but qualifications or elaborations of the truth that our fundamental concern is with how our world is in so far as we can affect it, our actions and not with certain personal antecedents valued for themselves.

This ordinary moral thinking, hardly at the level of moral philosophy, is typically forgotten or passed over in a salient condemnation of some killings of somehow innocent people. I have in mind such as the killings, by the Israeli crew-member in the helicopter-gunship, of the passer-by as distinct from the Hamas terrorist leader. This is contrasted, in terms of intention, with the Palestinian suicide-bomber's killing of an Israeli passer-by. The first killing is said to be right, the second wrong.

It is said the killer in the helicopter in some sense does not *intend* the death of the innocent passer-by, but only that of the Hamas leader, while the suicide-bomber *does* in this sense intend the death of the innocent Israeli. Of the two effects of his firing the rocket, the killer in the helicopter intended only one. There is therefore a difference in the two acts, the first being right and the second wrong. This is the doctrine of double effect.

It is not my main concern, but let us glance at it in passing. Against it, there is the easy and perfectly correct objection that the intention of the man in the gunship, ordinarily conceived, represents both the death of the Hamas leader and another probable death or deaths. For a start, we need to take the man in the gunship to be aware of the incidence of deaths of more or less innocent Palestinians—perhaps, as indicated earlier, that there have been about three times as many deaths of more or less innocent Palestinians as against more or less innocent Israelis.

The probable death is of course a foreseen consequence. Do you bravely say it was only a probable consequence? Well, *foreseen probable consequences*, as against foreseen absolutely certain consequences, are not rare or unusual, let alone suspect. They are by far the most common sort of foreseen consequences, the ones we are mainly concerned with in life, the ones we generally act on. The probabilities may be high. An innocent death owed to a rocket fired into a busy street is about as probable as the consequence of playing Russian roulette with someone else's head.

Therefore, in terms of intention as conceived in the rest of adequate morality, and presumably in every legal system in the world, the killer in the gunship *did* intend more than the death of the Hamas leader. He knowingly did and can be held to account for more than that—the death of the passer-by. So too, incidentally, does he add to the moral criminality of Sharon, the leader of his country.

Of course it can be maintained that there is a different sense in which the helicopter crew-member did *not* intend the death of the passer-by, also a clear one. *If* he could have killed the Hamas leader without killing a passer-by, we are to understand, he would have done this. But of course it is false that the suicide-bomber does not have such an intention. It must be taken as just as true of the suicide-bomber that *if* she could have acted effectively to try to liberate her people without killing a kind of innocent, she would have done this. The distinction, if different in detail from the other case, is as real and relevant.

No one can quarrel sensibly with this kind of refutation of the casuistic doctrine of double effect, so often put to such unspeakable use by ignoring facts of identical intentions. My main aim, however, is to add something to the refutation.

In brief, what is to be added is that while there are uses of our conceptions of moral credit and moral worth, mentioned above, there are also misuses of them. It is a misuse of the conception of moral credit to suppose that one can really begin to justify as right the action of the man in the helicopter by assigning to him the credit that if he could kill the one person without killing the other, he would do so. This is not our ordinary morality, but rather a self-serving misconception of it. It is not as if a double effect argument fails only because of its intrinsic weakness or indeed chicanery, but that it *begins* from a mistake.

Even if it were the case that the man in the gunship lacked an intention had by the suicide bomber, it does not at all follow that he would have been doing right, and that the suicide-bomber was doing wrong. There are no such connections. For example, there is no connection between having an intention that represents or pictures an *unidentified* human being, rather than a *seen and nearby* person, and the action's being right. Hosts of ordinary examples establish the contrary. And of course there is no significant general difference in intention.

To repeat, there *is* reason to reflect at more than one level about particular questions, one about innocents, that face any morality and are answered by particular moral propositions. That is to be granted, as it is also to be granted that it is insufficiently clear how things at different levels are related. But there is the overriding fact that what is right is at bottom a matter of our actions to change or keep the world in which we live, and that matters of credit and standing are no sure guides to this.

Any arguable morality will be like anything that deserves the name of being a court of law. It will disdain the defence of a killer that what he did was right because in a secondary sense he did not want to do what he did and what he knew he was doing. From the horror of killing the somehow innocent, there is no conclusion to be drawn except with the aid of or in the context of an adequate morality. Anything else is childish or at least suspect. It may be viciously self-serving.

VI. Conventional Views

It is also my conviction, as you have heard, that there is a possibility of rightness with respect to terrorism for humanity, and thus Palestinian terrorism, and no such possibility with other terrorism. If that has not been proved for you, which I grant, you have most of the elements that can go into an attempt at proof—the sort of proof possible in morality. Consider now another large thing that enters into resistance to any such thing. It is surely more effective than such propositions of argument as double effect.

In some societies, most importantly the United States, as already implied, it can seem that there is little or no assent to the possibility that terrorism for humanity is justified, let alone its actually being justified. So too with the others of the particular propositions with which we began, and which, as you have heard, give collateral support to the proposition about Palestinian terrorism and terrorism for humanity in general. It can seem that a large majority of people find them or say they find all but the one about 9/11 outrageous. There seems to be no assent, if there is a little lip-service, to the general morality in which the propositions are at home. Instead, a large majority of people appear to give assent to what can be labelled *conventional views*.

Whatever this fact really comes to, it contributes to a presumption. This is the presumption that what most people in our own societies think is right does at least have something to be said for it. In the fact of numbers and whatever goes with it, we are to suppose, there is a reason for thinking something right. There is no doubt this presumption has a grip on us. Anyway, it has had a grip on me.

Convention in moral thought, feeling and language, generally speaking, is a sameness or congruence in a society about what is right or who is to be credited with responsibility or who is decent. It seems a natural thing since it is not a code, and since people may follow it just because it has been followed before. The fact of convention is as old a society. So is the perception and valuation of it, and of how it comes about. Thrasymachus spoke of it to Socrates when he exposed the alternative truth, as he thought, that justice consists in the interests of the stronger. At the present moment of language in my own country, Britain, one part of the fact of convention is talked of in terms of governmental *spin*, which term in its tolerance is itself an instance of it. Spin is typically lying so done as make a denial of its nature possible later, maybe lying in order to get a people into a war or to increase your personal anticipation of having done right by your own dim lights.

Bacon, Burke, Mill and Marx gave different accounts of convention, Burke approving much of it under the name of *prejudice*. It is one thing clarified in detail by the great moral judge of this time, Chomsky. The fact of it has been properly studied by way of many related social facts. These are the facts of authority, legitimacy, legitimation, illegitimation, naturalization, consent, ideology, norm-construction, indoctrination in education, mystery and mystification, influence, propaganda, sacralizing, and demonizing.

To engage in the study of convention by these means is partly to engage in conspiracy theory. Plainly there have been and are conspiracies, which is to say secret plans to achieve or keep something about which at least a question arises. To deny all or even most conspiracy theory is to be oblivious of the history of monopoly and the pretences of free markets, relations between government and business or church and state, international trade-offs, hidden or obscured alliances, and so on.

What is more important with respect to the fact of convention is its being owed to the self-interest of dominant groups whose members act together not out of secret plan but partly out of a want of self-awareness, an excess of self-deception, and self-serving illusions having to do with the common good and the just society and the like. They have no need of a plan. Their interests fall together, which is the main fact about their endeavours, and these are served by their common convictions. They are more like a mob than a plot, if a mob with some decorum and with the rules on its side.

Is convention a larger fact now than it was in the past? Consider our culture of the past few decades, since about 1979. It has had in it, increasingly, profit in place of public service, competition and the pretence of it in place of cooperation, a new greed, the manufacturing of wants in place of satisfying them, buying raw materials and commodities from poor societies by victimization, market as morality, corporate engrossment, a sexualization of life that makes prostitution secondary, and so on. This culture, which does not have truth as its aim, is now a larger part of morals and politics. Governments are unable to see outside of it. So too, since about 1979, has there been a further domination of mass communications, which domination also does not have truth as its aim. It is rather an engine whose products are authority, legitimacy, and so on.

These two developments, at the very least a greater imbalance between sides of life, between profit-seeking and the other sides of life, and more of self-serving control or management of information and attitudes, may make the fact of convention a more consequential social fact now than it has ever been before.

VII. Factual and Moral Truths

Despite the explanations given of conventional morality in terms of authority, legitimacy and so on, the presumption that what most people think is something like right can have a grip on you. The presumption itself is very likely more efficacious, as already remarked, than any other attempt to resist most of the eight propositions with which we began.

The presumption first faces the necessity and difficulty of making clearer and qualifying the actual fact of numbers on which it depends. Generally speaking, that was said to be most people, maybe a vast majority, finding certain moral propositions mistaken or outrageous, and presumably the reasons for them mistaken. The generalization runs up against, for example, the public opinion polls showing that half the British people were somehow against the idea that war on Iraq was right.[17] It runs up against the fact that international charities such as the Red Cross and War on Want can effectively appeal to our bad conscience about Africa as well as our concern. It is also plain, about my own country, that the Palestinians have the sympathy of much of the population in their resistance to an army of occupation and suppression. The sympathy issues in such politicians' plans as the one in 2003, called the road map to peace.

Despite these several qualifications, it remains true that there is a fact, not simple, of kinds of majority-opposition in our societies to certain moral propositions. There are kinds and degrees of congruence in opposition to them or at least withdrawal from them. This is true of Palestinian suicide-bombing, which we have uppermost in our minds. It is true, somehow, of the killing of kinds of innocents. Why should the fact trouble those of us who are inclined to or committed to the morality of humanity and all the eight propositions?

The presumption of its moral importance, some say, in one way or another, has to do with the fact that two heads are better than one, and more heads are better than fewer. The community of scientists may be offered as an analogy. There are other expressions of the thing. Is the idea that more heads rather than fewer are a guide to relevant *truths of fact* as distinct from what can seem to be moral truths? Well, to be on the side of the common people is of course not to be committed to any such piety with respect to relevant propositions of fact. Science itself is the first of overwhelming obstacles to such piety.

No doubt, consistently with the realism about truth that traditionally has issued in the Correspondence Theory, there is pretty good evidence that it is raining in Texas if most Texans say it is. But there is extensive ignorance of the factual proposition about our natures that makes (1) anybody's wretchedness a stronger reason to him or her for something than (2) somebody else's satiety a reason for something else. It is more relevant than anything else with respect to the questions before us. To ignorance is to be added falsehood. That Iraq perpetrated 9/11 is not made less idiotically false by the fact that a majority of Americans believed it. So too with what has been remarked on already, the wretched falsehood by Blair that we were under immediate threat from Saddam, half-believed by many in my country for a while, and that this was the aim of the war.

In place of continuing this reminder of ignorance and mistake, absolutely necessary though it is in other contexts, let me qualify my scepticism about the connection between majorities or congruences and factual truths, and quickly draw a conclusion.

By way of qualifying the scepticism, can we not do more than *hope* that people come to believe factual truths about their politicians eventually, see whether they are straight or not? Have the British people not seen, differently, that the expropriation by privatization of their railways was not at all in their interest? Do all my neighbours in Somerset fail to see that it was not a good thing that their water fell into the hands of Enron? Have they not seen, in general, that what were called the public services were overwhelmingly in their interest? You may say that my hopeful examples of public knowledge are true to my politics, which is no surprise. But they serve as well as any to indicate a conclusion.

Taken together with what was said before, about kinds and degrees of public support or tolerance of radical propositions, we have the cautious conclusion about factual propositions that there is *no* clear, well-supported and significant generalization connecting majorities or congruences with morally-relevant truths of fact. I suspect a less cautious view is true, but it is unnecessary in order to defend the morality of humanity against conventional morality.

Are so-called *moral truths* different? We can have in mind not only such conventional denials of my particular propositions on Africa, Palestinian suicide-bombing, Iraq and so on, but also the recommendatory views and doctrines from which denials of the particular propositions issue. Here we face another reminder. It is a kind of consideration that could as readily have been used against the supposed recommendation of majority support for relevant propositions of fact.

It is not as if the many who hold the conventional moral propositions have thought them out or inquired into them. Nor have they been educated into them if education is different from indoctrination. They have not heard what can be said both for and against them, put them in a structure of argument, clarified the relevant concepts, or even heard an actual exposition of the conventional propositions by those who for whatever reason defend them. Those who hold the conventional propositions, as you have heard, have no adequate grasp of morally relevant factual propositions. They are unpracticed in the rationality of consistency. They have had no such instruction worth the name in the bits and pieces of patriotic language that help to identify what you can call a national consciousness. Nothing calls out for more analysis than talk of *freedom*, unless perhaps it is *the American way of life*.

What the many who incline to the conventional propositions have had, rather, is an induction into morality that indubitably is to be studied, in large part, in terms of all those ideas mentioned earlier—authority, legitimacy, legitimation, illegitimation, naturalization, consent, ideology, norm-construction, indoctrination, mystery and mystification, influence, propaganda, sacralizing, demonizing and so on. There can be little doubt about this.

The *forming* of Americans, to continue to speak of them on account of their importance, is owed in large part to an ongoing history of which the basic fact is economic power. To describe it more enlighteningly, it has to do with different grasps on the material means to well-being, the most important means to the great goods, and in particular on political power. The basic fact of economic power is that the top tenth of Americans have 17 times the incomes of the bottom tenth, and a few hundred times the wealth of the bottom *four* tenths.[18]

Again it is not hard to draw a cautious conclusion, in this case about moral propositions. There can be no clear, significant and well-supported generalization connecting majorities or congruences with moral propositions that have the recommendation, in brief, of *moral intelligence*. This moral intelligence is a matter of judgement owed to knowledge and of practice in inquiry, not watching television.

Add in some historical episodes, including the German population's tolerance of the genocide of the Jews. Add the discomfiting and indeed destructive thought that different societies existing now have different and inconsistent conventional moralities, including different attitudes to various instances of terrorism. They can't *all* be right.

For all these reasons, it can seem to be a kind of dream that there is a decent presumption that what most people in a society think is right at least has something to be said for it. Presuppositions of it are a kind of mess. And yet the dream lingers, in more heads than mine.

VIII. Democracy, and a Conclusion about Convention

Does the lingering of the dream have a lot to do with democracy? Democracy is also about majorities, and it does certainly have a recommendation over most of the actual governments it has supplanted. If the outcomes of democratic elections have a recommendation, then so too, you may say, do the factual and moral beliefs that issue in the votes of the people—i.e. conventional morality. Indeed any defence of democracy must assign *some* recommendation to the input-beliefs.

You may take the view that the main recommendation of democracy is that it leaves a people politically freer, or less politically unfree, than they are under certain alternative forms of government. More people get more of what they want—whatever happens to other peoples. But that recommendation is less impressive if conjoined with the admission that democracy is about as likely as not to derive from mistakes of fact and morality, including mistakes about wants. That the democratic election gives you freedom takes a knock from one of them issuing from such factual and moral beliefs that it produced Hitler as the winner.

You will guess that at least a general scepticism about democracy, or rather *our* democracy, is basic to a general scepticism about conventional views, and to support of the eight propositions with which we began. To stick to the present point, it is indeed possible to think that recourse to our democracy is of little use in trying to explain why conventional morality should be accorded a significant respect. Indeed the history of reflection on illegitimation, mystification, sacralizing and so on is mainly reflection about our democracy.

To me, for the reasons you know having to do with income and wealth mentioned earlier, the most important means to well-being, our democracy is *hierarchic democracy* at best, indeed *oligarchic democracy*. By proper comparisons it is government of, by and for inequality rather than for equality.[19] It is specifically not a decision-procedure that recommends the decisions made. In brief, it is not truth-governed.

You will anticipate that it also seems to me that the fact of convention, often but not always the fact of convergence on views that have a long history, gets no recommendation from the ideology of conservatism. An analysis of it in terms of its commitments to conserving things, its superiority to theory, its perception and promotion of a certain human nature, and its selective attachment to freedom and so on, can issue in a certain conclusion. That is not that it is uniquely self-interested, but that no recognizably moral principle supports that self-interest.[20]

Even so, does the dream still linger that there is sense in what most people think is right? I confess to having hoped to find something or other of interest to say about this, something more or less philosophical. Perhaps some cautionary light on the obvious exceptions to principles and nostrums about the value of *any* rules as against none. Perhaps some stronger generality about working to change the rules rather than breaking them, or something about giving up violence as a precondition to negotiation, or about negotiation now because you will have to negotiate in the end. Perhaps some toleration of the people's deference to governments and states, which things in their genocides and politicides have, as remarked before, killed so many people as to make deaths by terrorism numerically trivial.

But *is* there any more to be said of majority views in our democracies? Is there any more in popular perception and wisdom than that those with bad lives know what those lives are like and see through our shams? In the absence of some clear thought about the recommendation of conventional views, about the people and truth, it is hard to resist a boring conclusion. It is that the dream that there is sense in what most people think is a dream that itself is part of the convention. The convention applies to and gives to itself an authority, legitimacy and so on. The convention, for which there is so little to be said, is not only about Africa and Palestine and so on, but also about itself. We philosophers and the like remain victims of what we only *see* a little better.

IX. Actual Justification of Some Terrorism for Humanity

Of what else can be said here, one thing was more or less anticipated when it was remarked that from the felt horror of killing the innocent, no conclusion can be drawn but by way of some adequate morality.[21] This sort of morality was gestured at still earlier[22]—it is an articulation of a whole view as to how the world ought to be. It is to be added, or made more explicit, that there is the same need for such a morality in any strong reflections on killing the innocent.

This comes into focus immediately, by the way, with respect to both half-innocents and clear innocents—they must be understood in terms of *wrongful* killings or other actions by their own state or people. To know an innocent, you have to make a reflective judgement on the innocent's state or people. Clear innocents, as against half-innocents, are not by choice or consent benefiting or profiting from *wrongful* killings by their own state or their people.

It is plain that to enter into the questions we have been considering, something general and clear has to be thought about our basic moral concepts—right actions, moral credit, moral standing. It is as plain, to come up to where we are, that the only recommendation that conventional views could have is that they somehow express an adequate morality. Is it even conceivable, on final reflection, that we could have found a reason for going along with a majority if we did not have a hold on an adequate morality somehow to assign to them? The same question arises about trust in our democracy, indeed any democracy. It arises, more generally, about a residual inclination, despite the genocides and politicides, to support or accept state or governmental action, *official* action, as against other action.

Finally here, it is my own judgement that those who stand against most of the particular propositions with which we began cannot explain themselves by way of an adequate morality. But my present point is that nothing else will suffice. If you disagree with the propositions, what is the adequate morality by which you do so?[23]

The question of whether a campaign of terrorism for humanity is not only possibly but also actually justified comes down to whether it will work—whether it has a decent probability of gaining the end in question, or more likely one of a range of related ends, at a cost that makes the result worth it. Those of you who are superior to what is misconceived as *consequentialism*, and is sometimes absurdly understood as the idea that an end justifies any means,[24] will do well to reflect that the reasoning in question is of just the form recommended by the orthodox theory of the just war.

The terrorism for humanity that is most likely to pass this final test of rationality is liberation-terrorism, which calls up human and moral resources greater than any other terrorism. Palestinian terrorism, for example, was of the strength to see through and disdain the dog's breakfast of a Palestinian state on offer during the presidency of Mr Clinton. It will, I think, see through and disdain any other dog's breakfast.

You now have an idea of most of the materials for what proof can be given, in my view, of the moral right of the Palestinians and other peoples to their terrorism for humanity.[25] I myself have greater confidence in it than before the war on Iraq.

The lies on which that war was predicated, or at the very least the culpable stupidity of self-deception, has strengthened my confidence. I refer to that consideration of guilt by association mentioned earlier. To be against Blair is to be reassured.

Still, and sadly, this matter of confidence has more to it. It is not easy to escape contradiction, not easy to get to consistency. There is great reason to take terrorism as *prima facie* wrong, as a good definition makes it. It is possible to think that the factual questions in terrorism—centrally the question of whether and how it will work—are of yet greater difficulty than the moral questions. What of those terrorists for humanity who will never give up, not because they will win, but so that others may one day win? The moral questions, to revert to them, cannot be taken as entirely clear and readily manageable. You can understand a man who says his head blows up when he brings together the viciousness of the neo-Zionism and the murdering of an Israeli child.[26]

Do you, in the end, ask me how it is possible to contemplate rising over the horror of the killing of a child? How it is possible to rise over the horror to a justification of the killing? Well, I would like to have more confidence than I have, more than the war on Iraq has given me. But some things are clear, indeed obvious. There is also the horror that is the rape of a people. To avoid the shock of it, to be half-lulled by the unspeakable spokesmen on the television mouthing stuff about democracy and terrorism, is also to be in a state that is appalling.

It is also to be remembered that in a clear way there is nothing unusual about such a claim as that the Palestinians are justified in their terrorism. Exactly such a claim is made daily by and on behalf of the Israeli state—explicitly or, less honourably, implicitly. Certainly its spokesmen are not informing us that what they are doing is wrong, maybe necessary and wrong. And there is nothing in between wrong and right—there are not degrees of being right or of being wrong.

Do you stick to the judgement that both sides are wrong to kill? If you have an ordinary view on the issue that has resulted in the killing, the main and prior issue about Palestine, you should find it difficult to maintain your even-handedness about the killing. The ordinary view is that the Palestinians have an indubitable right to what is perfectly properly described as their homeland. Can you accord such a right to a people or a person and deny to them the only possible means of getting or keeping the thing to which you accord them the right? Deny them a means to which there is no alternative?

Evidently to do so is at best to accord them an empty right to the thing. It is, surely, not really to accord them a right at all. To grant someone a right, whatever else is involved, is somehow to support them in getting or having the thing. What support is given by saying a people has a right to what you then also say they have no right to get by the only possible means? Further, if the Palestinians do have a right to their terrorism, the Israeli state does not have a right to its terrorism. It cannot be that both sides are justified in what they are doing.

Do you say that to assert a moral right to some terrorism is to give up a hesitancy that is part of proper moral philosophy?[27] Well, claims of moral right, as watching television can remind you daily, are not abstract propositions, so to speak, or not only abstract propositions, but ordinary parts of conflicts, ordinary means to an end, weapons made use of to the fullest extent possible. If the side of humanity has always been served better by truth than the other side, it needs also to say the most for itself that can truly be said. To do less, in the face of those against it, is to fail in a kind of realism.

Is there arrogance in all this? Well, there is not much sense of personal ability or importance. There is a sense of the importance of the greatest of moral principles, that of humanity, the one not deformed or tainted by self-interest. As it seems to me, it stands alone.

Ted Honderich, University College London
March 4, 2004

Notes

1. My thanks to Ingrid Honderich for comments on this paper, which demonstrate that we are not in complete agreement. The sample of twenty million lost lives has to do with the worst-off tenths of population in Malawi, Mozambique, Zambia and Sierra Leone. See my *After the Terror* (Edinburgh University Press, Columbia University Press, 2002), chap. 1.

2. Mifta (Palestine Initiative for the Promotion of Global Dialogue and Democracy) website (March 15, 2003).

3. Palestinian Red Crescent Society website (June 30, 2003).

4. B'Tselem: The Israeli Information Center for Human Rights in the Occupied Territories website (May 31, 2003).

5. Barbara Harff, "Toward Empirical Theory of Genocides and Politicides: Identification and Measurement of Cases since 1945," *International Studies Quarterly* (1988); "No Lessons Learned from the Holocaust? Assessing Risks of Genocide and Political Mass Murder since 1955," *American Political Science Review* (2003).

6. On war and terrorism, and on such other matters as the definition of terrorism, killing the innocent, and humiliation as a cause of terrorism, see the exemplary paper by Virginia Held, "Terrorism as Small War."

7. Professor Ed Kent, personal communication.

8. Cf. Bernard Williams, *Utilitarianism: For and Against* (Cambridge University Press, 1973). See also my *Violence for Equality: Inquiries in Political Philosophy* (Routledge, 1989),

Ch. 1, or a revised edition under the title *Terrorism for Humanity: Inquiries in Political Philosophy* (Pluto, 2003).

9. Jonathan Glover, *Humanity: A Moral History of the Twentieth Century* (Jonathan Cape, 1999), chaps. 10, 11, 12.

10. There is more on morality in *After the Terror*, chap. 2.

11. Cf. "Terrorism for Humanity: A Book and Further Thoughts," *The Journal of Ethics* (2003), which piece is reprinted in my *Political Means and Social Ends* (Edinburgh University Press, 2003).

12. Cf. Bernard Williams, *Utilitarianism: For and Against* and *Moral Luck* (Cambridge University Press, 1982), *Ethics and the Limits of Philosophy* (Fontana, 1984). As footnote 9 also indicates, I have lately been struck by the wider implications, political and social, of moral philosophy primarily concerned with private lives.

13. Cf. Tim Mulgan, *The Demands of Consequentialism* (Oxford University Press, 2001).

14. Violence is physical force that injures, damages, violates or destroys people or things. Terrorism is violence with a political and social end, whether or not intended to put people in general in fear, and necessarily raising a question of its moral justification because it is violence—either such violence as is against the law within a society or else violence between states or societies, against what there is of international law and smaller-scale than war. For more on this definition see *After the Terror*, 91–100, and "*After the Terror*: A Book and Further Thoughts."

15. R. A. Duff, *Punishment, Communication and Community* (Oxford University Press, 2000).

16. There were about 365,000 Arabs and about 7,000 Jews in 1876 in Palestine, then a recognized Arab homeland with the same boundaries recognized by the Western powers mandate after World War I. There were about 500,000 Arabs and 50,000 Jews in 1900 in Palestine. After World War II, if both states called for by the United Nations had come into being, there would have been about 750,000 Arabs and 9,250 Jews in the Arab state, and 479,000 Arabs and 498,000 Jews in what would be the Jewish state. See *After the Terror*, Ch. 1. The given figures and others come from *The World Guide 2003–4* (New Internationalist Publications, Instituto del Tercer Mundo, 2003). Cf. Justin McCarthy, *The Population of Palestine: Population History and Statistics of the Late Ottoman Period and the Mandate* (Columbia University Press, 1990), and Norman G. Finkelstein, *Image and Reality of the Palestine Conflict* (Verso, 2001).

17. A Guardian/ICM opinion poll published in *The Guardian* (March 19, 2003) was that 51% of Britons were against war and only 35% supported it.

18. For a consideration of this and related facts, see *After the Terror*, chap. 1.

19. See also "Hierarchic Democracy and the Necessity of Mass Civil Disobedience," Conway Memorial Lecture, 1994, republished in *On Political Means and Social Ends*, and also *After the Terror*, chap. 4.

20. See my *Conservatism* (Hamish Hamilton, Westview, 1990; Penguin, 1991; Pluto, 2004).

21. See above, 28, final paragraph.

22. See above, 20, beginning of Section III

23. For a consideration of several candidates, see various essays, several pertaining to liberalism, in *On Political Means and Social Ends*. The demand that an adequate morality be provided in argument is my principal reply to at least intemperate Israeli critics of such views as the one in this chapter. Professor Jacob Joshua Ross of Tel Aviv-University, in his spoken paper on it at the conference, said it was like the Nazis' antisemitic instruction to Germans, derived from Bismarck, to "think with your blood."

24. "Consequentialism, Moralities of Concern, and Selfishness," *Philosophy*, 1996, reprinted in *On Political Means and Social Ends*.

25. See also "*After the Terror:* A Book and Further Thoughts," *Journal of Ethics* (2003): 176–180.

26. Dr. Jeremy Stangroom, personal communication.

27. Cf. *Violence For Equality: Inquiries in Political Philosophy* (Routledge, 1989), revised as *Terrorism for Humanity: Inquiries in Political Philosophy* (Verso, 2003). It is true that my convictions have become both more confident and more resolute.

Terrorism, Self-Defense, and the Killing of the Innocent

WHITLEY R. P. KAUFMAN

Abstract: In this essay I analyze and defend the common sense moral conviction that terrorism, i.e., the use of violence against civilians for political or military purposes, is always morally impermissible. Terrorism violates the fundamental moral prohibition against harming the innocent, even to produce greater overall good. It is therefore just the sort of case that serves as a refutation of consequentialist moral theories. From a deontological perspective, the only remotely plausible forms of justification for a terrorist act would be that it constitutes a form of justifiable punishment of the guilty, or that it is legitimate self-defense against an aggressor. But an examination of the fundamental moral and legal principles of punishment and self-defense demonstrates that neither of these claims can succeed. Since terrorism cannot be justified either as punishment or as self-defense, it cannot be morally justified at all.

I. Introduction

Perhaps the most widely accepted moral rule, both in wartime and peace, is the constraint against intentionally killing the innocent.[1] This rule is so powerful that some have called it absolute, and it is widely agreed that the constraint may not be violated even to produce a greater social good as a result: one may not, for example, sacrifice an innocent person even to save five other lives. Indeed, the most significant objection to consequentialist moral theories is precisely that they allow (at least in principle) for just such sacrifices. This intuition is of great significance in making sense of the activity usually labeled "terrorism," which I will here understand as the deliberate use of violence against civilians for political or military purposes.[2]

Our intuitive revulsion against acts of terrorism would seem to be directly attributable to the fact that the terrorist violates this most fundamental of constraints. In this essay, I will take for granted that killing the innocent cannot be morally justified merely because it leads to desirable overall results. The question then becomes whether there is any other sort of legitimate basis that one might invoke to defend the morality of terrorism. The only remotely plausible such basis, it seems to me, is a defense of at least certain cases of terrorism as acts of justified defensive force. My purpose in this essay, then, will be to address the question of whether terrorism can be defended as a form of justified self-defense.[3] For reasons of space limitations, I limit my discussion to terrorist attacks on what are ordinarily termed "innocent civilians" or "civilians" as opposed to attacks on soldiers (as for example in the U.S.S. Cole bombing), though this is not to concede that all attacks on soldiers are justified. I will also assume that even in wartime, all killing must be justified as a form of defensive force, albeit on a larger scale; as Warren Christopher asserts, even in wartime "there is no justification for intentionally harming those who are not involved in attempting to harm others."[4] I will argue in this essay that terrorism against civilians cannot be justified as a form of defensive force, and hence that it can never be justified at all.

This essay is of course aimed at those who accept the existence of such moral constraints both in peace and in war (including those codified in the Just War tradition). Obviously, those who reject such constraints, whether they be Realists, consequentialists, or advocates of the Holy War tradition, will not likely be swayed by this sort of discussion. Nor am I suggesting that terrorist organizations will necessarily respond to or acknowledge the sorts of arguments made here. (Timothy McVeigh, however, is an example of a terrorist who explicitly, though mistakenly, invoked Just War doctrine to justify his attack). Nonetheless, one should not underestimate the important effect of the development of a strong and widespread moral consensus that terrorism is impermissible. Achieving such a consensus is an important form of "soft deterrence" against terrorist acts (as opposed to hard deterrence, which involves the use of force against terrorists). In any case, this essay is meant as an argument that the moral constraint against killing the innocent renders terrorism always morally impermissible.

II. Defining "Innocence"

A first problem is of course to define the word "innocent." It is often claimed that the word "innocent" in such an argument either has no clear meaning or simply begs the moral question against terrorism: i.e. "innocent" simply means "those who it is not considered permissible to kill."[5] Yet there is a perfectly tolerable sense in which we distinguish the innocent from the guilty on the grounds of culpability, especially for purposes of punishment. The innocent person has not committed a moral or legal wrong, as the guilty person has. If capital punishment is justified at all, it can only be justified against the guilty. Yet of course the presence of guilt by itself is not sufficient to justify all forms of punishment; the degree of guilt must be taken into consideration as well. Thus capital punishment is surely not justified simply because one is guilty of any offense at all (a parking ticket will not do); the guilt must be proportionately serious as to justify the punishment. But then it is clear that terrorism is not justified as a form of legitimate punishment, because it kills those who are either wholly innocent of any offense (e.g. babies or young children) or innocent of any offense which would justify the penalty of death; indeed the terrorist typically aims to be largely indiscriminate in his aims, without particular regard for the victim's innocence or guilt (or for any procedural protections to establish guilt or innocence). At least then in this sense of "innocent" it appears that terrorism is wrong because it violates the constraint against intentionally killing the innocent.

III. Self-Defense Against the Innocent

However, it is widely believed that an important (perhaps the only) exception to the constraint against intentionally killing the innocent is found in the doctrine of self-defense. The traditional principles of self-defense are generally held to permit the use of homicidal force even against the innocent or nonculpable aggressor. Thus while the paradigm case of justified homicidal self-defense is the culpable aggressor—the murderous attacker—it is usually held that defensive force is also permissible even where the aggressor is legally and morally innocent. Two cases in particular stand out: the psychotic aggressor and the mistaken aggressor. The psychotic aggressor attacks without being able to help or control himself or in the genuine but insane belief that you are a deadly threat to him. In a court of law, he would not be adjudged guilty of any harm he committed under his psychosis; similarly, few moralists would find him morally guilty. If you are attacked by such a person (and you know that he is psychotic and therefore innocent), may you use deadly force to defend yourself if necessary? The standard view is that you may, and the same goes for the (reasonably) mistaken aggressor, someone who mistakenly believes you are trying to kill him, and so is trying to kill you first. In both cases, the innocence of the attacker does not rule out your killing him. Arguably, this is the single important exception to the general prohibition on intentionally killing the innocent.

To be sure, this conclusion is not universally accepted. Some ethicists argue that defensive force is *not* permissible against the innocent, but only against the culpable.[6] For that matter, pacifists such as Leo Tolstoy have claimed that defensive force is never justified, against the innocent *or* the guilty. A tradition stemming from Aquinas and shared by many ethicists today holds that defensive force is justified precisely because the intention is not to kill or harm but to *defend* oneself. Nonetheless, it remains the dominant view that deadly force may be used in self-defense even against innocent aggressors, and that this counts as an exception to the general rule against intentionally killing the innocent, (i.e., those who are not guilty of any moral or legal wrong).

Thus let us suppose for purposes of argument that the self-defense doctrine does sometimes permit the intentional killing of the innocent as well as the culpable aggressor. Nonetheless, any such permission remains strictly limited, as evidenced by the following four legal and moral restrictions on the use of defensive force. (These limitations are further evidence of the power of the presumption against homicide):[7]

1) Force may only be used against an *unlawful aggressor*
2) The use of force must be *necessary*
3) The amount of force used must be *proportionate* to the harm being averted
4) The attack must be *imminent*.

These four conditions are necessary and jointly sufficient for the use of defensive force. Although the interpretation of each of these is complex and controversial, it will be useful to present a brief summary of each of these conditions.

Unlawful Aggression: force can only be used against an aggressor, that is, one who is actually attacking you or threatening to attack. One may not, for instance, harm a bystander (one who is not an aggressor) in order to divert an attacker's attention. What does it mean for the aggression to be "unlawful"? First, one may not use defensive force against someone whose aggression is lawful, such as a police officer carrying out a lawful arrest of you (even if you know you are innocent). More importantly, to say the aggression is unlawful is simply to say that it is not legally justified. It is not to say that it is legally or morally culpable; thus, psychotic aggressors are unlawful, if not legally guilty of anything. Hence one may use force against an attacker except where his attack is legally justified (assuming of course that the legal system itself is not itself morally corrupt).

Necessity: one may not use force at all, let alone homicidal force, unless it is the only possible means of avoiding the threatened harm. Thus if one can simply hide, run away, or talk the person out of it, one is obligated to do so (with some few exceptions, such as the lack of an obligation to retreat from one's own home). One must also use the least amount of force possible to prevent the harm. Once the wrongdoer is disarmed or no longer a threat, one may no longer harm him. The necessity principle is not always easy to apply, for it does not require that one sacrifice other important values for the sake of avoiding force. (Does it, for example, require one to retreat from a place one is legitimately entitled to be in, to avoid having to use force?). In general, though, it is a tolerably clear requirement.

Proportionality: one may use only force proportional to that being threatened. If one is threatened with death or serious bodily harm, then the use of deadly force is justified. However, most commentators agree that one may not kill simply to prevent one's personal property being taken, given that life is a far greater value than property. There is of necessity a certain amount of indeterminacy as to what counts as proportionality. But it is usually held that deadly force is justified to prevent death, seriously bodily injury, rape, or kidnapping.

Imminence: the use of defensive force is justified only where the harm is actually present or imminent, about to happen. One cannot inflict harm based on the mere possibility of a threat in the future, nor may one inflict harm after the aggression has ceased. Defensive force must be used only at the very moment of the threat occurring, though of course it is not easy to say when mere preparation becomes an imminent attack.

Every one of these principles involves complexities of application that we cannot explore in detail here. Nonetheless, the basic principles of self-defense are in general sufficiently uncontroversial and well-established so as to allow us to continue our investigation.

IV. Terrorism and Self-Defense

If terrorism can ever be justified morally or legally, it appears that it would have to be justified as a form of defensive force, as the only possible exception to the prohibition against intentionally killing the innocent. But can an act of terrorism be justified under the above four conditions? It is easy to see that it cannot, for it patently fails at least two of the provisions: the Unlawful Aggressor and Imminence requirements.

First, it is simply not plausible that terrorist attacks are carried out against unlawful aggressors. Mere presence in the World Trade Towers, in a nightclub, in a church, or in other such locations ("soft targets") does not constitute one as an aggressor at all, let alone an unlawful one. Presumably few if any of these victims were even armed, and certainly did not present a direct threat of deadly force against anyone else which would justify the use of deadly force. Nor were they plausibly directing, commanding, or controlling the use of force through any of their agents at the time of the attack. The terrorist would have to justify his claim of self-defense on the grounds that his targets were in some extended sense engaged in an act of aggression, perhaps by being bond traders and thus participating in the global capitalist system by which the financial hegemony of the United States is used to oppress Arab peoples.

It is arguably true that most American adults have *some* sort of connection, however remote, to some purported grievances that Arab peoples hold against the United States. However, to use such tenuous (often merely financial) connections as grounds for the use of "defensive" force would stretch the concept of "aggression" so far as to make it essentially meaningless. Indeed, Osama bin Laden has called on his followers to kill all Americans, regardless of their particular activities or their loyalties, as if (absurdly) merely being American (or even present in America) were sufficient to make one an unjust aggressor. But bin Laden is hardly an exceptional case; indeed, (as Michael Walzer argues) it is part of the essence of terrorism that its violence is deliberately indiscriminate and random, not making distinctions among those who are a threat and those who are not.[8] It of course follows for the very same reasons that it cannot plausibly be claimed that terrorist acts take place against an imminent threat. Obviously, if the targets are not aggressors to begin with, they cannot be engaged in "imminent" aggression. Indeed, should a terrorist use force against someone engaged in an immediate and unjustified attempt to harm him, his use of defensive force would be justified, and not count as terrorism at all under my definition.

It thus appears quite clear that terrorism cannot satisfy all four requirements for the use of defensive force. Indeed, arguably it fails to satisfy *any* of the four requirements. It is quite doubtful whether the terrorist seriously pursues all nonviolent alternatives to achieve his ends, including diplomacy and negotiation. Nor is it likely that most terrorist acts would satisfy the proportionality requirement, especially given the rather hazy and unclear notion of harm which the terrorists claim they are trying to prevent. (Al Qaeda attackers sometimes assert as justification a general feeling of "humiliation" of the Arab peoples by United States dominance in the world; but such a feeling is hardly a proportionate basis on which to commit homicide).

The inevitable conclusion seems to be that terrorism cannot be justified as defensive force. Indeed, one might go further and suggest that it is precisely because a terrorist attack takes place against those who are neither guilty of a capital crime nor engaged in an unjustified attack that we both identify this use of violence as a form of terrorism and simultaneously condemn it. The intuitive sense that terrorism is wrong because it aims to kill the innocent is just a way of saying that it is a form of killing that is without any justification. Indeed, it appears to be justified only from the standpoint of a consequentialist outlook, according to which the end justifies the means, and the innocent may be sacrificed for the greater good. Thus Palestinian suicide bombers kill the innocent for the sake of promoting the cause of Palestinian independence. But even if one accepts the legitimacy of the ultimate end being aimed at, one need not accept that any means whatsoever (even those proportionate to the end sought) are justified. For this is just the fundamental moral constraint that we identified at the outset, that one may not kill the innocent even for a good end. Terrorism, in short, is simply murder.

V. War and Self-Defense

It is sometimes argued, however, that terrorists groups such as al Qaeda or even militia groups in the United States are at war or engaged in an insurrection against the United States, and that therefore their actions are justified. The implication appears to be that the rules against killing civilians are in some way relaxed in wartime.

However, such an implication is misguided. Arguably, the most fundamental legal and moral restriction in wartime is that of noncombatant or civilian immunity: those who are not soldiers or directly contributing to the fighting may not be targeted, no matter the circumstances. That is to say, the rules of self-defense govern the legitimacy of the use of violence even in wartime, and one may not attempt to kill those who are not engaged in an attempt to harm others, with all the restrictions on the use of defensive force such as proportionality, necessity, and imminence. On these grounds, it should be immediately obvious that events such as the 9/11 attack or suicide bombings of commuter buses in Israel are unjustified.

However, it might be objected that the line between combatant and noncombatant is not so easily drawn. Thus in wartime, it is widely held permissible to attack even those who are not engaged in a direct, present threat, such as munitions manufacturers in enemy territory or command and control centers. So might there not be a broader permission to use defensive force in the context of a larger war-like campaign of resistance against the United States?

Here it will be helpful to refer to Jeffrie Murphy's idea of the "chain of agency." Murphy distinguishes those who are the legitimate targets of force in war ("combatants") from those who are not ("noncombatants") by an application of the idea of defensive force. In war, one may use defensive force against not only those who are a direct, immediate threat against you or others, but also against those who are part of a "chain of agency" of the use of force:

> What I mean by this is that the links of the chain (like the links between motives and actions) are held together logically and not merely causally, i.e., all held together, in this case, under the notion of who it is that is engaged in an attempt to destroy you.[9]

Thus, for Murphy a military General is a legitimate target (even if he is not presently aiming a weapon at you) because he is directly engaged in a chain of violence, whereas a farmer or a taxpayer is not part of this chain (even if the farmer's and the taxpayer's actions are necessary to the war cause, since the farmer belongs to a "causal" but not a "logical" chain). To be sure, Murphy concedes, there are difficult borderline cases, such as workers in munitions factories. Murphy sensibly calls for a policy of circumspection: a person should be considered a "noncombatant until proven otherwise."

It seems to me that this is a very plausible extension of the concept of self-defense to the conditions of warfare, which is the use of defensive force on a much larger scale. But if this is correct, then once again the terrorist clearly cannot claim justification for his attacks on civilians. Financiers in the World Trade Center, however necessary to United States power and authority in the world, are not plausibly engaged in an act of aggression. Nor are Israeli teenagers in a dance club, worshipers in a temple or church, or government employees in Oklahoma City. And clearly bin Laden's claim that merely being American is sufficient to make one a legitimate target is wholly without moral foundation. Hence even if a terrorist group such as al Qaeda claimed to be in a state of war with the United States (a claim which is already problematic, given the internationally recognized moral and legal constraints on the conduct of war), that would not justify acts of terror against civilians under the rubric of defensive force.

It is true of course that history displays many examples of widespread, intentional attacks on civilians. The latter stage of World War II is a notorious example of the targeting of civilians by both sides, including the Allied firebombings of Tokyo and Dresden. However, to use such cases as justification for present acts of terrorism would be to draw on a moral *non sequitur,* for the fact that such legally and morally illegitimate actions were taken in the past obviously does not justify similar attacks in the present. It was wrong to firebomb Dresden, no matter how noble the cause. It remains wrong to attack civilians today.

It is also sometimes claimed that terrorism is no worse than war, in that in war many civilians are typically killed in the course of fighting. By most accounts, the United States attack on Afghanistan caused as many civilian casualties as the 9/11 attackers did. However, such a loss of civilian life does not contravene the prohibition against intentionally killing the innocent, in that such deaths are not intended but merely foreseen. Indeed, in wartime one is morally obligated to minimize civilian casualties.[10] The distinction between intended and merely foreseen of course remains controversial. But in any case it will not help terrorists, for it is widely agreed that intentionally killing civilians is impermissible; the most that can be justified is the merely foreseen deaths of some civilians. This is of no use to terrorists, for they will be obligated to show that there is a legitimate *intended* target and that the civilians were only an unintended byproduct. But terrorist groups such as al Qaeda have made it clear that killing civilians is their intention, not merely a foreseen byproduct. As we have said, there is no plausible candidate for a legitimate target in the World Trade Towers, an Israeli commuter bus, or an Indonesian nightclub.

One important example of a terrorist who attempted to justify his deed as an act of war is Timothy McVeigh. Following the Oklahoma City bombing, McVeigh claimed that the children (and other civilians) killed in the bombing were merely "collateral damage," military jargon for an unintended byproduct of a legitimate attack. He argued that the bombing was an act of war, no different than an attack on a command and control center in wartime. To engage in a detailed critique of McVeigh's justification is beyond the scope of this essay. Nonetheless it can be said that his statements are a jumble of confused and incoherent ideas, including the ideas of retaliation, preemptive attacks, and "sending a message" to the federal government.[11] None of these justifications (even if legitimate in Just War theory, which they are not) would pass Murphy's test; it is simply not the case that federal bureaucrats in Oklahoma City are or were directly participating in or commanding acts of aggression against the American people, let alone unjustified aggression. More fundamentally, his vague and simplistic assertion that the "federal government" was "becoming increasingly hostile," is not even remotely plausible as a legitimate basis for what is in effect a declaration of war by McVeigh against the United States government. No matter how sincere McVeigh may have been in his belief that he was justified, his claim of justified self-defense cannot withstand reasonable scrutiny.

VI. Killing Civilians in Self-Defense

From time to time there have been some theorists who have disagreed with the sorts of conclusions drawn here about self-defense. One of the most notable is Larry Alexander, who has urged that "innocent noncombatants" may be killed under the doctrine of self-defense.[12] Although Alexander does not present his conclusion as a defense of terrorism specifically, the principle that killing noncombatants may sometimes be justified in self-defense can easily be extended, as we will see, to terrorist violence.

Alexander makes the case that killing noncombatants can at least in some cases be justified as an act of self-defense. His argument depends on a particular account of self-defense, what he calls the "correct formulation" of the doctrine. His corrected version is as follows:

> X (a person or persons) may be killed in self-defense, regardless of X's moral innocence, if the defender perceives (reasonably) that:
> 1) there exists the requisite threshold level of danger or greater;
> 2) killing X will reduce that danger
> 3) more desirable courses of action, such as killing fewer or guiltier persons, or not killing at all, will not eliminate condition (1); and
> 4) more desirable courses of action will not reduce the danger as much as killing X.

It is not clear where Alexander gets this definition of self-defense, or on what grounds he considers it the "correct" formulation (he does not attempt a defense of it here). However, it is worth comparing it with the standard account given above.

Alexander's (3) and (4) appear to correspond to the Necessity condition of the traditional doctrine, which requires that force not be used unless no less harmful means of protecting oneself from harm is available. The traditional Proportionality requirement appears as Alexander's condition (1), a certain threshold of danger. (Presumably Alexander means the threshold is that the harm threatened is proportionate to the harm being used in defense). However, what is interesting is what the "corrected" doctrine leaves out: both the Unjust Aggressor and the Imminence requirement. Indeed, it is interesting that these are just the two requirements that, as we saw above, rendered terrorism impermissible. But why does Alexander omit them?

Perhaps this question can be answered by observing the effect of Alexander's reformulation of the self-defense doctrine. For what it does (in effect if not in intent) is to move it in the direction of a *consequentialist* account of self-defense, in at least the sense that it accepts those elements of the traditional doctrine that are consistent with a consequentialist theory (notably the requirements that the harm caused not be greater than the benefit received and that less costly alternatives be used first where possible.)[13] But it omits just those requirements that in effect function as deontological constraints against killing even where it would lead to good overall results, constraints limiting the use of force to defend against (1) immediate and (2) unjustified aggression. But under Alexander's version, one can use deadly force against anyone—innocent bystander, culpable aggressor, innocent aggressor—so long as it is the only available means to avoid a certain "threshold" of harm.

But this reformulated doctrine would entail disturbing consequences (the possibility of which Alexander ignores in his essay). A terrorist who felt that the only way to protect the Palestinian people was to get the world's attention by killing as many Israeli civilians as possible might conceivably be morally justified under Alexander's corrected self-defense doctrine. Indeed, killing the innocent in general would be justified, so long as it was reasonably expected to lead to avoiding a significant possible harm. Now perhaps Alexander would respond that his principle would in fact permit only very rare cases of terrorism, and that such examples as the World Trade Center attack and the Oklahoma City bombing would be ruled out as a matter of fact.[14] But even if true that assurance does not capture the strong moral intuition that such actions are ruled out in principle, not merely contingently. Such horrific events are not merely ineffective, they are morally inexcusable. They are wrong not because of their inefficacy to achieve a desired result but because they violate the basic moral constraint against intentionally killing the innocent. Hence Alexander's version of the principle of self-defense must be rejected and cannot be used to justify acts of terrorism.

VII. Conclusion

Acts of terrorism—intentionally harming noncombatants for the sake of some larger good—are not morally justifiable, nor can the doctrine of self-defense be used to legitimate terrorism. Terrorism is wrong because it violates the most fundamental moral principle, the prohibition against the deliberate killing of the innocent. Indeed, we typically use the morally-loaded label "terrorism" precisely when an actor attempts to justify killing the innocent in the name of a greater good or a (purportedly) legitimate cause. Even if self-defense is construed as permitting a single, limited exception to the rule against intentionally killing the innocent, it cannot be made the basis for legitimating terrorism, at least not without distorting the doctrine of self-defense beyond recognition; for the terrorist aims to harm civilians, those who are neither guilty of a crime nor engaged in an act of unjustified aggression. And if terrorism cannot be justified as self-defense, then it cannot be justified at all.

Whitley R. P. Kaufman, University of Massachusetts Lowell

Notes

1. One might add "against their will" in order to encompass suicide and euthanasia. But the powerful traditional presumption against either of these is evidence of the strength of the rule against killing the innocent, against their will or not. I also leave aside the question of abortion, a controversy which goes to the definition of when an entity is to count as a human person.

2. The problem of defining "terrorism" is notorious. See, e.g., Philip Heymann, *Terrorism and America*, 3 ff. My concern here is to analyze the phenomenon of directly targeting civilians, the practice which is usually called "terrorism," though my interest is not in the name one uses but the practice itself. By using the term "terrorist" I do not mean to prejudge the moral issue. Note also that Just War theory does not prohibit harming civilians as an unintended byproduct of a legitimate attack.

3. I follow here the awkward but universal convention of using "self-defense" to include other-defense as well as self-defense in the strict sense.

4. Warren Christopher, *The Ethics of War and Peace* (New Jersey: Prentice Hall, 1999), 161. See also Jeffrie Murphy, "The Killing of the Innocent," in *War, Morality, and the Military Profession* (Boulder: Westview Press, 1986).

5. In defense of the widespread use of the term "innocent" and "innocent civilian," however, is the fact that its original meaning from the Latin is simply "harmless," i.e., one who is not currently engaged in a harmful act, and hence cannot be killed in self-defense.

6. See, e.g., David Rodin, *War and Self-Defense* (New York: Oxford University Press, 2002); Michael Otsuka, "Killing the Innocent in Self-Defense," *Philosophy and Public Affairs* 23, 74–94.

7. See, e.g., LaFave and Scott, *Criminal Law*, second edition (Minnesota: West Publishing, 1986), Section 5.7.

8. Michael Walzer, *Just and Unjust Wars* (HarperCollins Publishers, 1977), 197.

9. Murphy, 346.

10. See, e.g., Walzer, 151–159.

11. See McVeigh's April 2001 Letter to Fox News (available at http://www.foxnews.com/story/0,2933,17500,00.html).

12. Larry Alexander, "Self-Defense and the Killing of Noncombatants: A Reply to Fullinwider," *Philosophy and Public Affairs* (1976), 411–412.

13. I do not mean to claim that the account is a straightforward form of consequentialism, but only that it shares significant elements with consequentialism that traditional moral theory would find objectionable.

14. It is at least plausible that terrorism can sometimes be objectively the only effective way of defending a people. See, e.g., Alan Dershowitz, *Why Terrorism Works* (New Haven: Yale University Press 2002), arguing that terrorism persists in the Middle East precisely because it has been an effective tool.

Evil, Ignorance, and the 9/11 Terrorists

TODD CALDER

Abstract: In this paper I consider the excuse of ignorance as a justification for acting in a way that would otherwise be evil. My aim is to determine when ignorance precludes us from evildoing and when it does not. I use the 9/11 terrorist attack on America as a case study. In particular, I consider whether the 9/11 terrorists were precluded from evildoing because they thought they were doing right and thus were ignorant about the true nature of their actions. The paper begins with a discussion of the nature of evil. I argue that the 9/11 terrorists were not precluded from evildoing by their ignorance because they were largely responsible for being ignorant about the true nature of their actions. They were responsible for their ignorance because they evaded acknowledging information that should have revealed to them the evilness of their plans. They were "self-deceptive evildoers."

People accused of evildoing typically offer some sort of justification or excuse for their actions. If successful, their justification or excuse precludes them from evildoing, since they cannot be condemned for a justified or excusable act. In this paper I consider the excuse of ignorance as a justification for acting in a way that would otherwise be evil. My aim is to determine when ignorance precludes us from evildoing and when it does not. I use the 9/11 terrorist attack on America as a case study. In particular, I consider whether the 9/11 terrorists were precluded from evildoing because they thought they were doing right and thus were ignorant about the true nature of their actions. The paper begins with a discussion of the nature of evil.

I. The Nature of Evil

In recent years several theories of evil have been offered (see, e.g., the theories of Claudia Card, Eve Garrard, John Kekes, Hillel Steiner, Ernesto V. Garcia and Laurence Thomas).[1] In this paper I do not give a detailed exposition and criticism of these theories. Instead, I present and defend a theory of evil which I have developed largely in response to these other theories. I call my theory the Desire Account of Evil because it differs from these other theories by contending that desires play a fundamental role in evil. According to the Desire Account two conditions must be met for an act to be evil: first, the act must involve someone else's significant harm, and second, the harm must follow from what I call an e-desire, i.e. from an effective desire for the harm for an unworthy goal such as one's own pleasure or entertainment value. By an *effective desire*, I mean a desire that is not outweighed by a stronger desire that our victim is spared the suffering, so that in the absence of inhibiting factors such as cowardice it would move us to act.[2] Together these conditions assert that we act evilly when we cause someone else significant harm from an effective desire for that harm for an unworthy goal.

Evil and Harm

The first condition for evil, that evil must involve significant harm, is accepted by most theorists writing about evil and is easy to defend. Evil acts must involve significant harm because much of the moral gravity of evil comes from the seriousness of the harm inflicted. So, for instance, while it would be evil to cause someone excruciating pain for one's own pleasure, the amount of harm normally inflicted by a light pinch on the arm could never be evil no matter how viciously it was inflicted.

Although most theorists agree that evil must involve significant harm, this condition is not entirely uncontroversial. In her paper "The Nature of Evil," Eve Garrard argues that evil acts need not involve much harm. As an example she cites the case of a tyrannical state that executes a young dissident by firing squad and then forces the grieving relatives to pay for the cost of the bullets. Garrard suggests that while the execution of the young dissident is wrong it is the charging for the bullets that strikes us as evil. Yet, Garrard contends, charging for the bullets involves very little harm especially as compared to the execution.[3] I disagree. Charging for the bullets inflicts a significant harm on the family of the dissident. This significant harm consists in the psychological trauma of being forced, not only to accept the authority of an unjust state but to play a role in the state's unjust execution of a family member. I contend that the charging for the bullets would not have been evil if it hadn't been psychologically harmful to the family. No evil is done unless someone gets seriously hurt.

Evil and Desire

The second condition for evil, that the harm must follow from an e-desire, i.e. from an effective desire for the harm for an unworthy goal, is more complicated and controversial and will need more argument and analysis than the first condition.

To show that e-desires are fundamental to evil, I will discuss the failings of John Kekes's theory of evil which attempts to characterize evil without making reference to the desires of evildoers.[4] According to Kekes, evil acts consist in causing serious, morally unjustified harm to other human beings.[5] No mention is made of the desires or motivation of the evildoer. By morally unjustified harm, Kekes means a harm that is avoidable, undeserved and not the best way of preventing a greater harm.[6] The central problem with characterizing evil in this way rather than by reference to the desires of evildoers is that our doing evil becomes largely a matter of circumstances external to us and quite possibly beyond our control. Consider first Kekes's condition that the harm must be undeserved. Rather than being a requirement for evil this condition seems to be completely irrelevant to the evilness of an act. Imagine a case where a victim deserves serious harm, say for instance because he is a serial killer, but that the perpetrator of his harm is really not concerned that the serial killer gets his just reward. Rather, she simply desires to take pleasure in causing someone else serious harm. I think in cases like these causing serious harm is evil even though the victim might deserve the harm.

It is also possible to inflict serious avoidable harm on an undeserving person without doing evil. For example, a dutiful prison warden or an executioner may cause a person serious harm that she does not deserve because she has been wrongfully convicted. If the warden or executioner is ignorant of her victim's innocence we would not say that she acts evilly by causing undeserved harm, for she had no malicious intent or despicable desire.

These two cases show that what is important for evil is the sort of desire from which the act is done and not whether the victim deserves the harm. Causing serious harm to a serial killer for pleasure is evil because one's own pleasure is not a good reason to cause serious harm. Acting from a despicable desire of this sort is evil even if the victim deserves the harm. On the other hand, it isn't evil to cause serious harm to an innocent convict if the harm is done from a desire to fulfill one's duty to mete out just punishment, since in that case the harm does not follow from a despicable desire.

Kekes's requirement that evil acts are not the best way to prevent greater harm is also neither necessary nor sufficient for evil. For instance, we might have good reason to believe that greater harm is being prevented by our harming someone when it is not. In these cases, it would be too harsh to call our act evil, for we have no despicable desire or intent. We have just miscalculated the relative amounts of harm. In other cases, an agent might, in fact, prevent greater harm by harming another, yet cause the harm from a despicable desire for that harm and not because it is the lesser of two "evils." In these cases it seems clear that the act might still be evil even though greater harm has been averted. Once again Kekes's account of evil fails by ignoring the motivational component of evil.

So we can see from the failings of Kekes's theory of evil that, no matter how serious, undeserved or inexpedient an act of causing significant harm might be, to be evil it must follow from an e-desire, i.e. from an effective desire for someone else's significant harm for an unworthy goal. I will now give an analysis of e-desires.

Unworthy Goals and Moral Theory

Let us first consider what it is that makes a goal unworthy of harm. The answer to this question lies in the relative values of the harm and the goal for which it is desired. Causing someone else significant harm for pleasure is evil because significant harm is obviously disvaluable to a high degree while any pleasure we might get from this harm is of questionable value.[7] Our own pleasure is not a worthy goal for which significant harm may be caused; the value (if any) which is derived from our pleasure in someone else's significant harm does not make things on balance more valuable. On the other hand, saving five from significant harm is a worthy goal for which to cause significant harm to one, since the disvalue of the significant harm is more than outweighed by the amount of disvalue that has been prevented. So a goal is worthy when the value of the goal combined with the disvalue of the harm is on balance more valuable than states of affairs where the harm does not occur. Of course in order to know whether a goal is worthy of a harm in any particular case we need the right theory of value plus other relevant information, e.g., what consequences will follow from the harm. I will not attempt to argue for any particular theory of value here, nor can I provide empirical information to determine the worthiness of a goal in each particular case.

I also want to be clear that I am not here assuming the truth of consequentialism. Nor is the Desire Account of Evil a consequentialist theory of evil. I am not assuming the truth of consequentialism because I am not making a claim about the rightness or wrongness of actions. For instance, it does not follow from what I have said about worthy and unworthy goals that it would be morally correct or justified to cause significant harm to one person to save five others from a similar harm. Instead, I only make the much weaker claim that to act from a desire to cause significant harm to one person to save five from a similar harm would not be evil. I believe this is a claim that even a deontologist could accept since it is a claim about the conditions for evil and not a claim about the conditions for right or wrong action.[8] Thus a deontolologist may insist that it is immoral to act on a desire to cause one person significant harm to save five others and yet concede that such an act would lack the despicableness required for evil.

The Desire Account of Evil is not a consequentialist theory because it does not judge the evilness of actions solely on the basis of the consequences (or the intended consequences) of the action. For instance, as I noted above while discussing the failings of John Kekes's theory of evil, while acting evilly we might rightly believe that we maximize the good by causing significant harm to one person, and thus, do what is right by consequentialist standards. However, we still act evilly if we desire to cause the harm for an unworthy goal such as our own pleasure and not to maximize overall goodness.

This is not to say that the Desire Account of Evil is in no way similar to consequentialism. There are at least two respect in which the Desire Account of Evil is similar to consequentialism. First, just as wrongdoing requires bad consequences for the consequentialist, evildoing requires significant suffering according to the Desire Account of Evil. If we have an effective desire to cause significant harm but fail to bring about the suffering, we fail at our attempt to do evil. However, our failed attempt at evil may still be indicative of an evil of character since incompetence doesn't make our characters any better.[9]

Second, consequentialists determine the rightness or wrongness of an action by comparing the total value or disvalue of an action with the total value or disvalue of alternative courses of action. In the same way, the Desire Account determines the worthiness or unworthiness of goals by comparing the total value or disvalue that would be created by causing significant harm with the total value or disvalue that would obtain if the harm did not occur. But this does not make the Desire Account consequentialist since the determination of the worthiness or unworthiness of goals is only one part of how the Desire Account determines evilness of action. Non-consequentialist elements affect the evilness of our actions as well, such as the reasons we have for bringing about the harm. In fact, we have just as much reason to call the Desire Account of Evil deontological as we do to call it consequentialist, since it follows from this theory that some acts are evil regardless of the overall value of the consequences.

It shouldn't be any surprise that the Desire Account of Evil is neither fully consequentialist nor fully deontological since these categories typically apply to theories of right action and the Desire Account is not a theory of right action. I will now turn to a discussion of what it is about desires that make them fundamental to evil.

The Nature of Desire

To desire some object or state of affairs is to want (or to have a pro-attitude towards) what we know or take that object or state of affairs to be like, and not necessarily to want what that object or state of affairs is actually like. In other words, if we believe A is X when it is actually Y, desiring A entails wanting X and not Y even though A really is Y. So, if, for example, I believe that by beating my wife I cause significant harm for an unworthy goal and I desire to beat my wife, then I desire someone else's significant harm for an unworthy goal. If instead I believe that beating my wife is an insignificant harm to her or that it would be for the best overall, e.g. because it would put her in her place, then it wouldn't really be proper to say that I *desire* significant harm for an unworthy goal even if that is the true nature of what I desire. Instead, we should say that I *desire insignificant* harm for an unworthy goal or significant harm for a *worthy* goal, or whatever the case may be, but that I am mistaken about the nature of what I desire.

It is important to think about desires in this way in the context of our discussion about e-desires, for we would not think that desires were fundamental to evil if we thought that the objects of our desires were actual objects or states of affairs rather than what we believe or take these objects or states of affairs to be like.[10] To illustrate this point, imagine there are two buttons I can push, a red one and a green one. If I push the green button I cause a stranger a significant amount of suffering. If I push the red button I cause a stranger a significant amount of pleasure. Unfortunately, I believe that the green button causes pleasure and that the red button causes suffering. So now the question becomes, what if I desire to push the green button? Do I desire a stranger's pleasure or do I desire her suffering? If the objects of our desires are actual states of affairs and not what we take these states of affairs to be like, then we must say that I desire the stranger's suffering. But that doesn't fit with the ordinary notion of desire. According to the ordinary notion of desire, we would say that I desire the stranger's pleasure but mistakenly choose the wrong button. In order to blame people for their desires we must suppose that the objects of our desires are what we take the states of affairs desired to be like and not the states of affairs themselves, since, for the most part, we aren't blamed for getting the facts wrong but rather for knowingly choosing what is bad or wrong.[11] Thus, if desire is fundamental to evil it must consist in wanting what we take an object or state of affairs to be like and not in wanting what the object or state of affairs is actually like.

Before turning to the relationship between evil and ignorance, let us first sum up what we have learned about the nature of evil thus far. To act evilly we must cause someone else significant harm from an e-desire. E-desires consist in wanting what we believe is someone else's significant harm for a goal that does not make up for the disvalue of the harm desired. At least one further qualification to the notion of e-desires is needed. This qualification will arise out of my discussion of evil, ignorance and the 9/11 terrorists.

II. Evil and Ignorance

Having discussed the nature of evil, we are now in a position to discuss the relationship between evil, ignorance and excuse. I have argued above that desires are fundamental to evil only if by 'desire' we mean the ordinary notion of desire. According to the ordinary notion of desire, to desire x means to want what we take x to be like and not necessarily to want what x is actually like. Given this feature of desire, it follows that to have an e-desire we must believe or acknowledge that what we desire is someone else's significant harm for an unworthy goal. But then what if we believe that the harm we desire is insignificant when it is significant, or that the goal is worthy when it is not? Does ignorance get us off the hook in every case? And if not, when does ignorance preclude us from evildoing and when does it not? These are important questions to answer, for most, if not all, evildoers purport to believe either that they don't cause significant harm or that the goal for which they cause the harm is a worthy one. These evildoers go wrong in one of two ways: they either fail to get the natural facts right, for instance, by thinking that a significant harm will lead to a great benefit when it will not, or else they fail to evaluate the facts correctly, for instance, by judging that their own pleasure is valuable enough to outweigh someone else's significant harm.[12] Aristotle makes a similar distinction between those who are ignorant of universals in practical syllogisms and those who are ignorant of particulars.[13] He argues that we are not pardoned for being ignorant of universal moral claims, such as that it is immoral to cause unjustified serious harm to another person. For Aristotle ignorance of this sort invites reproach. Being ignorant of particulars, on the other hand, such as that the consequences of a particular act would be someone else's serious harm, is reason to pardon wrongdoing unless the person is responsible for their ignorance.

I agree with Aristotle about the distinction between ignorance of moral universals and ignorance of particular natural facts. We are certainly not precluded from evildoing by wrongly judging that some unworthy goal, such as our own pleasure, is valuable enough to outweigh someone else's significant harm. Psychopaths are perhaps paradigmatic examples of those who cause significant harm under this form of ignorance. They are ignorant in the sense that they are poor moral evaluators. I also think there are times when we should be excused for getting the natural facts wrong about whether someone has been significantly harmed or whether great benefit will result from the harm. In the remainder of this paper I want to discuss in more detail the conditions under which ignorance of particular facts provides a legitimate excuse for causing significant harm. I also want to propose that in a great many cases those who are responsible for their ignorance about the significance of the harm they cause or the worthiness of the goal for which they cause the harm are self-deceptive evildoers. I argue that the 9/11 terrorists were more than likely evildoers of this sort.

Defensible and Indefensible Ignorance

Imagine that a boy has been indoctrinated since birth about the evils of Westerners (i.e., people from Western society), especially Americans, by the worst sort of Islamic extremists, such as those who recruit terrorists for al-Qaeda. While growing up this boy is repeatedly told that Americans are the enemy of Allah, that they are destroying the world, that they have no morally redeemable features and that it is God's will that they be destroyed by the faithful. Imagine further that this boy is isolated from Westerners and moderate Muslims, spending his entire youth in extremist Islamic schools and at al-Qaeda training camps. Without ever being confronted with good contrary evidence we could not expect him to believe anything other than that Americans are inherently evil and that he would be doing right by sacrificing himself in a terrorist attack against them.

If this were the profile of a 9/11 terrorist it would be difficult to call his actions evil since his belief in the worthiness of taking part in a terrorist attack against Americans would be reasonable or defensible. His belief would be defensible since, given the information available to him, it would seem to anyone similarly situated that taking part in the attack was justified.

However, it is unlikely that any of the 9/11 terrorists where subjected to this kind of systematic indoctrination, or to indoctrination systematic enough to make their false beliefs in the value of killing Americans defensible. This is not to say that the leaders of al-Qaeda did not take every opportunity to indoctrinate the 9/11 terrorists into believing that their mission was justified.[14] It is just that there was a lot of information readily available to the 9/11 terrorists that was contrary to the teachings of the al-Qaeda leadership. For example, we know that four of the nineteen hijackers had had extensive contact with Americans and Westerners.[15] Three of them, Mohamed Atta, Marwan Al-Shehhi and Ziad Samir Jarrah, lived and attended University in Hamburg, Germany, where they had friends who were not very different from most Americans. Furthermore, the Hamburg students arrived in America 16–18 months prior to the attacks to make preparations. The fourth Hijacker who had had years of contact with Westerners was Hani Hanjour. Hanjour studied English and went to flying school in the US since 1996.

The takfiri creed enjoins al-Qaeda members who are on missions in non-Islamic countries "to mask their true purposes even if it mean[s] breaching strict Islamic rules."[16] Some al-Qaeda terrorists were better at this than others. The Hamburg terrorist Jarrah was particularly good at fitting in with Americans. Jarrah was everybody's friend at the Florida Flight Training Center where he and the other two Hamburg students learned to fly. For example, he once brought a six pack of beer to his flight instructor after he had injured his knee, staying for hours to socialize. He also often cooked for his American roommates in Florida. There is a photograph of him enjoying Thanksgiving dinner with his American friends.[17]

Unlike Hanjour and the Hamburg students, twelve of the nineteen hijackers arrived in America from Saudi Arabia three or four months before the attack on tourist visas. Although these late comers didn't spend as much time interacting with Americans and other Westerners as did the organizers of their mission, they were also encouraged to fit in and to hide their true purpose. Most of them spent a lot of time working out at local gyms and practicing martial arts.[18]

Given the amount of time the 9/11 terrorists spent with Americans and other Westerners it would have been difficult for them not to realize that Americans, like other Westerners, had morally redeemable qualities such as the capacity for love, compassion and good will towards others – in short, that Americans are not thoroughly evil. This is particularly true of the organizers who seem to have had full knowledge of the plan well in advance.[19] Even if their friendly conduct towards

Americans was a deception, it would have been difficult for them to have had these cordial relationships while viewing all Americans as irrevocably evil.

In the face of their friendly contact with Americans and other Westerners, one thing that kept the 9/11 terrorists going and gave them the hardness to complete their mission was the idea, instilled in them by the al-Qaeda leadership, that they were carrying out the will of God and thus that they were acting for a worthy goal.[20] But how certain were they that they were carrying out the will of God and that the goal for which they intended to kill hundreds or thousands of Americans was a worthy one? Given their upbringing and the information available to them, was it reasonable for them to be certain that they were carrying out the will of God (Allah)? I say *certain* because the death and suffering of hundreds or thousands of innocents is so morally important that it would be reprehensible to take part in such an act without being certain of the worthiness of the goal for which they were taking part.

Each of the nineteen hijackers should have had doubts about the worthiness of the goal of their mission. Most, if not all, of them came from families that were opposed to extremist forms of Islam.[21] So it is unlikely that any of them was indoctrinated into militant Islam since birth. In fact, most of them were introduced to militant Islam in university. Furthermore, since they were mostly middle class university students, most of them would have been exposed to a variety of information from various sources about world events and the dictates of Islam.[22]

Ignorance and Self-Deception

Thus, I contend that the 9/11 terrorists could only have believed that they acted for a worthy goal by deceiving themselves about the strength of the evidence supporting this conclusion. However, there are at least three respects in which this contention needs further support. First, I must say more about what I mean by "self-deception." Second, in order to argue that the 9/11 terrorists deceived themselves about the worthiness of the goal for which they desired to kill hundreds or thousands of Americans, I must show that they had a motive for their self-deception. And third, I must argue that it was self-deception, rather than carelessness or negligence, that led the 9/11 terrorists to believe in the worthiness of their goal. I will address each of these concerns in turn.

By "self-deception" I mean to evade acknowledging to ourselves some truth "or what [we] would view as truth if [we] were to confront [the] issue squarely."[23] Self-deceivers are initially aware of moments where they shift their attention away from available evidence to something else, although they may not be aware of the overall project of their self-deception.[24]

In his book, *Moral Responsibility in the Holocaust*, David Jones lists five common tactics used in self-deception: (1) we avoid thinking about p (that is the proposition we want to avoid acknowledging); (2) we distract ourselves from thinking about p with rationalization, for instance by trying to insist that there is good evidence that not-p when there isn't; (3) we evade belief in p by systematically failing to make any inquiries about p, distracting our attention from p and ignoring available evidence of p; (4) we block appropriate emotional responses such as horror and assume an attitude of indifference towards p; and (5) we evade activities that would be appropriate for someone who believed p.[25]

Now that we have a better understanding of the nature of self-deception, the next question to ask is what motive the 9/11 terrorists could have had for deceiving themselves about the worthiness of killing hundreds or thousands of Americans. An answer to this question begins with the observation that, although many of the 9/11 terrorists were university educated, most of the hijackers lacked purpose and a sense of belonging.[26] Some, such as Mohamed Atta, who attended university in the West, felt alienated in his new surroundings. Al-Qaeda specialist Paul Williams writes that "Typical recruits for al-Qaeda are unmarried males between the ages of 17 and 25 ... Scouts usually choose youths who have been injured by ethnic conflict ... those who have been victims of beatings, or who have lost a father or brother in a demonstration, or who are without much hope of escaping a life of grinding poverty."[27] Of the late comers from Saudi Arabia, many were disaffected youths caught in the kingdom's recent economic downturn having graduated with degrees that didn't qualify them to do anything but religious studies.[28] Al-Qaeda gave them a sense of belonging, a brotherhood and a purpose. To maintain this sense of purpose and belonging, al-Qaeda members needed to turn away from evidence that opposed Osama Bin Laden's interpretation of the Koran and his view of Americans. They used self-deception to convince themselves of the worthiness of the goal of their mission.

But why should we believe that the 9/11 terrorists were self-deceptive rather than careless or negligent? My response is that killing hundreds or thousands of human beings is so morally important that the 9/11 terrorists could only have failed to consider, or appreciate the force of, evidence against the terrorist attack by being self-deceptive or monstrously indifferent to the suffering of others. That is, being careless or negligent about the justification for killing hundreds or thousands of human beings amounts to psychopathy. I think we make better sense of the 9/11 terrorists if we characterize them as self-deceptive rather than as psychopathic.

Ignorance and E-Desires

It is now time to revise my notion of e-desires in light of our discussion of evil, ignorance and self-deception. I have argued that, even though we do not truly *desire* significant harm for an unworthy goal in cases of self-deception, since we falsely believe that the harm is insignificant or that the goal for which we cause the harm is a worthy one, our ignorance is largely a matter of our own doing and thus is indefensible and does not preclude us from evildoing.

Our ignorance would be defensible if, *given the information readily available to us, it would seem to any unbiased person who had similar cognitive and deliberative powers that our false beliefs were true.*[29] The central idea of defensible ignorance is easy enough to understand: we cannot be expected to have information that does not exist or that is unavailable to us. However, more must be said about the role played by the cognitive and deliberative powers of unbiased people in defensible ignorance and about what I mean by "information readily available to us."

Since by my understanding of defensible ignorance we are judged relative to people with similar cognitive and deliberative powers, those of us whose cognitive and deliberative powers are highly developed are held to a higher standard than are those of us whose cognitive and deliberative powers are less developed. For instance, we should expect a supreme court judge to be better able to assess information relevant to the worthiness of a goal for which she desires to cause serious harm than a seventeen year-old high school drop-out. However, as a bare minimum, to do evil we must have the cognitive and deliberative powers required for moral agency. To be a moral agent we must be able to obtain correct information from the world through our senses (to the extent to which normal human beings can obtain correct information through their senses) and to draw basic inferences from this information.[30] People suffering from cognitive and deliberative deficiencies, such as those associated with schizophrenia, cannot obtain accurate information from the world and/or draw basic inferences; thus, they are not moral agents and are defensibly ignorant.

The notion of defensible ignorance, as expressed above, assumes that, given the same information and the same cognitive and deliberative powers, unbiased people will draw the same conclusions. If people with the same cognitive and deliberative powers draw significantly different conclusions from the same information this is the result of a bias. A bias is a preference for one conclusion over another based solely on self-interest or a desire that cannot be supported by reasons acceptable to nonbelievers. According to my notion of defensible ignorance, biases should have no weight in moral deliberation.

By "information readily available to us," I mean information that we could be expected to acquire given our abilities and our current environment. Just how much effort we can be expected to put into acquiring the relevant information depends upon the sort of action we intend to perform. Two factors that are particularly relevant are the moral significance of the proposed act and the amount of expertise required to make an informed decision about whether the goal for which we intend to cause harm is a worthy one. For instance, if we intend to kill hundreds or thousands of human beings because they are irrevocably evil and it is the will of God that they be killed, then we should make a considerable effort to find out whether these human beings are in fact irrevocably evil and whether it is the will of God that they be killed since deciding whether to kill hundreds or thousands of human beings is so morally important. Thus, if we have the opportunity to interact with our potential victims, we should consider very carefully whether their overall behavior is indicative of evilness. We should also seek out the advice of experts from disparate positions to determine which view makes most sense of the evidence. If after assessing the available evidence it is still unclear whether the group in question is irrevocably evil and whether it is the will of God that they be killed, we should refrain from killing since we must be quite certain before acting on such a morally significant decision. Our ignorance about the value of killing hundreds or thousands of human beings would certainly be indefensible if we turned away from, or made little effort to acquire, evidence that was opposed to the killing.

If we are considering whether to make a judgment about the worthiness of a goal which requires training or expertise that we do not have, we should either acquire the requisite training or expertise or else not make the judgment. For instance, I should not make a judgment about whether dumping some bio-hazardous material into a river will cause significant harm since I am not an expert in environmental science. If I do make such a judgment and I am wrong, my ignorance is indefensible even if I seek out relevant information to the best of my ability. To be justified in making this judgment I would need to first acquire the requisite training and then seek out the relevant information. This is not to say that to avoid being indefensibly ignorant we must become an expert in every field, but rather that we are required to refrain from making judgments when it should be obvious that we are incapable of making an informed judgment.

In sum, our ignorance is defensible only if it follows from a reasonable assessment of available information relative to our own cognitive and deliberative powers. Self-deceptive ignorance is indefensible and does not preclude us from evildoing because it does not follow from a reasonable assessment of available information, but rather, from a desire to avoid the truth about morally important facts. Thus, according to the revised Desire Account of Evil, we act evilly when we have an effective desire for someone else's significant harm (or for what cannot defensibly be believed is not significant harm) for what cannot defensibly be believed to be a worthy goal.

III. Conclusion

In this paper I have argued that ignorance is only a legitimate excuse for alleged evildoing in cases where the alleged evildoer is ignorant of particulars in practical syllogisms for defensible reasons. It is defensible to be ignorant of particulars when any unbiased person with similar cognitive and deliberative powers would be ignorant of these particulars given the information readily available. I have argued that ignorance of particulars is not a legitimate excuse for alleged evildoing if the ignorance has resulted from self-deception. I contend that the ignorance of the 9/11 terrorists was more than likely of the self-deceptive variety. Thus the 9/11 terrorists caused significant harm from an effective desire for that harm for what could not defensibly be believe to be a worthy goal. That is, they acted evilly.

Todd Calder, University of Western Ontario

Notes

1. Claudia Card, *The Atrocity Paradigm: A Theory of Evil* (Oxford: Oxford University Press, 2002); Ernesto V. Garcia, "A Kantian Theory of Evil" *The Monist: An International Quarterly Journal of General Philosophical Inquiry* 85 (2002): 194–209; Eve Garrard, "The Nature of Evil," *Philosophical Explorations: An International Journal for the Philosophy of Mind and Action* 1 (1998): 43–60; John Kekes, *Facing Evil* (Princeton: Princeton University Press, 1990); John Kekes, "The Reflexivity of Evil," *Social Philosophy and Policy* 15 (1998): 217–232; Hillel Steiner, "Calibrating Evil" *The Monist: An International Quarterly Journal of General Philosophical Inquiry* 85 (2002): 183–193; Laurence Thomas, *Vessels of Evil: American Slavery and the Holocaust* (Philadelphia: Temple University Press, 1993).

2. I get the term 'effective desire' from Harry G. Frankfurt, "Freedom of the Will and the Concept of a Reason," *The Journal of Philosophy* 68 (1971): 5–21.

3. Eve Garrard, "The Nature of Evil," 44–46.

4. I make this criticism of Kekes for a different purpose in a footnote in my paper, "The Apparent Banality of Evil," *Journal of Social Philosophy* 34 (2003): 364–376.

5. Kekes, "The Reflexivity of Evil," 17. See also, Kekes, *Facing Evil*, 45–64.

6. Kekes, "The Reflexivity of Evil," 17.

7. According to Aristotle pleasure has no intrinsic value on its own. Pleasure in a good activity is good and pleasure in a bad activity is bad. Aristotle, *Nicomachean Ethics*, trans. Martin Ostwald, (Upper Saddle River, New Jersey: Prentice Hall, 1999), Book X, Section 5, 1175a22–1175b35, 282–284. Others such as Thomas Hurka argue that even pleasure in a bad state of affairs has some value as pleasure. See his *Virtue, Vice and Value* (Oxford: Oxford University Press, 2001), 149–150. My sense is that pleasure in itself is always valuable but that when combined with other states of affairs it can make for the worst sorts of wholes. However, I will not argue for this position here.

8. I do not have the space here to argue that the moral concept of evil is distinct from the concept of wrongness. Roughly the idea is that even very wrong acts (according to whatever theory of wrongness you choose) may not be evil because they lack either the despicable motivation or the significant harm required for evil.

9. For more about the Desire Account of Evil Character see my "The Apparent Banality of Evil."

10. I thank David Copp and Charles Mills for pointing this out to me during the question period at the presentation of my paper "The Apparent Banality of Evil," *Eighteenth International Social Philosophy Conference*, University of Eastern Michigan, Ypsilanti, Michigan (July 26–28, 2001).

11. This is not entirely true. Very shortly I will consider circumstances where we are blamed for mistaking the facts.

12. I want to distinguish this sort of evildoer from the sort who judges that someone else's significant harm is very disvaluable and that his own pleasure is comparatively trivial, yet desires the harm for his own pleasure anyway. By contrast, the person I have in mind here thinks he is acting for the greater good but is mistaken because he evaluates poorly.

13. Aristotle, *Nicomachean Ethics*, Book III, Section 1, 1110b27–1111a20, 55–57; Section 5, 1113b30–1114a30, 65–67.

14. Jane Corbin, *Al-Qaeda: In Search of the Terror Network that Threatens the World* (New York: Thunder's Mouth Press, 2002), 208; Rohan Gunaratna, *Inside Al Qaeda: Global Network of Terror* (London: Hurst & Company, 2002), 88–89; Paul L. Williams, *Al Qaeda: Brotherhood of Terror* (New York: Alpha, 2002), 8–11, 151–161.

15. Corbin, Al-Qaeda, pp. 111–205.

16. Ibid., 154.

17. Ibid., 154–155.

18. Ibid., 205–214

19. Ibid., 178–190, 207.

20. Gunaratna, *Inside Al Qaeda*, 229–230

21. Corbin, *Al-Qaeda*, 208–210.

22. Ibid., 111–210.

23. Mike W. Martin, *Self-Deception and Morality* (University Press of Kansas, 1986), 13. Michelle Moody-Adams refers to ignorance of this sort as "affected ignorance." See her "Culture, Responsibility, and Affected Ignorance," *Ethics* 104 (1994): 291–309.

24. David Jones, *Moral Responsibility and the Holocaust* (Lanham, MD: Rowman & Littlefield, 1999), 81–84.

25. Ibid., 82.

26. Ibid.

27. Williams, *Al Qaeda*, 10.

28. Corbin, *Al Qaeda*, 208.

29. My account of the reasonableness or defensibleness of beliefs is inspired by Laurence Thomas's discussion of what makes a person's moral views defensible in his *Living Morally* (Philadelphia: Temple University Press, 1989), 9–10. I have also borrowed the terms 'cognitive powers' and 'deliberating capacities' from David Jones in his *Moral Responsibility in the Holocaust,* 28–29. I thank anonymous reviewers for *Social Philosophy Today* for their critical comments on my notion of defensible ignorance.

30. I give a similar characterization of moral agency in "Toward a Theory of Evil Acts: A Critique of Laurence Thomas's Theory of Evil Acts," in *Earth's Abominations: Philosophical Studies of Evil*, ed. Daniel M. Haybron, Value Inquiry Book Series (Amsterdam: Rodopi, 2002), 58. By basic inferences I mean for example modus ponens and universal instantiation.

Beyond Retribution: Reasonable Responses to Terrorism

RICHARD M. BUCK

Abstract: The very nature of terrorism and the context in which it typically occurs make responding to it much more complicated, morally speaking, than responding to conventional military attacks. Two points are particularly important here: (1) terrorism often arises in the midst of conflicts that can only be resolved at the negotiating table; (2) responses to terrorist acts almost always present significant risks to the lives and well-being of noncombatants. The history of the Israel-Palestinian conflict suggests that its resolution will only come through negotiation. However, Israel has an obligation to secure the safety of its citizens. In this context, responses to terrorism must be judged, morally speaking, by how well they balance the following competing aims: (1) protecting the lives of potential victims of terror; (2) protecting the lives of noncombatants living among the terrorists; and (3) preserving the possibility for negotiating the end of the conflict. My aim in this paper is to show that responses against terrorists need not be retributive in aim, and can therefore satisfy these competing demands.

I. Introduction

In a conventional war, a morally justifiable and useful strike at the enemy might be an attack on supply lines, armaments depots, or, in many cases, an attack against clearly identifiable combatants. But the very nature of terrorism and the context in which it typically occurs make responding to it much more complicated, morally speaking, than responding to conventional military attacks. Two points are particularly important here. First, terrorism often arises as a response to, and in the midst of, conflicts that can only be resolved at the negotiating table. Second, responses to terrorist acts almost always present significant risks to the lives and well-being of noncombatants. The current Palestinian-Israeli conflict is an example of a case in which both of these points are relevant: terrorist organizations such as Hamas and Islamic Jihad—that clearly pose a threat to innocent civilians—knowingly and willingly set up a base of operations inside densely populated urban areas, making it extremely difficult (if not impossible) for the state of Israel to protect its citizens and deter future terrorist acts without making noncombatants the unintended victims of a military response.

In addition, and perhaps no less important, the history of the conflict between Palestinians and Israelis suggests that its resolution will only come through meaningful negotiations. Armed struggle on the part of the Palestinians and military responses on the part of the state of Israel will only prolong the conflict and the suffering of noncombatants. However, the government of the state of Israel has an obligation to secure order and safety for its citizens; thus a response to terrorists is mandatory. But since the safety and overall well-being of Israeli *and* Palestinian civilians—the latter also being the responsibility of the Israeli government—will never be fully secured so long as the current conflict rages on, responses to terrorist attacks must be viewed as a short-term measure necessary to prevent harm to Israeli noncombatants, while at the same time paving the way for secure and meaningful negotiations. Thus, responses to terrorism must be constrained so that they do not intensify the conflict and make negotiations unlikely. In the end, the moral assessment of responses to terrorism must reflect how well these responses balance the following three *competing* aims: (1) protecting the lives of potential victims of terror; (2) protecting the lives of noncombatants living among the terrorists; and (3) preserving the possibility for secure and meaningful negotiations that will end the conflict.

In *Just and Unjust Wars*, Michael Walzer argues that military *reprisals* are one form of justified response to terrorism. On Walzer's view, reprisals "have the form of a warning: if our villages are attacked, yours will also be attacked."[1] It makes sense to ask how such a response might be justified. At first glance, it seems like the most plausible justifications would rest on a retributive or utilitarian/deterrence principle. In my view, neither option is promising. A utilitarian justification would condone too much suffering, while on a retributive justification such responses would effectively be forms of collective punishment. In my view, both of these approaches would offend some of our deepest moral commitments. My aim in this paper is twofold. First, I want to set out a principle by which we can judge the permissibility of military responses. Second, through the use of this principle I hope to show that responses against terrorists need not be retributive in aim, and can therefore avoid the problem of defending claims of collective responsibility.[2] My view is that military responses are justifiable only when they satisfy what I will call the principle of reasonable response. This principle is a modified version of what Walzer calls the principle of backward-looking proportionality, which he deploys as a standard for evaluating military responses during conventional warfare. On Walzer's view, the principle of backward-looking proportionality serves to justify military reprisals—a tit for tat strategy in which *proportional* military responses aim to deter future attacks. In my view, such a strategy is not appropriate when responding to terrorist attacks linked to—though not necessarily justified by—a current territorial or other international dispute. In these cases, a response to terror must serve to protect civilians from terrorist attacks while at the same time preserving the possibility of discussions and negotiations that are needed to resolve the dispute. Under these conditions, the justificatory strategy deployed by Walzer will not work, since reprisals will likely wear down the will of the parties to continue with negotiations. Thus, there is a need for an alternative account or principle of justifiable responses to terrorism, and I attempt to develop such an account in this essay. In discussing the application of my principle as a standard for judging military responses, I will use as case examples two operations conducted by the Israel Defense Forces against Palestinian terror groups. I hope to show that the principle of reasonable response offers us a standard by which we can distinguish morally acceptable and unacceptable military responses.

II. Terrorism: A Suggested Definition

Before I begin laying out my case for the reasonableness of military responses to terrorism I want to offer a definition of "terrorism." There is considerable disagreement in the literature when it comes to defining terror, and in a paper of this size I can do little more than present what I believe to be a plausible definition, one that captures what I believe to be most important about the acts and actors that we group under the label "terrorist." With that in mind I will define terrorism as the following: indiscriminate acts of violence, carried out against innocent civilians (or civilians whose guilt has not been established by the perpetrators), but directed at a third party, and undertaken in order to bring about a significant change in social or political structures.[3] Using the word "terror" instead of calling the agents simply "killers" or "murderers" indicates that the killing is simply a *means* of producing a climate of fear among the general population.[4] This is why the attacks must be indiscriminate or random. The terrorist will not be able to create a climate of terror if the general population has reason to believe that only select persons (government officials, army officers, or soldiers) are likely targets.[5]

Some further clarification is called for here. By "indiscriminate" I do not mean to suggest that terrorists never choose specific targets to attack. The use of "indiscriminate" is meant to suggest that as far as a terrorist is concerned, one potential target is as good as any other, in principle, and that the only reason for choosing this marketplace or that bus is the impact that the attack would have. Thus, other than the effect that the action will have on the terrorist's audience (usually the government), terrorists usually have no reasons to support their selection of victims. Simply put, the victims themselves carry no weight in the terrorist's decision to attack or not to attack. In the words of Michael Walzer, the victims of terrorists are targets because "they . . . share what they cannot avoid, a collective identity."[6]

III. The Problem of Response

Now that I have laid out a definition of terrorism, I will move to the problem of responding to terrorist attacks. In particular, I will be laying out a conception of a reasonable response to a pattern of terrorist attacks (as opposed to developing an account of a justified response to isolated incidents). I will focus on how a basically just government—a government that is committed to some reasonable conception of justice and human rights—should respond to persons and groups engaged in acts of terrorism as an essential strategy for achieving their aims or interests. These persons and groups engage in what I will call persistent terror.

Leaving aside tactical concerns, there are at least two pressing problems for any *legitimate* government facing a terrorist threat: protecting the lives of noncombatants and responding proportionally. Terrorists do not attempt to face off against their enemies. Since they aim to make foundational structural changes, terrorists engage in acts that are meant to influence those who have some have authority to make the changes they desire. But the victims of terrorism, as I have defined it, are typically not governmental officials. Even in cases where officers of government are targeted (as was the case when Israeli Tourism minister Rahavam Zeevi was assassinated by gunmen of the Popular Front for the Liberation of Palestine), the attack is typically part of a strategy of random attacks. Thus, civilians have good reason to be fearful of an attack and there is no way for the general population to reasonably protect itself.[7] Further, since stealth and deception are necessary components of terrorist strategy, terrorists intentionally set up operations among the general civilian population. Because of this, pursuing and responding to terrorists present significant risks to noncombatants and those carrying out the response.[8]

The first course of action of a legitimate government, in my view, is to use the resources of the existing criminal justice system. The aim of a basically just government should be to apprehend terrorists, collect necessary evidence against them, and try them publicly. In certain situations, it might be appropriate to invite international observers or set up an international tribunal.[9] But even when this strategy is implemented, it may still be extremely difficult to avoid killing noncombatants. This is because of the nature of engagement with terrorists: terrorists are difficult to locate, but even when they are found, often within densely populated residential neighborhoods, they are often more willing to die than be apprehended and tried. Such conditions make armed conflict unavoidable. In the end, a strict adherence to a policy of apprehension *only* may fail to stem the tide of terrorist violence. In addition, an increased and more intense police effort would surely compromise the freedom and well-being of noncombatants (though the terrorists must bear some of the blame for this). It is because of these conditions that responses to terrorism present the most difficult moral challenges. I will now elaborate on the two challenges listed at the beginning of this section, starting with the problem of protecting the lives of noncombatants.

Protecting Noncombatants

According to Michael Walzer, the second principle of the war convention—a set of norms, professional codes, religious principles, and legal precepts that serve as our standard for judging military conduct—is that noncombatants cannot be attacked at any time.[10] Article Three of the Geneva Convention Relative to The Protection of Civilian Persons in Time of War also forbids the targeting of those not involved in combat. But both conventions are standards for conduct during conventional warfare (i.e., where war has been declared and the armies of two nations are squaring off). For example, those who recognize the Geneva Convention as a normatively binding document must believe that it is possible in conventional warfare to distinguish between combatants and noncombatants. But when combatants mix into the general population, like terrorists do, it becomes increasingly difficult to distinguish between combatants and noncombatants. As I have already pointed out, from the perspective of terrorist organizations, this is not an unfortunate or unavoidable outcome; indeed, it is an essential component of their strategy. Thus, responses to terrorist attacks and activities often involve risking harm and causing harm to non-combatants. In morally assessing these responses we must determine whether harming or risking harm to non-combatants is ever justifiable.

I think it is clear that targeting noncombatants or *structuring* responses in such a way that it would be impossible to distinguish between combatants and noncombatants is morally unacceptable.[11] By definition, noncombatants play no role in carrying out the actions that have brought on the response and cannot, therefore, be held morally responsible for them.[12] To argue that noncombatants can be *targeted* or that no great precautions need be taken to avoid killing them is to effectively "argue," as terrorists do, that people may be killed simply because of who they are, not because of what they have done.[13]

But I do not think that we can condemn a response *simply because* noncombatants are killed. Part of the reason for this is that the nature of terrorist acts makes it difficult to distinguish between combatants and noncombatants. And for this reason, terrorists can be held morally responsible for noncombatant deaths that occur if their actions indeed make it impossible for those carrying out the response to protect noncombatants. Indeed, I would argue that in some situations those carrying out the response are *causally* though not *morally* responsible for noncombatant deaths that may occur. Later in the essay I will offer a set of conditions that must be met in order to justify a response in which noncombatants are killed.

Proportionality

Michael Walzer claims that military reprisals (one form of response) must be governed by the principle of backward-looking proportionality.[14] According to this principle, responses are directed at a previous crime. This is in contrast to the forward-looking view according to which responses are directed at the prevention of future crimes and are, therefore, only indirectly limited by previous crimes (insofar as previous crimes give the authorities some idea of what kinds of crimes might be committed in the future and thus what kinds of crimes they will need to try to deter).[15] The proportionality of the response, then, is determined by the act that has been committed, not by what might be accomplished in the future by means of the response. Nor is proportionality to be determined by the justice of the cause in support of which the response is carried out. Thus, as Walzer puts it, the purpose of reprisals is "not to win the war or prevent the defeat of the cause, but simply to enforce the rules."[16]

The advantage of the principle of backward-looking proportionality, then, is that it creates a limit that clearly excludes the intentional killing or targeting of noncombatants. These strategies for military reprisals are ruled out because they violate any military convention worth defending.[17] In addition, it avoids the snares of retributivism on the one hand—which would require complicated explorations into claims of collective responsibility (and in any case, seems to increase the amount of suffering in the world)—and utilitarianism on the other—which would possibly allow the killing of innocent civilians if this were to promote the best consequences of all available actions. In my view, backward-looking proportionality is an example of a *restorative* principle of combat, since it requires that responses re-establish the standing of the prohibition against targeting noncombatants instead of simply punishing those who willingly break it.

However, including conventions as part of the principle of backward-looking proportionality (BLP) may make it difficult to use this principle in the moral assessment of military responses to terrorism. As I understand Walzer's view, the idea that a convention is a necessary component of a justifiable response suggests that all the parties to conflict adhere to the convention to some degree. As Walzer puts it, "responses [are a form of] reactive deterrence . . . If there is no convention there can be no response."[18] Conventions are typically in place to govern warfare of the ordinary type, and a response that aims to enforce the convention is a response to the mode or means of an attack which violates the convention and not the attack itself.[19] But when responding to a terrorist attack, it is the attack itself (i.e., the terrorism) that generates and justifies the response. Indeed, we call the attack terrorist, in part because it occurs outside the bounds of the war convention. Because of this, one might argue that the principle of backward-looking proportionality does not apply to engagements with terrorists.

Revising BLP: Toward a Principle of Reasonable Response against Terrorists

As I indicated in my introduction, responses against terrorists present special difficulty because they typically involve a greater risk to the lives and well-being of noncombatants. To be sure, this increased risk is caused, in large part, by the terrorists themselves because they operate and hide in densely populated areas and are knowingly and willingly putting the lives of noncombatants around them in danger. Thus, terrorists are at least morally *blameworthy* for putting the lives of those people at risk, and they may, in some cases, be morally *responsible* for the deaths of noncombatants that occur during a response. But neither the responsibility terrorists bear for compromising the safety of the people they live among nor their culpability for the psychological and physical harm they cause to their victims can excuse those carrying out a response from moral responsibility for the harm caused to noncombatants. However, both the present danger to potential victims and noncombatants and the obligation of any legitimate government to protect its citizens require decisive action. And as the demand for action increases, so does the potential risk to noncombatants. How are we to balance these competing concerns?

What I suggest is a revision of BLP to what I am calling the principle of reasonable response. According to this principle, responses are still directed at the action committed, but there are three additional conditions that a response must satisfy:

1. The aim must also be to apprehend or otherwise incapacitate those responsible for previous actions. The second of these options is justifiable only in the following circumstances: (a) attempts to apprehend the responsible parties would cause more harm to noncombatants than the incapacitation of the responsible parties; (b) attempts to apprehend the responsible parties have failed.
2. Due care is taken to (a) avoid killing and (b) minimize the suffering of noncombatants (suffering here means a substantive and negative impact on well-being broadly construed).
3. In all other respects, the nature of the response is such that any harm that does occur does not erode the possibility of future good faith negotiations aimed at resolving the conflict.

Although the principle of reasonable response clearly retains the spirit of BLP, the two principles differ in that on the revised principle justification is both backward and forward-looking. The crucial concern here is the possibility of future good faith negotiations between noncombatants and those who authorized the response. In some cases, such as the current Israeli-Palestinian conflict, a resolution to the conflict will have to emerge out of the ruins of numerous attacks and responses, and it is unlikely that indiscriminate responses will encourage noncombatants to come to the negotiating table in good faith. While I think it too demanding to require that all responses be structured so as not to *upset* noncombatants, among whom we hope to find negotiating partners, it is certainly reasonable to argue that responses not destroy all hope for a reasonable dialogue between the parties to the conflict.

One important advantage of the principle of reasonable response is that it does not rest on the tenuous distinction between intended consequences and foreseen results. That is, I am not claiming that the deaths of noncombatants, even if foreseen, are not morally troubling so long as they are unintended. Instead I want to argue that a response can be justified even in the event noncombatants are harmed or killed, but only if due care is taken to minimize the suffering of noncombatants and the operation as a whole is structured in such a way that it would be deemed reasonable by those who were put at risk or suffered as a result of it. To be sure, the standard "due care" is not precise, and there will be disagreement over whether this standard was satisfied in any given case. More importantly, there will likely be disagreement over the *criteria* of due care, particularly in cases where there is a significant risk to non-combatants. In such situations the question of how much care must be taken to avoid harm to non-combatants must be addressed. Admittedly, it will be very difficult to establish a set of conditions for due care that all reasonable persons would accept. However, I would suggest that a government has demonstrated due care in responding to terrorists if the response poses a greater risk to its own combatants than to any *non-combatants* in the target area. This standard does address the question of how much care should be taken to avoid harm to non-combatants because it requires that a government show more concern for the lives and well-being of non-combatants than for the lives and well-being of its own soldiers. Since we can assume that a basically just government would place significant value on the lives of its own soldiers, this standard demands that a great deal of value be placed on the lives of non-combatants.

As I have noted above, it is very likely that there will be significant debate and disagreement over whether the standard of due care has been met in a given case. But unlike claims about intentions which involve complicated and controversial *philosophical* judgments, claims about the due care standard can be sorted out in part by appeal to empirical judgments resting on facts available through careful investigation. Thus, claims about due care are less likely to generate considerable and irresolvable disagreement than claims about intentions. Simply put, claims about measures taken to avoid non-combatant casualties are more readily justifiable even to those who suffered as a result of the response.[20]

IV. Operation Defensive Shield and the Battle in Jenin[21]

Now that I have presented the basic idea of the principle of reasonable response, I want to show how it can be applied to cases in which *some risk* to noncombatants is unavoidable, and there is a good chance that some noncombatants will be killed. If the principle is to be useful to us it should help us to clearly distinguish between morally acceptable and unacceptable uses of force in these situations. Specifically, my aim is to show that a response is justifiable in at least some cases where there is some risk to the lives and well-being of noncombatants and some noncombatants are killed or harmed as a result of the response.[22] In what follows I will examine two operations conducted by the Israeli Defense Forces (IDF) against Palestinian terrorists. In my view, both of these cases constitute unjust responses, though they differ in the severity of the moral wrong committed. I hope to show that the principle of reasonable response can demonstrate the difference between these two cases.

On Tuesday, April 2, Israeli tanks began to move into the town of Jenin as part of Operation Defensive Shield. which began on March 28 in Ramallah when the IDF surrounded the headquarters of Palestinian Authority president Yassir Arafat. Jenin was a priority for the IDF because many of the previous spade of attacks that began in September, 2000 were carried out by residents of the city who were members of one of three main terrorist groups: Al-Aqsa Martyrs Brigade, Islamic Jihad, and Hamas. Most recently, a Hamas cell based in Jenin had dispatched the man who detonated a bomb in a hotel in Netanya, killing twenty-eight people as they sat down to a Passover Seder. The IDF operation was, in part, aimed at the capture of three men: Mahmoud Tawalbe, Thabet Mardawi, and Ali Suleiman al-Saadi, also known as Safouri. All three held leadership positions in the local Islamic Jihad cell, and all three had been responsible for planning terrorist attacks.

The IDF plan was to move in from three sides, thus surrounding the camp. In order to avoid civilian casualties, the IDF decided against an air-strike. Instead the plan was to use a combination of navy seals, engineers, tanks, and heavily armed bulldozers to carve a path for the tanks. For their part, the Palestinian fighters had lined the streets with booby traps—some with as much as 250 pounds of explosives—and had dug tunnels between houses so that they could remain hidden while moving around. The battle included street to street fighting and, as one would expect, noncombatants were caught in the crossfire. But Israeli officials claim that they never entered a home without shouting out a warning, and Palestinian accounts support this claim. Indeed, one Palestinian witness reported that he heard an Israeli officer yell, in Arabic, "People in the house get out; we don't want you to be hurt." On some occasions, this strategy was effective and doubtless saved many lives. Nevertheless, noncombatants were killed. In addition, the Israelis damaged hundreds of homes with the D-9—a twenty-foot tall fifty ton armored bulldozer. The IDF used the D-9's (about twenty of them) to clear paths for the tanks and detonate booby traps. The D-9's certainly destroyed some houses; according to Human Rights Watch more than 140 homes were destroyed and some 200 others were damaged. But it is not likely that the D-9's buried many people. (It takes the D-9 at least thirty minutes to demolish a home; anyone inside a house hit by a D-9 would have had ample time to escape). Indeed, even Palestinian military officers conceded that it was probably the booby traps set by Palestinian gunmen that buried some of the noncombatants alive. All told, approximately sixty Palestinian dead were pulled from the rubble. Forty-nine Palestinians were reported missing.

Was the IDF operation in Jenin a justified repsonse? There is no doubt that noncombatants were killed during the operation. The first question is whether the operation targeted noncombatants or involved unreasonable risks to them. I think we can answer no to the first question. There were approximately 1300 people remaining in the camp when the IDF troops arrived, and it is likely that fewer than 100 people were killed, some of whom were fighters. Further, there is nothing about the method used by the IDF to suggest that the operation aimed at killing as many noncombatants as possible. What about the risk to noncombatants? Given the location of the operation and the nature of the conflict, a certain degree of risk to noncombatants has to be assumed. The IDF attempted to *minimize* the risk by notifying noncombatants that they were approaching—thus putting their own lives in greater danger—and giving them the opportunity to leave the house. However, the number of homes destroyed by the IDF was excessive, which may suggest that greater care should have been taken to avoid such extensive damage; this would surely constitute significant harm to the well-being of those whose homes were destroyed.

Reviewing the details of the operation, I think a convincing case can be made that the operation in Jenin satisfied some the requirements for a reasonable response. The aim of the operation was to apprehend the men responsible for planning several previous and future terrorist attacks in Israel, thus the first part of the principle of reasonable response was satisfied. In addition though, and in my view more importantly, the operation was structured in such a way that noncombatants were not targeted and all due care was taken to avoid harming noncombatants. In view of this, I think, we can make the case that the operation in Jenin was not narrowly retributive in aim, and was conducted in such a way that due attention was given to protecting the *lives* of noncombatants in Jenin. However, the operation caused considerable *harm* to hundreds of Palestinian noncombatants whose homes were destroyed. To this extent, the response would seem to be disproportionate. However, we need to keep in view the normative import of the condition of proportionality, in virtue of which the principle of reasonable response is both backward and forward-looking. The backward-looking concern is the well-being of Palestinian civilians, and the requirement of proportionality is meant to constrain responses so that the well-being of Palestinian civilians is protected. The forward-looking consideration is the preservation of the conditions necessary for future meaningful negotiations between Israelis and Palestinians. With these two concerns in mind, we can say that the destruction of homes was excessive and therefore morally unacceptable. However, if the Israeli government recognized this and made restitution by paying the cost for rebuilding Palestinian homes, and further compensating Palestinians for loss of possessions, the forward-looking requirement of the principle of reasonable response would have been satisfied, because the Israeli government would have taken significant steps to assure that the harm caused during the operation did not undermine the possibility of future good-faith negotiations.

V. A Case of Retribution? The Assassination of Salah Shehadah[23]

On the night of July 23, 2002 an IDF Air Force Jet dropped a one-ton bomb on a residential building in a crowded Gaza City neighborhood. The target of the attack was Salah Shehadah, a founder and current leader of the military wing of Hamas. Shehadah was killed in the building, along with fourteen other residents, nine of whom were children. Over one hundred others were injured.

Since its founding and at the time of the attack, Hamas was ideologically committed to the destruction of the state of Israel and the creation of the Palestinian Islamic state in its place. Thus, Hamas had categorically rejected coexistence and peace with Israel. In furtherance of its aim, Hamas had carried out hundreds of terrorist attacks against Israeli civilians, including suicide bombings. Both the IDF and the Palestinian Authority knew that Shehadah was the mastermind of several of these attacks and was continuing to plan attacks from his Gaza headquarters. In fact, in the period leading up to the attack on Shehadah, Israel had received warnings that Shehadah was planning a large-scale attack. Israeli intelligence suggested that the most likely target of the attack would be the Katif Bridge, which leads from Jewish settlements in the Gaza Strip over Palestinian population centers. Israel had been planning an attack on Shehadah for six months, but it had postponed the attack eight times because the cabinet and IDF officials were concerned about the possibility of harming noncombatants living near Shehadah. Moreover, on July 19, 2002, a mission in progress was called off (and jets ordered to turn back) because the IDF learned that Shehadah's daughter was with him in the target location. The mission of July 23 was carried out on the basis of what Israel assumed to be correct information that Shehadeh was not with his family at the time.

The IDF actions *leading up to* the attack of July 23 do demonstrate a concern to avoid killing noncombatants. However, there are two factors about this operation that make it morally unacceptable according to the principle of reasonable response. First, the plan of the operation—dropping a one-ton bomb on his building—suggests that there could not have been an attempt to apprehend Shehadeh, which would also have prevented him from planning or carrying out the operation that the Israelis had been warned of. The intent clearly was to incapacitate (that is, kill) Shehadeh, even though the conditions for this approach had not been met. Second, even if the IDF had good reason to believe that the building in which Shehadeh was located was empty of civilians (which turned out not to be true), there was also good reason to believe that dropping a one-ton bomb into a residential area would cause tremendous harm to noncombatants. Thus, due care was not taken to minimize bystander casualties. And since one could surely predict that the attack would cause noncombatants to suffer tremendously, one would have to argue that all those killed and harmed were in some way morally and criminally responsible for the actions of Shehadeh and his group. Absent evidence that Shehadeh's neighbors helped to carry out his plans or offered other material support, the only basis for such an argument is the claim that one can hold a group of people responsible for an action in virtue of who they are (i.e., their ethnicity or nationality). In addition to appealing to features of persons that are morally arbitrary, the argument would also serve to justify the terrorist activity that provoked the military response. Thus, although it's clear the IDF did not intend to kill noncombatants, the attack did not satisfy the principle of reasonable response. Furthermore, even if by some miracle no noncombatants had been killed and damage to the general well-being of noncombatants had been minimal, the fact that the IDF did not do all it could to minimize risk to noncombatants during the response compromised the long-term goal of preserving the possibility of meaningful negotiations.

VI. Conclusion

My aim in this paper was to develop a principle or set of conditions which if met would make a response against terrorists justifiable even when noncombatants are harmed or killed. While I think the principle can be usefully applied in many cases, there are surely those cases where the likelihood of causing significant harm to noncombatants would be too great to justify a response, even when all due care has been taken to avoid or minimize harm. I think these situations are rare, but when they do arise, a basically just government must be prepared to recognize them, pull back, and reevaluate their options.

Richard M. Buck, Mount Saint Mary's College

Notes

1. Michael Walzer, *Just and Unjust Wars* (New York: Basic Books, 1977), 218.

2. To mount a retributivist defense of a response that causes harm to those not involved (actively or in a supporting role) in the terrorist act, one would have to make the case that all those harmed are members of a group capable of collective action. But this would be to attribute responsibility in the same way that terrorists do—on the basis of a collective identity that cannot be avoided.

3. This is meant to be a definition of *contemporary* or recent terrorism (of the last thirty years). This kind of terrorist is to be distinguished from what Michael Walzer calls "professional revolutionaries" who engaged armed struggle against an existing government but observed a code that prohibited, among other things, the killing of ordinary citizens who were not engaged in the oppressive or otherwise harmful activities of the state. For a discussion of this distinction and examples of professional revolutionaries see *Just and Unjust Wars*, 199–201.

4. I do not mean to suggest that terrorists are not murderers. They are, but they are not simply murderers or killers because the killing is just one piece of a larger plan. A murder *simpliciter* has no end beyond the act of murder itself.

5. I also want to point out that in some cases one can reasonably argue that terrorists have no good reason to believe that they are in fact doing anything more than creating a climate of fear among the general population. I believe the current state of affairs in Israel is a good example of such a case. At least one of the main terrorist groups in play, Hamas, is openly opposed to any peace treaty with Israel. As I read this (fairly, I think), Hamas would not be content with the withdrawal of the IDF from all of the disputed territory

6. *Just and Unjust Wars*, 200.

7. The case was slightly different with Zeevi, as his attack was believed to be retaliation for the killing of a member of the PFLP.

8. I do not think that a just response requires the soldiers carrying out the response to be willing to take losses in order to avoid civilian casualties.

9. According to Allison Jaggar, this is the preferred option. See her "Responding to the Evil of Terrorism," *Hypatia* 18 (2003). I offer a critique of her view later in the essay.

10. *Just and Unjust Wars*, 44, 151.

11. I think this is implied in Walzer's principle.

12. According to this definition, anyone who aids terrorists by providing shelter, food, or other material support before or after an attack is considered a combatant.

13. See *Just and Unjust Wars*, 200.

14. I assume this principle would govern all military responses to terrorism, though the aim of the response might vary.

15. Ibid., 211. This would be a classical utilitarian position, though it's clear that some contemporary utilitarians would distance themselves from it.

16. Ibid., 212.

17. There are, of course, other reasons one may use in defense of the claim that the targeting of innocent civilians is immoral. The most obvious, which avoids the metaphysical snafus of human rights claims, is the dignity of the victims and the fact that in targeting innocent civilians, terrorists treat them as means rather than as ends. I will deploy this reason later in the essay when I argue against the view that one should negotiate with terrorists.

18. *Just and Unjust Wars*, 212.

19. Ibid., 216.

20. I cannot go into any detail here about how such a public justification of a response could be carried out. Suffice it to say that public justification of epistemological claims is a much more difficult task.

21. The following account of operation Defensive Shield is based on the following: Mark Oliver, "Israel Steps up Attacks," *The Guardian* (April 3 2002); Arieh O'Sullivan, "Three Soldiers Killed in Jenin," *Jerusalem Post* (April 7, 2002); Arieh O'Sullivan, "IDF Tightens hold on Jenin, Nablus," *The Jerusalem Post* (April 8, 2002); Oren Shahor, "Jenin Fighting Invites Casualties," *Jerusalem Post* (April 10, 2002); Matt Rees, "Untangling Jenin's Tale," *Time*, May 2002.

22. It will be important to distinguish between deaths that *occur* during the response (e.g., if a terrorist accidentally kills noncombatants) and deaths that are caused by some action of those conducting the response.

23. The following account of the IDF air strike in Gaza City is based on the following: "Israeli Jets attack Hamas," *The Guardian* (July 23, 2002); "12 Dead in Attack on Hamas," *The Guardian* (July 23, 2002); Janine Zacharia and Gil Hoffman, "US Condemns 'heavy-handed' Action," *Jerusalem Post* (July 24, 2002); Melissa Radler, "Security Council Rakes Israel for Hit," *Jerusalem Post* (July 26, 2002); David Rudge, "Shehadeh was Planning Mega-attack," *Jerusalem Post* (July 26, 2002).

Selective Disobedience on the Basis of Territory

OVADIA EZRA

Abstract: This paper presents the view of the Israeli "Refusal Movement" known as "Yesh-Gvul." This movement began when Israel started a war in Lebanon in 1982. Some Israeli reservists refused at the time to join in that war on the basis of the concept of *jus ad bellum*. In 1987, when the first Palestinian "Intifada" (uprising) began, the Yesh Gvul movement expanded the forms of disobedience it supported, and acknowledged the legitimacy of the refusal to do military service in the "occupied territories" and detention camps in which Palestinians were incarcerated. In 2000, when the second "Intifada" began, Yesh Gvul decided on an additional expansion of the forms of disobedience it supported in expanding the right of disobedience to those who totally refused to serve in the Israeli army. In this paper I want to present a more detailed defense of the justification of these three phases of disobedience that Yesh Gvul supports.

This paper deals with a unique version of civil disobedience that was developed in Israel during the last two decades. It refers to the refusal of reserve soldiers to perform certain military duties, where the main criterion according to which they obey or refuse orders is geographical. They refuse to perform military service in the occupied territories, and through this they combine their political protest against the occupation and their conscientious disobedience to any immoral or evil activities in which they may become involved as part of their task as soldiers in the occupied territories. The boundaries of this refusal were changed according political changes in Israel, and in this paper I follow these changes, both chronologically (from the refusal to take part in the war against Lebanon in 1982 to the refusal to be drafted into the Israeli Army in 2000) and theoretically (from selective disobedience to absolute refusal to be drafted to the Israeli army), and I present their political and moral justifications.

I. Historical Background Of The Idea Of Military Disobedience

Refusing to take part in military actions for reasons of conscience or politics has become familiar in democratic countries during the last two generations. The pacifist movement that gathered momentum after World War I created massive pacifist disobedience among specific religious as well as non-religious groups and individuals during World War II. Since it was widely assumed that the latter war was morally justified, the only moral reason which was regarded as acceptable for refusing to take part in that war was a reason of conscience.

During the late 1960s and early 1970s, refusing to take part in the Vietnam War received its justification on the basis of the norms for *jus ad bellum* (justice leading up to the war). The refusal of young people to join the army and serve as soldiers going to Vietnam was the result of their judgment that the government's decision to go to that war was unjustified, and that "the use of military resources of the United States in Vietnam and elsewhere suppressed the aspirations of the people for political independence and economic freedom."[1] Some soldiers who went to Vietnam refused specific orders given to them on the basis of the norms for *jus in bello* (justice in the course of warfare). This time the refusal was the result of the soldiers' objection to the way that this war was being conducted by the United States. In any event, both manners of judging the morality of war raised arguments and reasons for justifying non-participation in military actions or for refusing to obey certain orders during wartime.

II. The Refusal To Take Part In The War Against Lebanon (1982)

In the current discussion I want to present the view of the Israeli "Refusal Movement" known as "Yesh-Gvul" ("there is a limit" or "there is a frontier," since the Hebrew word "Gvul" means both). This movement started—as in the case of Vietnam—when Israel started a war in Lebanon in 1982. Some Israeli reservists (including myself) refused at that time to join in that war on the basis of the norms for *jus ad bellum*; in our opinion, the reasons for declaring that war were not sufficient, and hence, that war was an unjust war, in which we refused to participate.

Disobedience on the basis of *jus ad bellum* can be justified insofar as it "requires that we make judgments about aggression and self-defense."[2] A just war can be considered legitimate when its aim is to protect the state from external attack or to avoid aggression that may impose an existential danger on the defending state. Reserve soldiers who established Yesh-Gvul thought that none of these justifications was applicable for justifying the Israeli invasion into the state of Lebanon. In a manner similar to that of U.S. soldiers who refused to go to Vietnam, Israeli soldiers who are not pacifists and usually serve as reservists in fighting units regarded the international border as their limit, and they refused to serve beyond it.

The justification for their refusal resulted both from internal reasons and from international reasons. The internal reasons were based on the fact that the Israeli military forces were used, for the first time in Israel's history, for purposes that could not be considered as self-defense. Beside this violation of what Michael

Walzer calls "the logic of war" (with reference to the moral conventions and norms of wars), those who refused to serve thought that the Israeli government thereby endangered the consensus regarding the legitimacy of the army and of military service in Israel as a whole. Using the army for aggression, occupation of territories and violation of the sovereignty of another state were not part of the consensus about the legitimate reasons for using the Israeli Defense Forces.

The reasons of an international nature for refusing to take part in the Lebanese war were connected with the infringement of the respect for the sovereignty of the Lebanese government and the Lebanese people and the respect due to the freedom of the Lebanese citizens and their rights to self-determination, freedom and autonomy. Another reason for the refusal to serve in Lebanon was a respect for the UN decisions calling for Israel to immediately withdraw from Lebanese territory. These decisions were ignored by the Israeli government.

In any event the refusal to take part in the war in Lebanon was basically political and fulfilled the acknowledged requirements of civil disobedience. First and foremost, those who refused considered their act as "a non-revolutionary encounter with the state."[3] This means that they did not challenge the legitimacy of the legal or the political system as a whole but only a certain part of it, namely the decision to occupy Lebanon. Second, their act was not violent in any way. Being non-violent, their act "expressed disobedience to law within the limits of fidelity to law, although it is the outer edge thereof."[4] They expressed their fidelity to the law in another way, i.e., "by the willingness to accept the legal consequences of one's conduct."[5] In addition, their act was public and was a consequence of political considerations, not of self-interested reasons or reasons of convenience. They stressed that the aim of their disobedience was to bring about a change in the policy of the government, and that their act was addressed to the public principles and public sense of justice. In this sense we can say that the refusal to serve in the Lebanese war was a clear act of civil disobedience and followed the conventions of such an act that were formed and developed in the discussions about the Vietnam War. The refusal to serve in Lebanon was not innovative or novel, either conceptually or ideologically. Even though there was selective disobedience on the basis of territory in the Lebanese war, one can consider this disobedience—again like the Vietnam case—as justified according to the accepted norms for *jus ad bellum*.

III. The Refusal To Perform Military Service In The Occupied Territories (1987)

In 1987, when the first Palestinian "Intifada" (uprising) began, the Yesh Gvul movement expanded the forms of disobedience it supported, and it acknowledged the legitimacy of the refusal to do military service in the "occupied territories" and in the detention camps in which Palestinians were incarcerated. Those soldiers who refused to serve in the occupied territories made their refusal on a geographic basis alone. They considered the international border before the Six Day War as the limit beyond which they would not serve. They were willing to do any military service within this border. However, they also refused to serve as guards or as wardens in detention camps where Palestinian prisoners were imprisoned, whether these camps were inside or outside the international borders.

The grounds for justifying these refusals were both moral and political. The moral aspect was associated with the injustice involved in denying political freedom to millions of Arab residents even after twenty years of occupation. Here, again, their position was similar to the Declaration Of Conscience Against The War in Vietnam, which stated that "all people of the earth, including both Americans and non-Americans, have an inalienable right to life, liberty and the peaceful pursuit of happiness in their own way."[6] The political reason was the desire to influence both the government and public opinion to put an end to the occupation.

If we look for an ordinary justification for a refusal on the basis of territory, we can apply *jus in bello* constraints. *Jus in bello* requires us to make judgments "about the observance or violation of the customary and positive rules of engagement."[7] Considering the requirements of *jus in bello*, those who refused to serve in the occupied territories could say that the means by which the occupation—as a state of war—was conducted were considered to be morally unjustifiable. However, this will not cover the whole story, since many of those who refused and still refuse to serve in the occupied territories refuse to do any kind of military service in those territories, even duties which do not involve contact with the civilian population. For example, as a medical orderly who is sometimes required to take care of the injuries to Palestinians as part of his duty, I refuse to take part in any activity connected with the military involvement in the occupied territories, since I consider it as serving the occupation in a certain way. Hence I refuse even to go to the territories as a soldier. So the point here is mainly connected to the fact that the territory where I refuse to serve is occupied, and not necessarily with the way the occupation is conducted. The geographical considerations play a significant role in the decision whether or not to do military service within a certain area.

The assumption that a certain area is occupied, and the moral belief that no one should deny anyone else's freedom or autonomy and that no nation has the right to negate another nation's right to self-determination, all jointly imply the placing of specific restrictions on one's actions or involvement in this area. These restrictions are established by the requirement for consistency in one's actions. I believe that taking part in the military action taking place in these territories is actually and physically carrying out the occupation, and hence it is striking at the Palestinians' rights to freedom, authority and self-determination. One cannot object to and politically resist the continued occupation for the rest of the year, and then serve for one month of reserve military service in the occupied territories and in effect acting as the subjugator. Such a position is inconsistent with and sometimes even opposed to a good conscience. If one holds a certain position, such as objecting to the occupation of certain area, he/she must follow the required conclusions of his/her position. In this case, this means that he/she will refuse to carry out the occupation, especially by the most substantial and concrete expression of the occupation: military service.

This conclusion can be derived from another consideration connected to consistency. The conjunction of one's objection to the occupation of territory and to the denial of people's freedom and liberty, and the Golden Rule, should lead the one who holds such a position to refuse to perform any military service in the territories. One who will not tolerate living himself under occupation should not do to others what he will not allow others to do to him. Considering all human beings as equal and acknowledging their rights to equal treatment and their rights to treatment as equals should convince him/her not to be their subjugator. In answer to the question whether one wants everyone else in the same situation to act the way one does, the answer is "Yes!" He/she can generalize the maxim that commands him/her not to take part in acts that violate others' freedom, even at the cost of his/her personal freedom. In the case that the authorities who wish to use him/her in order to violate the freedom of the occupied civilians now use force against him/her and violate his/her freedom, he/she does nothing but express solidarity with the victim. Here the choice is not between victimizing the other and victimizing oneself but between victimizing the other and being victimized by a third party. Morally speaking, the latter is the correct choice, since in this case the moral blame rests on the third party and not on the victim.

With regard to military service that is not in the territories (that is within the borders of Israel before the Six-Day War) those who are not pacifists will agree to perform most military tasks, except that of serving as guards and wardens in prisons where Palestinian prisoners of war are incarcerated—for the same reasons that they refuse to serve in "the big prison" of the occupied territories themselves. In such a case one may ask what is the difference between being the actual or concrete subjugator on one hand, and on the other hand being part of the army whose other soldiers who could have been replaced by those who serve within the international border (and thus are available to go to the territories) are the subjugators? This question points directly to the uniqueness of the idea of selective disobedience on the basis of territory. The person who is not a pacifist can ask him/herself whether the specific task one is being asked to fulfill contradicts his/her conscience or moral principles, and whether the performance of this task can be morally justified. In case he/she believes that it is necessary to maintain the army, for example for reasons of the nation's self-defense, and his/her fulfillment of that specific task is coherent and consistent with the requirements of the nation's self-defense, one should perform that task. Refusing to take part in any military action (which does not carry out the occupation) while expecting others to fulfill that task will not be fair towards those who do serve, and the person who refuses to perform that task can be considered as "a free rider." In this case one will be violating the Golden Rule while expecting others to do what he/she should not do. One also cannot generalize the maxim that tells him/her not to serve while he/she still thinks that the service is necessary. If everyone will follow that maxim, the aim that justifies the performance of that task will not be achieved, and in the event that the aim is self-defense, the aim that will not be achieved may even be the survival of the state. The most complicated question is what to do when one who is not pacifist thinks that every military task in which he/she may be involved serves the occupation in one way or another. This dilemma will be discussed towards the end of this paper in the presentation of the third stage of the Yesh-Gvul position.

However, there is also the political aim of the public act of military disobedience. On the personal level it expresses a feeling of obligation in accordance with Martin Luther's bold and defiant declaration: "here I stand; I can do no other."[8] This, in effect, says that the person who refuses will not tolerate either the continuing violation of human rights by his government or the world's silence about it. The one who refuses protests loudly and clearly in front of the other citizens and declares that he/she is not anymore taking part in what he considers to be a crime. He also appeals to world public opinion, saying that their act of ignoring the continuous violation of the Security Council decisions regarding the end of the occupation imposes a certain amount of responsibility for this injustice on their part. However, such an act has also its meaning and significance in the internal public sphere. Its aim is to bring about a change in the government's policy, and to encourage it to end the occupation. In this sense it is not only a protest; it is also an attempt to influence the politicians and bring them to reconsider the moral and political aspects of the occupation, with the hope that this will cause them to reassess the moral and political costs and implications of the continued occupation.

But the public act of military disobedience has also a hidden message. The refusal is carried out only after the normal appeals to the political majority have been made in good faith and have failed. The legal means of changing the government's policy have proven to be of no avail. Attempts to have that policy changed, as well as legal protests and demonstrations against the occupation, have had no success. All the legal means have been exhausted, and since the minority (which is opposed to the state's current policy) considers the state to have convicted itself of wantonly unjust and overtly hostile aims,[9] it cannot anymore expect us to acquiesce indefinitely to the terms it imposes upon us.[10] We now appeal to our last resort: disobedience. According to Martin Luther King, Jr., this is supposed to be the fourth and final step of any nonviolent campaign, i.e., direct action. (The three steps prior to this are collection of the facts to determine whether injustices exist, negotiation, and self-purification).[11]

However, in the event that the policy will not be changed we also warn the state that others may join us in our disobedience, since the principles and values which justify our defiance are shared by many more who, although still dutifully but reluctantly obeying, will hopefully not continue to do so forever. Such an expectation that others would follow the act of disobedience was expressed by Henry David Thoreau, when he was arrested for civil disobedience in July, 1846. According to the legend Emerson came to visit him and asked: "Henry why are you there?" In response Thoreau asked: "Waldo, why are you out there, and not in here?"[12] We believe that besides being committed to these values and principles, those people are also committed to us, and once we have crossed the line and breached the law, they will not leave us to pay alone the price of drawing public attention to the injustice involved with the continued occupation. They may reach the conclusion that the occupied territories are beyond the borders of the consensus, upon which Israeli society has been established. Many other people may follow Martin Luther King and declare, "We will not obey unjust laws or submit to unjust practices we are ready to suffer when necessary and even risk our lives to become witnesses to the truth as we see it."[13] This, we hope, will disturb and concern the authorities, who still wish such a consensus to continue to exist. They have to take into account the fact that the occupation is undermining the legitimacy of the Israeli government and its institutions, which may be left with the support of only a small part of the population.

IV. The (Absolute) Refusal To Be Drafted To The Israeli Army (2000)

The second "Intifada" which started in 2000 brought members of Yesh Gvul to consider an additional expansion of the forms of disobedience it supports and to decide to expand the legitimacy of disobedience also to those who refuse to serve in the Israeli army at all. Yesh Gvul now recognizes such a refusal, whether it results from pacifist or other moral reasons (such as freedom of conscience or political motives) as falling under the rubric of a respect for the desire of an individual not to play any part in an army which is involved in war crimes. Those who now refuse to do any kind of military service in Israel claim that so long as the occupation is continued, being in any way part of the army serves the occupation in one way or another. The fact that the occupation has already lasted for 36 years, with no sign that there will be a change in the government's attitude towards it, causes people who object to the occupation to escalate their nonviolent confrontation with the authorities. They realize that the hidden message of those who refused to serve in the occupied territories has not been received by the government. Sixteen years of refusing to serve in these territories have not affected the government's policy, and the brutality of the occupation has even been exacerbated.

At the heart of the decision to escalate and expand the range of disobedience is the assumption that the new form of the Israeli occupation, in the attempt to crush the Palestinian uprising, transgressed many moral borders and constraints. In order to reduce potential damage and injury of Israeli soldiers, the Israeli army started to use a strategy of excessive striking power. For example, it initiated the use of fighter planes and helicopters to kill militant or armed Palestinians. These weapons are indiscriminate, inevitably killing or injuring many innocent bystanders in addition to the main target (e.g., the 1000 kg bomb that killed a Hamas leader also killed 15 civilians, including 9 children). Another method is the use of bulldozers to demolish houses where suspected armed Palestinians may hide. This definitely saves the lives of Israeli soldiers, but it destroys the lives and hopes of the Palestinians who live nearby, who lose their houses as well. Those bulldozers are also used to uproot many orchards and trees within which Palestinians could hide in the attempt to attack Israeli targets. Another way of reducing Israeli damage is the expropriation and forfeiture of Palestinian houses that can be used by the army for observation posts or for controlling the area. They also expropriate and forfeit Palestinian land in order to build the wall of separation that may make it more difficult for terrorists to enter Israel. However, this wall also separates children from their schools, farmers from their land, and people from their clinics and hospitals. All these steps are not compatible with the requirements of just war theory that demand the proportionality in the use of power and the immunity of civilians and their property. More importantly, they do not fulfill the moral demand to respect the life and welfare of innocent people who are not involved in terror or crime.

Those who found this new strategy of the Israeli army immoral, or even unjust in terms of a just war theory, decided that what is required is a change in their strategy, which involves escalating their struggle. They therefore concluded that leaving the protest at the same level, i.e., refusing to do military service only in the occupied territories, cannot be effective any longer, as it only continues the current unbearable situation. Hence, they have expanded the range of their refusal to any sort of military service. By doing so, they challenge not only the legitimacy of the occupation but also the legitimacy of being part of military forces involved in a continuous violation of both human rights and the Security Council decisions. They claim that any contribution to the military forces inevitably supports, or at least involves complicity with, the occupation, and hence it should be considered to be illegitimate.

This claim challenges the idea of selective disobedience on the basis of territory, since the refusal to military service is here absolute, and does not result from pacifist considerations. Here those who disobey refuse to do any military task, even within Israel, on territory which is undisputed. Without the occupation they would agree to do such military tasks, but since they believe that in the current situation they help the Israeli army whose legitimacy in the current situation they deny, they refuse to join the army. Here we should inquire into the question whether there is any need for the army other than for carrying out the occupation. A negative answer to this question cancels the dilemma, since even the disbanding of the army as a whole will still be consistent and coherent with the principles, goals and ends of the person who refuses to join the army. Unfortunately, this is not true in the Israeli case, and the issue of the legitimacy of joining the army requires further considerations.

Thus, if one believes that there is still a need for the existence of military forces, but the use of most of these forces in most cases is morally wrong, he/she should inquire into the question of personal responsibility for a nation's actions and for the nation's maintenance. The first issue refers to the question of the extent to which one can be responsible for his/her nation's actions. Of course, one is responsible for his/her personal actions, and hence, when one is directly involved in performing war crimes he/she bears the full responsibility. However, this is the extreme case, where the circle of responsibility is the most inner and includes the direct and immediate agent who acts. Hence, this is the easiest and clearest case to deal with. One should not be involved in war crimes in any way, under no circumstance. The wider circle of responsibility is when one is indirectly involved with war crimes or other immoral actions, for example by acting as a guard or soldier in an area where others—belonging to his/her army or even to the same military unit—are involved in immoral actions. In this case the idea of selective disobedience on the basis of territory means that the extent of responsibility this person bears is high enough to justify disobedience. Thus those who think that participating in military actions in the occupied territories imposes a certain amount of responsibility on their part, which can put at least part of the blame on what is going on in the territories upon them, will not serve in the territories in any military task at all.[14]

Now, there is another claim, which is that when one is serving in the army, even if not in the territories, he/she belongs to the same army which is involved in immoral actions and thus, even if indirectly is responsible for the consequences of these actions. Such a claim can even be supported by the claim that by serving *within* the international border, the one who does so enables the army to send someone else to the territories, someone who would otherwise have had to fulfill the task inside the international border (which has now been performed by the one who refuses to go to the territories).

This claim has to be carefully considered since if one considers the military service in the occupied territory to be morally wrong, and, even indirectly, this person's service within the international borders enables the army to send someone else to fulfill the immoral task. Such a person bears, at least partly, the responsibility for what he/she considers to be immoral. It is not quite clear that the extent of responsibility that justifies disobedience ends at the direct embodiment of the occupation (i.e., by physically serving in the territories), as the idea of selective disobedience assumes. It is clear that the person who does not go to the territories is less responsible for what happens there, but it is doubtful whether he/she is not responsible for them to the extent that that should guide him/her to refuse to any military service at all.

The idea of selective disobedience can answer this question in two different ways, even though both answers are not decisive. The first answer refers to the question of the chain of reasons whose conjunction imposes accountability on the person who does not him/herself serve in the territories, but only enables the army to send another soldier instead of him/her. A closer look at the chain of reasons, at the end of which the soldier decides not go to the territories, shows that in its middle there is the decision of the person who finally went to the territories, and this decision imposes the indirect accountability upon the person who did not. This means that we actually impose accountability on the one who does not go to the territories, due to someone else's decision or choice. If the one who did go to the territories would have refused as well, the one who refused in the first place would not bear any responsibility for immoral actions. However, this is only a partial answer, and I doubt if it is sufficient to convince the person who believes that the circle of responsibility to the military actions in the territories includes any sort of military service. This is because there will always be found a soldier who will after all go to the territories, and his/her possibility of going there was indirectly created by the one who served inside the international borders.

The second answer the idea of selective disobedience can give to the above claim relates to a wider issue regarding the responsibility of the individual for his nation's action. One can say that even those who do not go the army at all still contribute to the occupation by paying taxes to the government, which sends the army to the territories and covers the expanses of the occupation. According to this claim everyone who pays taxes to the occupying state is in some sense and to a certain extent responsible for the immoral actions done by the state's army. Such a position was held by Henry David Thoreau, for example who decided not to pay his poll tax because he did not want "to support a government which was engaged in unjust war (with Mexico) and which upheld the institutionalized practice of slavery."[15] This wide circle of responsibility imposes responsibility, accountability and blame—at least to a certain extent—even on those who are not citizens (for example residents who did not vote for that government, but work and pay taxes in that state—even if only VAT—Value Added Tax). Through this reasoning the circle of responsibility imposes responsibility even on those who object to the policy of the government but still pay taxes (even if not voluntarily, for example when their income tax is deducted directly by their employer, or when the VAT is included in the price of anything they buy—including food). Expanding the idea, one who helps to finance the occupation in any way imposes responsibility even on those who buy products from the occupying country, since the companies which produce these products pay taxes to the state's government (which can be used for financing the occupation).

This means that if we expand the circle of responsibility, according to the idea that any indirect contribution to the occupation imposes a responsibility on the one who supports the occupying state or its government, we can get into absurd or impossible situations, such as blaming most of the world for the occupation. This is because most of the countries buy products from or sell products to Israel, and the VAT, which is paid for these products by those who buy them, supports the occupation. In such a case, when we consider the whole world as responsible for the occupation, we cannot distinguish between those who are directly involved with war crimes and those who are remotely or passively involved. The measure of responsibility on each party will become obscure and vague, and may blur any moral blame or responsibility. Thus, those who hold the idea of selective disobedience think that the circle of responsibility that can justify disobedience should include only those who do military service in the occupied territories, and physically carry out the occupation.

However, those who do not go to the army at all can say that such a decision about the correct circle of responsibility is somewhat arbitrary and definitely cannot be accurate. The extent to which every soldier contributes the occupation is hard to measure since, for example, those who belong to the air intelligence and give instructions to the fighter pilots who bomb targets in the territories are almost as responsible as the pilots themselves (not to mention that the home bases of these pilots are not in the territories at all, even though their mission is in the territories). The difficulty to point at the exact measure of responsibility to military actions done by the army in the territories causes people who deny the possibility of serving in the army without contributing to the occupation to refuse to go to the army for any mission. This follows Henry David Thoreau's idea saying, " it is not a man's duty, as a matter of course, to devote himself to the eradication of any, even the most enormous wrong; he may still properly have other concerns to engage him, but it is his duty, at least, to wash his hands of it, and, if he gives it no thought longer, not to give it practically his support."[16]

In any event, those people who do not go to the army at all, and refuse to do any military service, make sure that their act remains within the limits of civil disobedience and does not deteriorate into a revolutionary act.[17] This means that their act remains "an act of protest, deliberately unlawful, conscientiously and publicly performed" and "invariably nonviolent in character."[18]

Considering themselves to be still part of Israeli society, those who have to do compulsory service have therefore requested a civilian alternative to military service, in order to bear their fair share and not to enjoy any advantage compared to those who do go to the army. Their request has so far been rejected, and all they are offered is the option of either going to the army or going to prison. As a reply to this offer, they follow Herbert Marcuse's quotation of Maurice Blanchot, in the last pages of the book *One Dimensional Man*, about the Great Refusal:

> What we refuse is not without value or importance. Precisely because of that, the refusal is necessary. There is a reason which we no longer accept, there is an appearance of wisdom which horrifies us, there is a plea for agreement and conciliation which we will no longer heed. A break has occurred. We have been reduced to that frankness which no longer tolerates complicity.[19]

Ovadia Ezra, Tel Aviv University

Notes

1. "Declaration Of Conscience Against The War In Vietnam," in *Civil Disobedience*, ed. Hugo Adam Bedau (Indianapolis and New York: Pegasus, 1969), 160.

2. Michael Walzer, *Just And Unjust Wars* (New York: Basic Books, Inc, Publishers, 1977), 21.

3. Michael Walzer, *Obligations: Essays On Disobedience, War And Citizenship* (Cambridge, Massachusetts: Harvard University Press, 1970), 24.

4. John Rawls, *A Theory Of Justice* (Oxford: Oxford University Press, 1972) (paperback), 366.

5. Ibid.

6. "Declaration Of Conscience Against The War In Vietnam," 160.

7. Walzer, *Just And Unjust Wars*, 21.

8. Quote is taken from Walzer, *Obligations*, 3.

9. See Rawls, 373.

10. Ibid, 383.

11. These steps are mentions in Martin Luther King, Jr.'s "Letter from Birmingham Jail," taken from Jonathan S. Bass, *Blessed Are The Peacemakers* (Louisiana State University Press, 2002, paperback edition), 239.

12. This citation is taken from Mark Stephen Howenstein, *The Moral Limits of Legal Obligation: Contrasting Conceptions of Civil Disobedience from Freedom to Necessity*. 1993. A dissertation submitted to the University of California at Berkeley. UMI dissertation service, 228.

13. This is a citation from Dr. King's speech in Oslo, when he accepted the Nobel Peace Price, 1964. It was published in the *New York Times*, 12 December 1964. The current quote

is taken from Carl Cohen, *Civil Disobedience* (New York and London: Columbia University Press, 1971), 40.

14. Hugo Adam Bedau proposes a principle to measure a person's responsibility to his/her government's acts. He suggests that "a person becomes responsible for the acts of another (person, government) if and only if (and to the degree that) he (a) has authorized the other to act, or (b) he has enabled that other to act, (c) knows how that other has used his position and authority to act, and (d) he continues to do (a) and (b), i.e., he does not act to revoke the authority granted or to prevent its abuse. See: Hugo Adam Bedau, "Civil Disobedience And Personal Responsibility For Injustice," in *Civil Disobedience In Focus*, ed. Hugo Adam Bedau (London and New York: Routledge, 1991), 61.

15. This citation is taken from Howenstein, 228.

16. Henry David Thoreau, "Civil Disobedience," in Bedau, *Civil Disobedience* (1963), 33.

17. On the difference between civil disobedience and revolution see Cohen, 42–48.

18. This definition is taken from Cohen, 40–41, but its principles are shared by most theorists of this issue.

19. Herbert Marcuse, *One Dimensional Man* (London: Routledge & Kegan Paul Ltd, 1964), 256 (n).

Part II:
Terrorist Motivations, Democracy, and Human Rights

Terrorism and the *Root Causes* Argument

ALISTAIR M. MACLEOD

Abstract: Without attempting a full-scale definition of "terrorism," I assume (for the purposes of the argument of the paper) (1) that terrorist acts are politically motivated, (2) that the political goals of terrorists are both diverse and (morally) a "mixed bag," (3) that terrorist acts inflict deliberate harm on innocent civilians, and (4) that they are therefore to be condemned even when the goals they ostensibly serve are defensible goals. The various versions of the "root causes" argument seek to *explain* the phenomenon of terrorism, not to *justify* it. Nevertheless, anti-terrorism strategists must take these explanations seriously and be prepared to adopt a suitably broad view of the causal factors that may be involved. Exclusive concentration on the motives of terrorists is a mistake. Also important, for example, are the attitudes of (non-terrorist) members of populations in which there is sympathy for the goals of terrorists without any endorsement of their methods.

I. Introduction

The recent 9/11 terrorist attacks in the United States have led to a so-called "war" against terrorism in which little attention seems to have been paid to the question of the "root causes" of terrorism. Indeed, the question itself has often been indignantly rejected. Those who have dared to raise it are often depicted as unacceptably "soft" on terrorism. They have been routinely represented—misrepresented, I shall claim—as unwilling to condemn terrorist acts as roundly as they deserve to be condemned. Charges of these kinds are based on regrettable misunderstandings of the "root causes" argument. The misunderstandings are regrettable because, correctly interpreted, the argument has an indispensable role to play in the fashioning of effective strategies to combat the threat of terrorism.

I shall try to sidestep the controversies that swirl around the proper definition of "terrorism." Two clarificatory remarks, though, are perhaps worth making.

The first is that the many correct uses of the term are probably best understood, following Wittgenstein, as forming a "family" the members of which exhibit resemblances of different (but overlapping) kinds.[1] It is consequently not to be expected that necessary and sufficient conditions will be specifiable for its application in all contexts.[2]

The second remark is that the sorts of terrorism relevant to the argument of the paper can be identified (at least approximately) by noting four of the assumptions I shall be making.

(1) The first assumption is that "terrorist" acts are *politically motivated*. By this I mean that the perpetrators of such acts view them as instrumental to the achievement of political goals of some sort. Innocuous—and seemingly unchallengeable—though this assumption is, its significance is sometimes ignored, perhaps in the belief that unqualified denunciations of terrorism might be endangered if attention were to be given to the underlying objectives of terrorists. Jean-Bethke Elshtain comes very close to contesting the assumption in her recent book, *Just War Against Terror*.[3] In a section of the first chapter entitled "What is a Terrorist?" she writes that "[the word] *terrorist* is twisted beyond recognition if it is used to designate anyone anywhere fighting for a cause."[4] She adds, in a second passage (a page or so later), that "[t]errorists are not interested in the subtleties of diplomacy or in compromise solutions. They have taken leave of politics. Sometimes elements of movements that resort to terrorism—say, the Irish Republican Army—may also develop a political arm and begin negotiating a political solution. No political solution is possible, however, when the terrorism is aimed at the destruction of innocent civilians—*when that itself is the goal*"[5] (emphasis supplied).

Now there is perhaps a way of reading the first of Elshtain's claims—the claim that the term "terrorist" is being misused when it is applied to people who are "fighting for a cause"—that does *not* challenge the assumption that terrorist acts are conceived by their perpetrators as instrumental to the achievement of a political goal of some kind. Thus the use might be open to objection because "fighting for a cause" is not a *sufficient* condition of being a "terrorist." There are, after all, lots of ways of "fighting for a cause" that do not involve resort to terrorism. This is true enough, but the very obviousness of the point casts doubt on the suggestion that this is what Elshtain has in mind. Moreover, the vehemence with which she dismisses the use to which she is objecting—the term is being "twisted beyond recognition," she writes—would be difficult to understand if she were simply setting to one side so *obviously* indefensible a definition. It is difficult to imagine anyone not realizing that "mounting a terrorist campaign" is a rather special case of "fighting for a cause." On the more interesting question whether "fighting for a cause"—striving to achieve an important political goal—is normally an essential part of what "terrorists" must be supposed to be up to when they plan, or execute, "terrorist" strikes, Elshtain's answer seems to be equivocal at best. What she says in the passage quoted strongly suggests that she would *not* be prepared to concede that "fighting for a cause" is normally a necessary condition of being a "terrorist"—that is, that normally a "terrorist" must be seen, *among other things*, as someone who resorts to terrorist acts in pursuit of a political goal of some sort.

The preferred interpretation of the second passage that I quoted from Elshtain's book is also rather difficult to pin down. On the one hand, she is conceding that a terrorist organization sometimes has a "political arm" through which a negotiated political solution may be sought. This clearly presupposes that such organizations *are* "fighting for a cause"—that is, that they have political goals of some sort that they are committed to trying to achieve. Yet, on the other hand, Elshtain represents terrorists as having "taken leave of politics" and as *aiming* (sic) at "the destruction of innocent civilians." The passage closes with the claim that "the destruction of innocent civilians" is "itself" *the goal*. This last claim shows part of what is at stake in trying to determine whether terrorist acts ought normally to be regarded as politically motivated acts. Elshtain's view—and it is a view that surfaces at various junctures in her book—seems to be that terrorists kill innocent civilians because that is, for them, an end in itself, not because it is instrumental to the achievement of a political objective of some kind.[6]

(2) There is a second assumption I shall be making—one that is closely related to the assumption that acts of terrorism must normally be seen to be politically motivated. It has two parts. The first is that the political goals that motivate terrorists may be of many different sorts. The second is that it is a mistake to think that they are all evil. On the contrary, when the goals in question are subjected to moral scrutiny, some turn out to be clearly defensible, others clearly indefensible, and yet others problematic or controversial.

Consider, first, the diversity of the political goals pursued by terrorist organizations. The Tamil Tigers in Sri Lanka, for example, want (or at any rate, wanted until very recently[7]) to form their own independent state. Hindu Nationalists want an end to India's secular constitutional arrangements. Some Palestinian suicide-bombers want to force the Israeli government to withdraw its forces from the West Bank and to dismantle illegal settlements. The terrorist campaign waged over several decades by the Irish Republican Army was designed to secure the incorporation of Northern Ireland into the Irish Republic, while the aim of the terrorist campaign sponsored by Ulster Protestant extremists was to ensure that Northern Ireland remained part of the United Kingdom. Various terrorist groups in Latin America in the 1960s and 1970s wanted to rid their societies of oppressive dictatorial regimes. And so on.

I also suggested that the political goals terrorists can be presumed to be pursuing may be good, bad, or indifferent and that it is consequently a mistake to think that it is a defining feature of terrorist acts that the goals they are ostensibly designed to serve are evil. Of course, terrorists may sometimes be subject to condemnation *both* because of the ends they are pursuing *and* because of the lengths to which they are prepared to go in the selection of means to those ends. But it is important to allow for the possibility that the goal they are pursuing is an unobjectionable (perhaps even a worthy) goal. When this is the case, there may still be a decisive moral objection to terrorism, but it will have to be seen as an objection only to the means being adopted in pursuit of the desired goal.

In the examples I have just cited to illustrate the great variety there is in what terrorists hope to achieve by terrorist campaigns, the objectives are quite a mixed bag. On the one hand, some are quite clearly morally defensible, and others, equally clearly, morally objectionable. Ridding societies of oppressive but powerful dictatorships, for example, is an uncontroversially desirable objective, while changing constitutional arrangements with a view to sanctioning religious intolerance is a morally objectionable objective. On the other hand, there are objectives that are not assessable either as clearly defensible or as clearly indefensible. For example, keeping Northern Ireland within the United Kingdom and establishing an independent Tamil state in Sri Lanka are objectives about which—notoriously—there is apt to be deep disagreement, even among reasonable people.

Recognizing that terrorists generally have political goals they want to achieve when they resort to terrorist acts and recognizing that the goals may sometimes be morally unobjectionable does not require it to be supposed—needless to say—that the end justifies the means. Indeed, as has already been noted, the basis for condemnation of acts of terrorism does not simply evaporate in cases where it can be shown that the goals being pursued are morally defensible. On the contrary, recognition of the worthiness of a goal can be combined, without the slightest inconsistency, with emphatic condemnation of the means adopted.

(3) It has to be admitted, however, that once terrorist acts are seen as having, in the eyes of their perpetrators, merely *instrumental* value, the question is bound to arise whether there are ever circumstances in which resort to terrorism might be thought to be morally *defensible*. This brings me to the third assumption underlying my discussion—which is that I want in this paper to bypass this controversial question as well. Thus, I shall make no effort to determine whether terrorism might be thought to be defensible when some demonstrably horrendous injustice cannot be eliminated without resort to acts of terrorism. Consider, for example, the role terrorist acts might play in a slave-owning society in inducing slave-owners to free their slaves. I shall simply assume that terrorist acts, in all the circumstances relevant to my discussion, are morally wrong—wrong, indeed, without qualification.

(4) A fourth assumption I shall make is that "terrorist" acts are acts that cause deliberate harm—generally, grievous harm—to *innocent civilians*.[8] I shall not try to determine, consequently, what is to be said about the characterization of politically motivated acts that involve the destruction of public or private property—of oil refineries or public monuments, for example—when care is taken not to endanger human life. I shall also not try to classify acts of politically motivated violence that target government officials or military personnel, when injury (or worse) to innocent civilians is studiously avoided.

II. Relieving Terrorists of Blame Is Not the Issue

It is to misinterpret the intended force of the "root causes" argument to suppose that it is designed either to protect terrorist acts and their perpetrators from moral condemnation or to suggest that the condemnation ought to be heavily qualified.[9] Sponsors of the various versions of the "root causes" argument are endeavoring to get clear about what might serve to *explain* or *account for* terrorism as a complex socio-political phenomenon. Their interest is *not* in the normative questions that would have to be dealt with in the course of setting out in detail just why there is so powerful a moral objection to terrorist acts and why, consequently, it is so difficult even to imagine situations in which this objection might be thought to be overridden.

Since the thrust of the "root causes" argument is explanatory and not normative, it is disconcerting to find how frequently the proper allocation of blame for terrorist acts is thought to be what is at stake in the discussion of "root causes." Those who exhibit an interest in the "root causes" of terrorist acts are not infrequently taken to be committed to exonerating the perpetrators as well as those who helped in the planning of the acts.[10]

However, the charge is thoroughly groundless. As has already been noted, to take an interest in the "root causes" of terrorism is to be committed to determining the merits of various approaches to the *explanation* of terrorism, whereas blame-allocation questions are a small and notoriously problematic sub-class of the many *normative* questions posed by terrorism. Of course normative questions of various sorts do indeed arise once we have before us plausible hypotheses about the "root causes" of terrorism. They arise simply because questions have to be faced about the appropriateness of the various policies that may have to be adopted if terrorism, seen in the light of these hypotheses, is to be effectively countered. However, it is obviously neither the case that these normative questions are themselves questions about "root causes" nor that the answers to them can be inferred from hypotheses about "root causes." For example, if it turned out to be the case that terrorists and their supporters are to some degree simply ignorant of the actual attitudes and motives of those whom they regard as "the enemy," normative questions would of course have to be faced by the architects of anti-terrorist strategies about how to set about combating this sort of ignorance. Yet such questions would clearly not themselves be questions about the "root causes" of terrorism, nor could the appropriateness of the required anti-terrorism strategies be regarded as mere corollaries of the hypothesis that "ignorance" plays a role in generating terrorist acts.

III. Getting Clear about the Motives of Terrorists is Not Enough

Even when the "root causes" argument is seen (correctly) as part of an attempt to explain, rather than to justify, terrorism, its force is often misconstrued through sponsorship of an excessively narrow view of its intended scope. Thus, it is to interpret the argument too narrowly to suppose that it directs attention—either exclusively, or principally—to the reasons for which *the terrorists themselves* have actually committed this or that terrorist act.[11] Questions about the beliefs, desires and dispositions of the perpetrators of terrorist acts (and questions, too, about the beliefs, desires and dispositions of the individuals or groups directly implicated in the planning of such acts) no doubt have their own importance in any serious attempt to understand the nature of the threat terrorism poses. However, exclusive (or disproportionate) emphasis on these questions can help to obscure the importance of broader causal factors that the "root causes" argument is also designed to highlight.[12]

A striking recent example of almost exclusive reliance on too narrow a version of the "root causes" argument is to be found in the recent book by Jean-Bethke Elshtain[13] to which reference has already been made. Elshtain recognizes, in her discussion of the reasons for the 9/11 attack, that getting clear about the motives of the Al Qaeda terrorists is crucial to the fashioning of effective anti-terrorism strategies. She consequently quotes quite extensively from key statements made by Osama bin Laden when she is building her case for the view that the attack had its origins in a certain fundamentalist interpretation of Islam[14] and in the hatred this interpretation generates in its adherents for America and its ideal of freedom. She is particularly insistent that bin Laden must be taken at his word and that consequently there is no mystery about the nature of his motivation. The aim of the 9/11 attack, she claims, was to express hatred of America by killing as many Americans as possible.

Critics of this account are likely to feel that she gives too little attention to questions about the broader political objective(s) bin Laden probably hoped to achieve by *means* of the attack. I sympathize with this criticism, as is perhaps already clear from what I have said about the importance of seeing terrorist acts as politically motivated. However, the more significant point is that Elshtain's account also reveals a deficiency in her general approach to the articulation of the rationale for defensible anti-terrorism strategies. She assumes that getting clear about the nature of the reasons *the terrorists themselves* had in planning and executing the 9/11 attack is to be in possession of the only kind of explanation needed both for the understanding of the nature of the terrorist threat and for the devising of an appropriate response.

It is important to challenge this assumption, not because a clear view of what motivated the terrorists themselves is not relevant to the fashioning of an appropriate response—it clearly *is* relevant—but because it does not provide either all we need to know to understand the threat posed by terrorism or all we need to bear in mind in trying to develop effective strategies to counter it.

In suggesting that more is needed if a judicious response to the threat of terrorism in the modern world is to be devised, I do not mean merely, or mainly, that the terrorist threat ought not to be too closely identified either with the threat posed by the Al Qaeda organization or with the threat posed by militant forms of fundamentalist Islam. Although this is not its central shortcoming, it is a deficiency of Elshtain's view that it virtually *equates* devising an effective anti-terrorism strategy in the post 9/11 world with figuring out how the threat posed by Islamic fundamentalism is to be countered. It is of course natural that she should want to give a good deal of prominence to the threat posed by Al Qaeda and by militant "Islamicism" in the wake of the 9/11 attack. Nevertheless, the so-called "war against terrorism" that was triggered by the attack has a broader set of objectives, at least in part because not all the forms of terrorism that threaten the modern world can be blamed either on Al Qaeda or on "Islamicist" fundamentalism. Terrorism in Northern Ireland, or in Israel, Gaza and the West Bank, or in Sri Lanka—to take obvious examples—cannot be understood in the terms laid down by Elshtain.

But there is a more fundamental reason for thinking that too blinkered an account of the threat of terrorism—and therefore of appropriate responses to this threat—is being offered by Elshtain in her book. It is that, even if the focus on Al Qaeda-related—or "Islamicism"-grounded—terrorist acts is to be maintained, the motives of the terrorists themselves provide only part of the explanation for the threat this sort of terrorism poses. The reason is that a sustained terrorist campaign cannot be conducted without the tacit sympathy or support[15] of the populations from which terrorist organizations recruit their members.[16] It is consequently important to be clear about the attitudes and aspirations, the resentments and animosities, *of the members of these populations*, despite the fact that they themselves cannot be regarded as terrorists (at any rate on any plausible understanding of the term "terrorist").

A mistake similar to that made by Elshtain is to be found in the short piece placed on the web under the title "A crime or an act of war?"[17] by Christopher Morris. He notes that mounting a credible response to the 9/11 attack calls for a clear distinction to be drawn between strategies aimed at *retribution* for the attack and strategies designed to *deter* similar attacks, and between both and strategies aimed at *preventing* such attacks in the future. Of these three objectives, much the most important, in Morris's view, is the third—prevention of terrorist attacks in the future. It is a reasonable view, surely. Merely retributive strategies may do nothing to diminish the threat posed by terrorism; indeed, they may simply heighten the risk of further terrorist attacks by antagonizing terrorist strategists. And terrorist organizations are notoriously difficult to deter. But while the emphasis on prevention of terrorism is of course salutary, Morris takes an unduly narrow view of what counts as "prevention" in this context. He poses the "prevention" question in a way that limits it to preventing "potential terrorists" from committing acts of terror, adding that "our most important, and urgent, aim should be to incapacitate all who threaten to attack our cities and people in the ways that the WTC killers have." While preventing terrorist attacks—the general objective of a sensible "war on terrorism"—certainly involves, in part, trying to "incapacitate all who threaten to attack our cities and people in the ways the WTC killers have," it *also* requires sensible responses to the fact that large numbers of people within the populations to which the terrorists belong sympathize with the political objectives ostensibly served by their acts. The members of these sympathetic populations are not themselves terrorists—and very few of them are even "potential" terrorists—yet their support for the political objectives, even if not for the methods, of terrorist organizations plays an indispensable role in enabling terrorist groups to survive and to keep on fashioning and implementing terrorist campaigns.

IV. A Broader Interpretation of the "Root Causes" Argument Is Needed

It is necessary, consequently, for a suitably broad interpretation of the "root causes" argument to be adopted. Among the broader causal factors to which the argument draws attention, some of the most important have to do with the attitudes, sentiments, beliefs, concerns, discontents, etc., not of the terrorists (or their sponsors) themselves, but of the societies (or populations) from which they emerge. For example, most Palestinians in the West Bank or in Gaza cannot plausibly be said to be "terrorists" (no matter how loosely, or expansively, we permit the term to be used). Nevertheless, their grievances—the sense they have that in various ways they have been, and continue to be, subjected to unjust treatment—form an important part of the backdrop to any plausible understanding of the "suicide-bomber" phenomenon. Again, the rank-and-file citizens who make up the so-called "Arab Street" cannot plausibly be described as "terrorists," yet their attitudes and concerns are crucial to any proper understanding of the ability of terrorist groups like Al Qaeda to recruit (new) members. Yet again, most ordinary Tamils in Sri Lanka are not terrorists, but their attitudes and aspirations nevertheless form an indispensable part of any comprehensive explanation of the resort to terrorism of the Tamil Tigers.

V. Practical Implications of the "Root Causes" Argument

Care must be taken, of course—in coming to grips with the force of the "root causes" argument—to offer a reasonably complex account of the ways in which a better understanding of some of the "root causes" of terrorism might contribute to the adoption of fruitful approaches to the combating of terrorism. For example, it matters to the mounting of an appropriate (and potentially effective) response to the threat of terrorism whether the sense of grievance of the members of societies (or populations) that "spawn" terrorists is taken to be (1) wholly justified, or (2) wholly unjustified, or (3) partly justified, and partly unjustified, or (4) justified (wholly or partly) only *in a sense*—in the sense, that is, that although the individuals and groups in question have cause to complain, their complaint is wrongly targeted. Thus, where the sense of grievance is wholly justified, part of an effective anti-terrorism strategy will have to take the form of adopting measures aimed at eliminating the sense of grievance by eliminating the underlying injustices. Where the sense of grievance is wholly unjustified, the attempt must be made to foster a better understanding of the policies that are thought—mistakenly, *ex hypothesi*—to be unjust or demeaning. Where the sense of grievance is partly justified and partly unjustified, modification of the policies responsible for the resented injustices must go hand-in-hand with better presentation (and defense) of the policies that are mistakenly *believed* to be unjust. And where the sense of grievance is justified only in the special sense that, while the aggrieved individuals and groups have plenty to complain about, their complaints are wrongly targeted, pains need to be taken to convince those who see themselves as victims of injustice that the sources of their undeniably miserable circumstances are being misidentified.

VI. Further Versions of the "Root Causes" Argument

The version of the "root causes" argument I have just been describing is one it is important to emphasize for two reasons. First, it shows how sympathy with the political goals of terrorist organizations on the part of people who do not endorse their methods can make an indispensable contribution to the success of terrorist campaigns. Second, it points the way to policies that might advantageously be adopted by those who are seeking to prevent terrorism. It should not be thought, however, that there are no other versions of the argument, or that these other versions are not relevant to the devising of anti-terrorism strategies. Let me in conclusion illustrate two further directions in which investigation of the "root causes" of terrorism might fruitfully be conducted.

One possibility is that long-standing injustices of which the members of a society are perhaps not fully aware—injustices about which, consequently, they have not yet begun to complain in any serious or sustained way—may over time contribute to the emergence of discontents of just the kinds that terrorist groups can readily exploit. It might be thought, for example, that it is only a matter of time before the widening gap between have and have-not nations begins to generate, among the have-nots, a sense of grievance against the haves—a sense of grievance of just the sort that terrorist organizations might be able to take advantage of. A prudent pre-emptive "strike" in the "war against terrorism" might consequently be one that aims, in a variety of imaginative ways and on a variety of fronts, at reducing these economic inequalities.

Another possibility is this. There may be reason to think[18] that there is an ominous correlation between the sense of powerlessness felt by victims of entrenched injustices and their willingness to contemplate desperate strategies for the improvement of their lives. It might consequently be wise for anti-terrorism strategists to be reticent about using the (military or economic) power they have in ways that add to the despair of the oppressed. A world in which powerful countries use their wealth or their military might in ways that are perceived to be arrogant, arbitrary, or insufficiently sensitive to the injustices that are often among the "root causes" of terrorism is likely to be a more dangerous world because of the desperate reactions it may generate on the part of the powerless.

VII. Conclusion

There has been a great deal of emphasis, in the conducting of the so-called "war against terrorism," on the need for better intelligence—by which is meant, overwhelmingly, better intelligence about the identity, the membership and the plans of terrorist groups around the world. If the "root causes" argument deserves more attention than it has so far received from anti-terrorism strategists, what may be needed even more than better intelligence is better research—research of all the kinds that might be relevant to the acquisition of knowledge about the "root causes" of terrorism. I have advanced the claim, albeit only in very general terms, that terrorist campaigns are facilitated and assisted by support within the societies to which terrorists belong for the political goals served by these campaigns. Further research is clearly needed to document the forms this support can take. It is already evident, however, that it takes instructively different forms in different societies. Anti-terrorism strategies that reflect this kind of research are consequently likely to be diverse in content and structure. Many of the most promising of these strategies will be part of a war on terrorism only in a plainly metaphorical sense of the term "war."

Alistair M. Macleod, Queen's University

Notes

1. Ludwig Wittgenstein, *Philosophical Investigations*, 66.

2. Attempts to define "terrorism" by specifying necessary and sufficient conditions for its use turn out either to be stipulative or to cover only a favored sub-class of the correct uses of the term (often without proper acknowledgement of this limitation of focus).

3. Jean-Bethke Elshtain, *Just War Against Terror* (New York: Basic Books), 2003.

4. Ibid., 18.

5. Ibid., 19.

6. Although Elshtain quotes approvingly from Michael Walzer's *Just and Unjust Wars* (New York: Basic Books, 1977) in the section of Chapter 1 entitled "What is a Terrorist?" there is

nothing in the passage she quotes from Walzer that is at all incompatible with recognizing that terrorist acts are (normally) politically motivated. Thus when Walzer writes (*Just and Unjust Wars*, 197) that terrorism's "purpose is to destroy the morale of a nation or a class, to undercut its solidarity," he is tacitly conceding that to understand terrorism we have to try to account for the fact that a nation or class is being targeted in this particular way. The required explanation will typically highlight the political goal terrorists hope to achieve by "undercutting the solidarity" of the particular nation or class in question.

7. Whether the negotiations between the warring parties undertaken in 2003 will yield the kind of "federal" solution that seems to offer the most promising exit from the current stalemate, it is still too early to say.

8. Since my aim in this paper is to highlight the importance of pursuing questions about the "root causes" of certain familiar kinds of terrorism, I am precisely *not* endorsing any definition of "terrorism" that makes the targeting of innocent civilians a necessary condition of the characterization of acts as "terrorist" acts.

9. If the full significance of this claim were to be spelt out—something that cannot even be attempted here—it would have to be noted, among other things, that there are as many versions of this misinterpretation as there are versions of the condemnatory judgments the "root causes" argument is alleged to be designed to undermine or qualify. There are differences, for example, between judgments that focus attention on terrorist *acts* and judgments that highlight the *motives* from which they are performed, and between both and more general judgments in which the *character-traits* of terrorists are dissected and assessed.

10. They are sometimes also taken to be laying the blame for the terrorist acts on the victims of these acts. This is a rather curious—and arguably unrelated—addition. After all, an argument that purported to show that the perpetrators of terrorist acts are blameless might also be designed to show that *no one* was to blame. And in any case, even if there were still room for blame once the perpetrators had been exonerated, the victims of the terrorist attack would be neither the only nor the most obvious candidates for blame.

11. A plausible case can be made for the view that explaining an act of terrorism in terms of the terrorist's own reasons for committing the act is to be contrasted with—instead of being regarded as a special case of—explaining it in terms of *root* causes. (The avowed reasons of the perpetrators of terrorist acts might be conceded to be among the *causes* without being identified as the *root* causes.) On this view, Elshtain's would *not* be "too narrow" a version of a "root causes" explanation. Rather, it would not be a "root causes" explanation *at all*.

12. The point here does not hinge at all on the distinction often drawn between explanations of actions in terms of the agent's own reasons and causal explanations of behavior. For one thing, even when the focus is on an agent's own reasons for some action, these reasons can readily enough be regarded as providing (at least part of) a causal explanation for the action. (The impulse on the part of some philosophers to deny this is poorly motivated if it reflects endorsement of a model of "causal" explanation for which there must be a 100% correlation between *explanans* and *explanandum*.) For another, some of the "root causes" of terrorism that are overlooked when there is an exclusive emphasis on the explanatory value of the beliefs, attitudes and motives of terrorists themselves will be found to include

the beliefs, attitudes and motives of the *non*-terrorist members of the communities that provide terrorists with a base of operations.

13. That is, *Just War Against Terror.*

14. It is an interpretation she thinks can be ascribed with confidence to bin Laden and his associates. "Islamicism" is the term she uses to refer to this fundamentalist interpretation of Islam.

15. There can be—and (I suspect) there typically is—"sympathy and support" because the *political goals* ostensibly served by terrorist campaigns are thought to be desirable (perhaps even urgent) goals by members of the community who disapprove of terrorist *methods.*

16. While it is an important task for historians and social scientists to provide empirically adequate accounts of the many different ways in which, in different societies, the members of terrorist organizations are "assisted" by the members of the communities from which they spring, it seems safe to assume that the success of terrorist organizations is always to some degree indebted to the kind of community support they receive.

17. Christopher W. Morris, "A Crime or an Act of War?" (This is one of a number of short articles to be found on a web page maintained by Larry Hinman, San Diego, under the title *Philosophers Speak Out about War, Terrorism, and Peace.* Most of the articles were posted in 2001, shortly after 9/11.)

18. Whether there really is reason to think this is perhaps one of the research tasks yet to be undertaken systematically by sponsors of the "root causes" argument.

An Evaluation of the "No Purpose" and Some Other Theories (Such as Oil) For Explaining Al-Qaeda's Motives

DOUG KNAPP

Abstract: Various causal factors have been offered to explain the motives behind the Al-Qaeda terrorist attacs on 9/11 and at various other times and places throughout the world. Quite often the reasons or purposes are said to include political, economic, religious and ethnic factors. Often historical factors, such as colonialism and neo-colonialism, as well as nationalism, poverty, class divisions and modernization, are included. But some scholars and political figures, quite inconsistently at times, assert that there is no discernable purpose or purposes in these attacks. It is argued, for example, that the sheer magnitude of the death and carnage in the 9/11 attacks suggests no rational purpose in the minds of the perpetrators. The implication is that the Al-Qaeda attacks are allegedly purely irrational. In contrast, I argue that there are flaws and inconsistencies with this No Purpose Theory, and that oil, moreover, shouldn't be omitted (as it often is) from any plausible broad explanation of the complex mix of causal factors. Needless to say, to suggest that Al-Qaeda had reasons is not to suggest that the reasons were necessarily good or morally justifiable. Then again, among these reasons it is necessary to sort out the goals from the violent tactics so as to discover why, in particular, many Arabs and Muslims sympathize with some of the goals.

This whole issue is important because, among other things, if the No Purpose Theory is assumed to be accurate, it would, at least for the problem at hand, eliminate from serious consideration in one fell swoop literally all of the other possible factors (political, religious, economic, etc.). This would be so in spite of the initial reasonableness of the notion that many of these factors have at least some weight or other. But if, contrary to what the No Purpose Theory says, items such as oil are shown to be actually causally important, and are consequently on the table for more extended and open discussion, then there at least would be a better opportunity for more successfully tackling these problems and ameliorating the risk of future terrorist attacks. At least so I will argue.

I. Introduction

Some of the main, general causal or motivational factors that have been cited for al-Qaeda terrorism include religion (such as pan-Islamism), a history of colonialism and neo-colonialism, economic and resource issues (such as oil), ethnicity, nationalism, modernization and globalization, poverty and class divisions. Biological reproductive dispositions, power, and the associated cultural characteristics (as reflected, say, in disparate rates of population growth between Muslims and non-Muslim, or the disparate percentages of young men constituting a population bulge[1]), as well as race and gender can be considered to be additional influences. Not on the usual list, but should be, is human induced environmental degradation. An indication that this should be on the list is the reference Osama bin Laden makes in one of his fatwas (i.e. religious edicts) to the Mideast deserts that he says were created by Allah. He seems to have no knowledge that many of the deserts were human induced.[2] (Presumably non-Middle Easterners are pretty much in the same boat concerning the lack of ecological knowledge in light of the common global practice of over-cutting, overgrazing, overdrawing and over-harvesting.)

Not part of the above list, which I take to be a quite good list of plausible causal factors, is the view that the perpetrators of the 9/11 attacks and other al-Qaeda attacks had no purpose at all in mind—not political, economic, religious or otherwise. For ease of reference, I'll hereafter call this position the No Purpose Theory. The implication of this theory is that pure irrationality or pure emotion or pure evil was the cause. In contrast, I argue that there are inconsistencies and omissions in this No Purpose Theory, and that oil, moreover, shouldn't be excluded (as it often is) from any plausible broad account of the actual complex causal mix. Of course to say or imply that al-Qaeda has reasons for its terrorism is not to suggest that the reasons are necessarily good or morally justifiable reasons. Indeed, perhaps a good label to describe the wrongness in the 9/11 attack is "crime against humanity," which in a Rome Statute of the International Criminal Court is an umbrella term under which specific acts such as murder, extermination, enslavement, forced deportation of a population, torture and other crimes are included.[3] Murder would here be an appropriate sub-designation. But the moral and historical analysis should not stop with this because there have been plenty of acts of crimes against humanity to go around. Virtually any country that has been around awhile, I would argue, would have some history of engaging in acts that are crimes against humanity. And the U.S. is no different I contend. Also, there is the difficulty, but the need, of making sense of tit-for-tat situations where one nation or ethnic group engages in terror, let us say, in a fight for a homeland, and the other side responds in kind. One of my claims is that while we must protect ourselves, we should also be open to examining how we ourselves, in part, may have actually contributed to bringing about the 9/11 attack.

This whole issue is important because, among other things, if the No Purpose Theory is assumed to be accurate, it would, at least for the problem at hand, eliminate in one fell swoop from serious consideration literally all of the possible major factors (political, religious, economic, etc.) cited above. This is the case because one would reasonably expect that no coherent political or economic motive would emanate from pure irrationality or madness. Thus, there would then be less incentive, assuming for the moment that it might be needed, to reevaluate the history and the values associated with U.S. geopolitical interests in the Middle East; also, there would be less need to try to understand why various reliable polls have shown that large numbers of Arabs and Muslims may not be sympathetic with the violent tactics of al-Qaeda, but are sympathetic with aspects of its goals.[4] Plus there would be less incentive to look for nonmilitary solutions. What would be the point in negotiating with someone who is completely mad, or with those who are even remotely sympathetic with the completely mad?

II. Various Versions of the No Purpose Theory

The versions of the no-purpose theory that will be analyzed here include the positions of (1) several Harvard scholars associated with the Kennedy School of Government, (2) writers Thomas Friedman and Frederick Forsyth, and (3) representatives or allies of the current Bush administration, including President Bush, Secretary of Defense Donald Rumsfeld, Secretary of State Colin Powell, and Saudi Arabia's Foreign Minister, Prince Saud.

At a Harvard University forum on November 5, 2001, in the aftermath of al-Qaeda's 9/11 attacks, Ashton Carter of the Kennedy School of Government argued as follows:

> It's very difficult, in many of those [al-Qaeda] cases, to figure out what their political motivation is—whether there is [sic] a political motivation, and whether there's any way of building a bridge to that political motivation. When the PLO began, when the IRA began, you could at least imagine some reconciliation of that underlying situation. But when we talk about mass terrorism, we may be dealing with truly fringe motivations that's very difficult even to understand, let alone deter, or to bargain with.[5]

At the same forum Middle East specialists Jessica Stern and Eva Bellen defend the same line of argument. Stern emphasizes the expressive or emotive as opposed to the instrumental or rational explanation of al-Qaeda's motives:

> One way to summarize the distinction that helps us understand Al Qaeda is to say that bin Laden's objectives are really expressive, not instrumental. Those groups that have set instrumental objectives are not [sic] going to carry out catastrophic attacks, because such attacks will never achieve those objectives, whereas groups that are expressing anger can continuously change their mission statement.

Bellen further develops this notion of al-Qaeda's mission statement or goals as regularly and randomly shifting, a point which allegedly buttresses the idea that al-Qaeda's motives are purely or mainly expressive or irrational. Bellen says that at one time al-Qaeda's goal is to target a Christmas market in Strasbourg, at another time the Eiffel Tower, at another time the World Trade Center. At one point, Bellen continues, the objective is forcing the U.S. out of Saudi Arabia, at another time defending Palestinian rights and Iraqi children, at another defending the Islamist cause in Kashmir. "The demands shift because the terrorists' goal is really not to solve any one of these problems, but rather to express anger."[6]

This type of analysis did not originate in the aftermath of the 9/11 attacks. Thomas Friedman posits a similar No Purpose stance when describing in 1999 the attempt by al-Qaeda's Ramzi Yousef to cause the collapse of the Twin Towers through a bombing in 1993. The main objective of that attack failed, but the explosion did occur and six people were killed and over a thousand were injured. Friedman summarizes the motives as follows: "They want a lot of people dead. They are not trying to change the world. They know that they can't, so they just want to destroy as much as they can."[7] Novelist and columnist Frederick Forsyth recently argues the same way: "We [al-Qaeda terrorists] do not want anything of you but your deaths. In thousands, in hundreds of thousands and eventually in millions. We say this because we hate you. We hate you with an all-consuming passion, not just for what you have done (though that is bad enough) but for what you are."[8]

Very recently government officials used a No Purpose Theory to explain an al-Qaeda attack in Saudi Arabia. In response to the May 12, 2003 suicide bombings at the residential compounds for foreigners in Riyadh, Saudi Arabia, bombings which killed 35 people including 9 Americans, the Saudi Foreign Minister, Prince Saud, described the terrorists as "people who only hate, only kill, and for no purpose whatsoever." At the same press conference U.S. Secretary of State Colin Powell concurred with Prince Saud: "I don't attribute [the al-Qaeda attack] to the Israeli-Palestinian conflict, I just attribute it to terrorists. We should not try to cloak their terrorist activity, their criminal activity, their murderous activity in any trappings of political purpose. They are terrorists."[9]

III. Critique

I first return to the previously mentioned Harvard forum in November, 2001. It is noteworthy that not all of the forum participants assumed such an entirely sharp division between anger and reason, or between expressiveness and instrumentality, where al-Qaeda operatives allegedly manifest the former but none of the latter. Responding to Ashton Carter's claim of there being no political motive, Philip Heymann says, "I agree that you have to include a category of sheer destructiveness without obvious motivation, though it always carries some message. Everything carries some message."

Heymann is more on target I contend. There should be a category of motivation involving "mainly destructiveness" if not "sheer destructiveness." With this amendment presumably this category would take into account the possibility

An Evaluation of Some Theories for Explaining Al-Quada's Motives

of pure instances of mental illness or psychopathology where there would be no evidence of significant overlapping political or religious motivation. But al-Qaeda operatives do not fit in such a category. Extensive evidence supports the notion that both religion and politics are influential for al-Qaeda. In fact there is evidence that suicide bombers in general, not just al-Qaeda bombers, are not mentally ill. For example, Nasra Hassan, a relief worker in Pakistan who interviewed some 250 failed suicide bombers from 1996–1999, found that none was dysfunctional or mentally ill, or behaved as if they had "nothing to lose."[10] Presumably the degree to which false beliefs, or delusional systems, are present in the minds of the terrorist would not be that much different than the degree in the general population, or at least among fundamentalists in general. Moreover, historical examples of mass or catastrophic terror can be cited to show that mental illness need not be present, or typically is not.

Consider the case of Timothy McVeigh, who bombed the Alfred P. Murrah Federal Office Building in Oklahoma City in April, 1995. His goal was to kill as many of the "enemy" as possible, namely heavy-handed government bureaucrats who would too often use, McVeigh believed, illicit lethal force at places such as Ruby Ridge. He wasn't categorized as mentally ill, and the anger that he felt would presumably be best described as a cool and controlled anger, rather than a blind anger. This is a plausible assumption given the detailed, methodical and instrumental thinking that is necessary to plan and accomplish such an attack. Similarly, given that al-Qaeda members often make detailed plans for attacks for two or four or even five years into the future, it is implausible that "an all-consuming" hatred is the motive. It is clear, moreover, that the choice of 9/11 targets had economic, military and political symbolic significance. Bin Laden said as much after the attack. From al-Qaeda's perspective, presumably if the White House had been struck and if the President or various Cabinet members had been killed, that would have been of greater significance in their eyes (and ours too I am sure) than if there was a larger loss of life with some other selection of a combination of targets.

Not only can examples for overthrowing the No Purpose view be found with individual terrorists such as McVeigh, but also with state terrorism. The U.S. government's policy surrounding the Trail of Tears from 1830–38 can be taken as representative. Considering only the first two-year phase of the more extended forced removal of several American Indian tribes from sites in Mississippi, Alabama, Georgia and Florida to present-day Oklahoma, the number of deaths through starvation, cold weather and the like was estimated to be over 4,000.[11] It's true, the very cold weather was not intended, but rescue efforts were not organized. An acknowledged important motive was the desire by white settlers to acquire the fertile farmland. Here I set aside the rebuttal that on other occasions there were terrorist tactics used by the other side against the settlers. My main point is that this was mass terrorism and did involve discernable motives. Also, historian Henry Steele Commager[12] ably develops the idea that the carpet, incendiary bombing of so-called "open cities" by both the Allies and the Axis powers during WWII was a type of state terrorism. And on the same topic, Ted Honderich[13] cites the British terror bombing (which was called just that) against the Nazis in WWII as presumably a justifiable method, at least early in the war, of preventing or forestalling a German invasion of England. Some of course would want to deny that there even is such a thing as state terrorism, especially when committed by democratic governments, but surely that is just one attempt among several to win the argument merely through using an unnecessarily narrow definition of terrorism. Basically it is a type of question-begging. The type of indiscriminate violence so characteristic of terrorism has often been the tool of states as well as individuals and small groups.[14]

For the Allies the carpet bombing as well as the eventual nuclear bombings at Hiroshima and Nagasaki, rightly or wrongly, did presumably have the intent of bringing about more quickly an unconditional surrender. Plus various historians argue that sending an unmistakable message to the Soviet Union about our willingness to staunchly defend the U.S. sphere of influence was also a factor. Whatever the best position on that may be, or whatever the morality of insisting on an unconditional as opposed to a conditional surrender,[15] one can see that when a large number of the enemy, be they military or civilian, were killed in a particular bombing mission, let us assume the large number itself would surely not necessarily suddenly obliterate the political motives in the minds of the pilots 30,000 feet up or in the minds of the planners or commanders on the ground. Yes, once the tit for tat of open bombing between Germany and England got under way in WWII, civilian deaths on both sides came to be expected, sad to say. But that fact did not undermine the political resolve and purpose of the combatants.

This explanation, if it has merit, again illustrates that al-Qaeda's policy is not historically different enough in the history of war and terrorism, and one should not conclude that no reasoned, political purpose was present in the minds of the 9/11 terrorists. One should not conclude, as all of the above No Purpose theorists do, that the large numbers themselves involved in, say, the 9/11 attacks is firm evidence that al-Qaeda's motives are only expressive (emotive), and not instrumental (rational). But these authors also base their claim on another premise, namely that the 9/11 attacks couldn't possibly contribute to a viable solution. However, as will be subsequently argued, this contention may lie, at least in part, on the mistaken assumption that al-Qaeda was attempting a sweeping global change, rather than a more limited one for which, in some ways, the jury may still be out. If, for example, bin Laden's goal was to create a split between the Saudi monarchy and the U.S., then it is reasonable to say that we should wait and see. Even if it should turn out that no rift develops, one can easily imagine how such a rift could occur given currently strong dissension within Saudi Arabia. So, one can still see where reasonableness (defined neutrally) should hinge more on probabilities than only on final results, and one should keep open the possibility of a limited regional solution, at least from al-Qaeda's perspective.

One way of plausibly construing Heymann's remark that "everything carries a message" is to recognize that in the absence of a finding of a type of mental illness, understood in the traditional sense of hallucinations and the like (for which there is no evidence that I can discern in the 9/11 perpetrators), it is reasonable to give substantial weight to the written and oral communiqués of al-Qaeda as indicating, or at least strongly suggesting, the kinds of actual motivation. This is not the place to go into great detail on this issue, but the 1998 fatwa (religious edict) issued by bin Laden and others, "Jihad Against Jews and Crusaders: World Islamic Front Statement," can be taken to be very representative of this type of evidence. Moreover, in light of the distinction between perpetrator, on the one hand, and sympathizer or supporter on the other hand, even if it turned out that al-Qaeda members themselves didn't really seriously believe what was written by bin Laden in the communiqués and fatwas (itself not a very plausible position), Arab and Muslim sympathizers may well take the reputed goals seriously, and that situation would be enough reason for us here in the U.S. to do the same. This would be one legitimate and important way of construing or applying Heymann's point that "everything carries a message." Even if it were to be the case that al-Qaeda's targets and mission statements varied randomly, perhaps for mere political expediency (something difficult to prove), the more important question or "message" would be whether in the real, geopolitical world and especially in the minds of Arabs and Muslims at large there actually is a kind of coherency and weightiness raised by the terrorists' stated goals or aspects thereof.

IV. The Three Major Grievances

The grievances presented in the 1998 fatwa relate to three major concerns, which were already recapped by Professor Bellen above. The problem with her summary is that the impression is given that nowhere were these three main concerns linked together as they obviously are in this fatwa. Here is a somewhat more detailed summary. First is the demand that there be a cessation of the stationing and activities of U.S. troops in Saudi Arabia and on the whole Arabian Peninsula. Large increases in U.S. troop strength commenced especially with the 1991 Gulf War. This troop presence, contends bin Laden, conflicts with the Islamic dictate that there should be no religion other than Islam on the Peninsula. Plus, bin Laden refers to the Saudi military bases which were used as a staging area for U.S. bombing raids into what I interpret to be the no-fly zones in Iraq. This and other military activity, it deserves note, are among the various reasons why bin Laden says the Saudi monarchy does not embody "true" Islam. The clear implication is that the Saudi government needs to be replaced.

Second, bin Laden cites the economic sanctions and military actions against Iraq, commencing, as did the first major grievance, with the Gulf War. Some estimate that perhaps a half million children died as a result of the sanctions. (In light of the suffering and death of Iraqi children during the time period in question, should we here in the U.S. consider the 9/11 and other attacks, at least in part, as a type of tit for tat as a result of the consequences of the sanctions? In his trial for the 1993 bombing of the World Trade Center, Ramzi Yousef in 1997 also explicitly makes this connection with the plight of Iraqi children.[16])

Third, bin Laden contends that U.S. support for Israel is one-sided or biased. This grievance goes deeper than just opposition to U.S. complicity in Israeli occupation of and settlements within the West Back, Gaza Strip and Jerusalem. Israel is portrayed as a type of client state which serves U.S. economic interests in the Middle East in general. Still, it is perhaps noteworthy that the 1998 fatwa doesn't explicitly deny Israel's right to exist. Perhaps bin Laden was compromising with the Palestinian nationalists who were accepting a two-state solution, which implies Israel's right to exist. (Be that as it may, there seems to be some truth to the supposition that the type of unconditional support, military and otherwise, that the U.S. provides to Israel can be viewed as a fallback geopolitical position. Should alliances with various oil-producing Arab countries become tenuous, access to relatively inexpensive oil can still be strategically preserved with the closer cultural (and racial?) identity with Israel.) Hereafter I will refer to the above three major political/religious complaints dealing with the Peninsula, Iraq and Israel simply as the "The Three Major Grievances."

The communiqué clearly uses religion in support of the desire to expel from the Peninsula all U.S. troops and other infidels (nonbelievers and secularists), and finally in support of the demand from Muslims for martyrdom missions, which would target Americans who are either military or civilian. As a reward, the martyrs would be assured of a special place in Paradise.

Now, in spite of the general religious framework of this fatwa, it is not difficult to discern the geopolitical elements, something with which many Muslims and Arabs, secularists and non-secularists, would be inclined to do.[17] By reading between the lines, ultimate economic motives, especially those related to oil, can be discerned. In this 1998 fatwa bin Laden rails against the U.S. forces, which, like "locusts," are "consuming its [the Arabian Peninsula's] riches."[18] It is clear that the riches bin Laden has in mind relate mainly not, say, to olives, but rather to oil. Later in the fatwa the "economic" aims of the U.S, along with U.S. support of Israel and control of the Peninsula, are condemned. Moreover, bin Laden was previously very explicit about the oil issue in a 1996 interview in which he said, "The presence of the American Crusader forces in Muslim Gulf states . . . is the greatest danger and [poses] the most serious harm, threatening the world's largest oil reserves."[19] And in a subsequent interview bin Laden warns that the price of a barrel of oil should be $144.[20]

Perhaps at this time a brief exploration of the implications of a sizable increase in the price of crude oil is worth exploring. After all, the Saudi monarchy and OPEC regularly negotiate for increases. Of course their proposed increases are not anywhere near the figure that bin Laden was demanding. But given the internal pressures within Saudi society—unemployment, restive youth, discontent with the leadership, a history of Wahhabism (a puritanical version of Islam)—it is not unrealistic to suppose that large revenue increases from oil could help to alleviate some of these problems, at least for a time. Of course the U.S. would strongly resist such significant increases. Under current circumstances political fates could fall quickly with even just a $10 increase in the cost of a barrel of oil. Still, one can ask whether it would actually be in the U.S. long-range interests to be generally supportive of such price hikes even if they are not in the range that bin Laden had in mind. One can imagine under the right conditions how this could be beneficial to the U.S. and the world at large. It could be plausibly argued that if the petroleum, auto and related industries were not subsidized to the huge extent that they now are (consider, e.g., the expensive infrastructure of highways, right-of-ways, environmental costs, etc., not to mention the huge military costs of assuring access to oil internationally), then a rationale for quickly beginning a transition to renewable energy sources, such as solar and wind, would not be unreasonable. Hart and Spivak,[21] for example, estimate in early 1990s dollars that subsidies for highways and parking alone come to between 8 and 10% of the U.S. gross national product. If there were a fuel tax on this (instead of currently drawing it from other sources of taxation), the authors estimate the tax would add approximately $3.50 to the price of a gallon of gas. Plus if the "soft" costs such as pollution cleanup and emergency medical costs were included, the additional gas tax would be up to $9.00 per gallon. And if, as I suggested, military costs as well as global warming effects were also factored in, the tax obviously would be still higher. Sure, one of the consequences of no longer subsidizing fossil fuel would be a significant rise in the price of gas. But if a serious national effort were made to concurrently reduce taxes in other areas such as income tax,[22] to enhance the infrastructure of public transportation and what has come to be called traditional neighborhood development (where housing, work, and amenities are in closer proximity), and to seriously implement conservation measures, then a political and economic transition to a state of less dependence on foreign oil may be possible. And that in turn could begin to address basic economic issues associated with terrorism, I would argue. This is not the time to explore this further. Suffice it to say that a bipartisan proposal by Timothy Wirth and others explores some of these possibilities and is worthy of consideration.[23] Very importantly, the argument that "There is no alternative, militarily and otherwise, to guaranteeing cheap oil" would at least be called into question.

V. The Oil Factor

Another type of evidence that supports the importance of oil as it relates to al-Qaeda's motivation, at least as an ultimate cause, are the explicit statements made not only by bin Laden but also by U.S. officials which assert a willingness to use military force in defense of U.S. oil interests in the Middle East. The assumption here is that if the U.S. expresses such military willingness, then al-Qaeda will be more willing to respond in kind, especially if it perceives that nation states, such as Saudi Arabia, are unable or unwilling to do so. Also, if the U.S. actually has furtively intervened in the past in the political affairs of various Mideast countries, then this too would contribute to the deep anger or hatred of the U.S. by ordinary Middle Eastern democrats as well as by al-Qaeda and its sympathizers. Fairness requires that the U.S. not so intervene, even though it has the power to do so, the argument might go. The following list (not intended to be complete) of actions or statements by former U.S. presidents or agencies help substantiate this claim.

- President Roosevelt and King Ibn Saud met on a U.S. warship in the Suez Canal in February 1945 following the Yalta conference which ended WWII and formed a "compact" which was basically a type of quid pro quo between the Saudi royal family and the U.S. Essentially, the U.S. agrees to protect the monarchy against foreign and domestic threats to power and in return Saudi Arabia helps protect U.S. geopolitical oil interests. Oil, so crucial in winning WWII and subsequently so important to the U.S. economy in general, was in limited supply in the U.S. Southwest, and there also was a limited supply in Mexico and Venezuela. During the War the State Department was directed to do the detailed study, and in 1945 Herbert Feis concluded, according to Daniel Yergin in *The Prize*, "In all surveys of the situation the pencil came to an awed pause at one point and place—the Middle East." (Saudi Arabia has approximately one-fourth of the world's oil reserve. In contrast, the U.S. has 3% of global reserves but consumes close to 25% of these reserves.)[24]

- In 1979 President Carter declared that the U.S. would protect its vital interests "by any means necessary, including military force." This is now called the "Carter Doctrine" and it is still in effect. Britain provided most of the military and police protection for the Saudi Arabian royal family up until 1971, when the U.S. assumed that role. In 1973 there was a six-month oil embargo during which we now know through the release of British intelligence papers the U.S. seriously contemplated using military force to seize Middle Eastern oil fields.[25] In 1979 the Shah of Iran was overthrown, the Soviet Union moved into Afghanistan, and, as Michael Klare notes, Islamic militants "staged a brief rebellion in Mecca" against the monarchy. All of these things helped prompt Carter's declaration.

An Evaluation of Some Theories for Explaining Al-Quada's Motives

- The continuance of the Carter Doctrine is illustrated by President Reagan's comment to reporters in 1981, "We will not permit [Saudi Arabia] to be an Iran." Then, under President Bush the elder came the Gulf War of 1990–91 after which not only was Iraq forced out of Kuwait, but residual U.S. troops have remained indefinitely in Saudi Arabia which has become a sore point not only with al-Qaeda but also with moderates.

- A number of administrations, utilizing the CIA and so forth, have actually intervened, often secretly and violently, to eliminate, keep or install a leader to our liking in the Middle East. Such interventions have occurred in various parts of the world,[26] but the Middle East will be the focus here. Often key underlying oil interests can be discerned. For example, the U.S. and British intelligence agencies coordinated the overthrow of the democratically elected government of Muhammad Mossadeq in Iran in 1953. Prime Minister Mossadeq's downfall can be attributed to his spearheading the effort to nationalize the sole oil company then operating in Iran, a British owned company. The shah of Iran, Muhammad Riza Pahlavi, was soon after restored to power, and ruled very brutally[27] for a quarter of a century. But soon after the Shah's restoration, foreign ownership of oil was also restored, with the British and the U.S. each owning 40%. Plus, the CIA inspired a coup in Iraq in 1963.[28] Less secretive of course is the ongoing U.S. support of the repressive Saudi Arabian government. It is true, Saudi reforms are being attempted, but critics can fairly say such reforms are not substantial and are long overdue.

- Finally, it is widely recognized that the U.S. was very slow in criticizing Saddam Hussein for using chemical gas warfare against Iran and the Kurds in the 1980s. The answer has been shown to relate to the then concurrent secret negotiations between the U.S. and Iraq to obtain an oil pipeline to run from Iraq to the Gulf of Aqaba, Jordon.[29]

In light of the above background material dealing with The Three Major Grievances and with the above explicit statements and actions by both al-Qaeda and U.S. leaders and agencies, it is plain how implausible it is for the No Purpose theorists to say or imply that there is no political, economic or religious purpose behind the 9/11 and other attacks by al-Qaeda. The implausibility carries over to the remark of Secretary of Defense Donald Rumsfeld when he told a radio audience that "regime change" in Iraq had "nothing to do with oil."[30] But as research by the Institute for Policy Studies found, when Rumsfeld was in private office, in 1998, he wrote a memo to the White House on January 26, 1998, acknowledging the connection: "If Saddam does acquire the capability to deliver weapons of mass destruction . . . a significant portion of the world's supply of oil will all be put at hazard."[31] Perhaps what he really meant was that a significant portion of the world's inexpensive oil will be put at hazard. Sure, Iraq might be considered a totally separate issue from the main focus in this paper, which is al-Qaeda's motivation. Still, even if Iraq and al-Qaeda have not been so closely linked as the Bush administration has alleged, both Iraq and al-Qaeda surely figure in the U.S.'s strategic oil interests in the Mideast, and here I am trying to make the case that al-Qaeda, at least in part, is motivated to respond to this U.S. strategic interest. So in this way Iraq and the Bush Administration's views on Iraqi oil are relevant to the topic at hand. Presumably to engender a terrorist response from al-Qaeda, various non-economic factors, such as politics and religion would necessarily come into play. But it is possible, given the weight of the evidence, that oil is one additional important and even necessary factor that has helped initially create or foment the terrorism.

Some commentators, such as George Will and Thomas Friedman,[32] may say that because U.S. citizens are not currently lined up at the gas pumps, or because we are not militarily threatening Venezuela from which we currently obtain substantially greater amounts of our foreign oil, oil therefore is not an important cause or indeed is not part of the causal mix at all, and therefore it is unrelated to current military actions in the Middle East. However, this is to confuse the difference between proximate and ultimate causes. Long-range strategic planners surely look to where the biggest reserves lie, and are likely to recommend policy based on those interests even when there is no current proximate crisis where, say, there's a queuing up at the gas station. Such commentators, at least for purposes of this argument, pretend that energy strategists do not think beyond a few weeks or months at a time. Plus, even if U.S. imports from the Gulf are relatively low, the imports of our allies, such as Japan and Western Europe, are now relatively high. And protecting their interests is in our interest. Moreover, Klare cogently argues that assuring high levels of Persian Gulf imports, no matter from us or our allies, does tend to keep the price of oil lower, thereby indirectly aiding the U.S. economy.[33] But my current case against Friedman, the Kennedy School and the other No Purpose theorists is still very general in some ways, and so some specific points still need to be argued.

VI. Al-Qaeda's Goals: More Regional Than Global?

A crucial part of the No Purpose argument rests on the assumption, a mistaken one I hope to show, that al-Qaeda was actually trying to defeat the U.S. militarily and soon bring Islam to the whole world (including an Islamic Republic to New Jersey, to cite an example by Thomas Friedman). But that is not al-Qaeda's goal, at least not for any foreseeable future. Of course if it were a goal of al-Qaeda, it would be a completely unrealistic goal, given the current balance of forces and current patterns of belief within the U.S. and throughout the world. If, moreover, this were al-Qaeda's present goal, then Friedman would at least be partly correct when he writes, to repeat, "They are not trying to change the world. They know that they can't, so they just want to destroy as much as they can." I say "partly correct" because Friedman is obviously wrong concluding "They are not trying to change the world." Even if one tries to change the world in a completely ineffectual way, there still is plainly an attempt to change the world. Surely given the effort that al-Qaeda has made in various detailed attacks, it is reasonable to suppose it is trying to change something, perhaps the region if not the world all at once. Along this line of thought, an important and compelling point was recently made by Michael Doran. Doran effectively argues that al-Qaeda is more immediately interested in uniting the whole Islamic community, the umma, not in conquering and then converting the non-Muslim West or the world at large to Islam.[34] Klare essentially made a similar point when he argued, to repeat, that the 9/11 attacks were designed to destroy the compact that was forged in 1945 between the then King Ibn Saud and FDR. Such an unraveling of the oil/military compact, if it occurred, need not imply that al-Qaeda envisions an inevitable speedy chain reaction resulting in an Islamic globe. However, without having the U.S. military or police protection, the Saudi monarchy obviously would be more vulnerable in various ways. But the results still could be, and likely are intended to be, mainly regional in effect rather than global. Further evidence for the regional emphasis comes from comments by a higher-up al-Qaeda operative who was captured early in 2003. He indicated bin Laden wanted to recruit Saudis for the 9/11 attacks because that would strain relations between the U.S. and the monarchy.[35] Plus, notice that this possible goal of uniting the Islamic community regionally fits well with the material in The Three Major Grievances already summarized. The First Grievance, recall, demanded that the U.S. troops exit Saudi Arabia and the entire Peninsula. In other words, the U.S. military exit would be a first, necessary step in uniting and achieving greater harmony in the Muslim community. And Grievances Two and Three concerning Palestine and Iraq can reasonably be interpreted in the same way. If sanctions against Iraq were lifted (as they have been), there would be less malnutrition and death of children of the Muslim community, and if the U.S. ended its military support for Israel, the tempo for freeing the entire Peninsula of U.S. bases and uniting the Islamic umma would be speeded up, bin Laden assumes. Notice that there is no call for the formation of an Islamic Republic in New Jersey or other new Islamic Republics throughout other parts of the world, and there is no eventual call to bring the whole U.S. military to its knees. It is of course true that if those things were to happen, and if other Middle East states beyond the Peninsula were to become "genuinely" Islamic, bin Laden would not be saddened. But it is clear that bin Laden's brand of Islamism does not require a quick, grand solution, something which both Friedman and the Kennedy School scholars seem to suppose.

The proper specific response to Jessica Stern's point about the supposedly random and emotive ("experiential") selection of targets now becomes clear. The

Strasbourg market at Christmas, the Eiffel Tower and the World Trade Center—all of them, and presumably many more too—relate to Western powers that do provide aid, military and the like to the allegedly illegitimate Islamic governments or to Israel. So the site selection should not be understood to be devoid of reason or instrumentality. Admittedly, the entertaining of Kashmir by al-Qaeda as a current battleground goes beyond the focus (of Grievance One) on the Peninsula. But the conflict there presently involves active military or guerrilla conflict where al-Qaeda and other Islamists think they can make a difference in the near term concerning who controls what territory. From this perspective, they may be right. To be sure, the battle there is not Islamists versus Christians and Zionists. The battle in Kashmir, I gather, is Islamists versus different "polytheists" or infidels, namely Hindu. But it still is envisioned as a battle for "true" Islamism, and therefore not devoid of political or religious motives as Professor Bellen mistakenly assumes.

VII. The Bush Administration Version of No Purpose

Various statements from members of the Bush administration assert that the 9/11 attacks and similar attacks were simply irrational acts, or due only to blind rage, with no political or social purpose in mind. Perhaps the clearest example of this was provided earlier in the quote from Secretary of State Colin Powell who said that the May 12, 2003 attack in Riyadh, Saudi Arabia had absolutely "no trappings of political purpose." A less clear version of the No Purpose Theory can be discerned in the address by President Bush shortly after 9/11. This view can be called a Hybrid version, and I will argue it is bound to be inconsistent. President Bush cannot consistently hold at one and the same time (as he does) that the No Purpose Theory is and is not true. He cannot consistently contend at the same time that there is No and there is Some Purpose. He cannot legitimately say or imply that there are religious and political motives (while omitting any mention of economic or oil motives, it deserves mention) and at the same time hold that pure irrationality or madness or evil was the cause.

On the one hand, Bush acknowledges various political and religious purposes. Bush asserts that "its [al-Qaeda's] goal is remaking the world—and imposing its radical beliefs on people everywhere."[36] Moreover, Bush rightly says that al-Qaeda intends to destroy the alliances that the U.S. has with other Mideast countries, such as Egypt, Israel, Jordan and Saudi Arabia. On the other hand, al-Qaeda, through its acts of sacrificing human lives, abandons "every value except the will to power," which, at least in terms of the ostensible desire for power just for power's sake, suggests a No Purpose Theory. Presumably what Bush means is that every "decent" value is abandoned. But then one can question whether this is really accurate since it would imply, e.g., that there are no general values or areas of concern to which Arabs, Muslims and people in general would identify. Within the Three

An Evaluation of Some Theories for Explaining Al-Quada's Motives

Major Grievances it has already been suggested that there are such general values or legitimate areas of concern, even if it is assumed that violent tactics undermine these goals. One does not have to be an al-Qaeda supporter or sympathizer to be concerned about Iraqi children, Palestinian rights to a homeland, or long-standing U.S. military support for an autocratic Saudi Arabia.

Yet another example of the tension and inconsistency with the hybrid approach is Bush's claim that "These terrorists kill not merely to end lives, but to disrupt and end a way of life." This has the implication, at least on one plausible interpretation, that al-Qaeda operatives kill merely to end lives, an interpretation which would fit with the No Purpose Theory.[37] But then in one and the same sentence there is the assertion of some political or social purpose, namely the purpose of disrupting and ending a way of life. Admittedly one can interpret the first part of this sentence differently to mean there is not any gratuitous killing when lives are ended in combat. But then Bush would not be as derogatory or condemning as he here intends, and the killing, moreover, would not differ in any significant way from the killing by soldiers in other wars, such as WWII, of which both Bush and I would not disapprove. So the inconsistency remains.

Another important point with respect to al-Qaeda motives in the passage at hand is that President Bush makes no reference here or elsewhere to any of the content of the Three Major Grievances. But given the importance of the fatwas for discerning possible motives, one could legitimately expect discussion of the matter. Admittedly Saudi Arabia is mentioned, but only with respect to security and not the liberties such as religious practice, speech, press, association, women's rights, parliamentary procedures—liberties which many competent observers say are wanting there. Instead, Bush resorts to the alleged envy by al-Qaeda of the American "way of life." But if envy did not prevent bin Laden from having a close military alliance, implicitly if not explicitly, with the U.S. CIA in Afghanistan in the fight to expel the Soviets in the 1980s (and it didn't), then one should not be so quick to assume that envy plays a leading role in causing the 9/11 attack. Besides, if some questionable mix of envy/hatred of democratic liberties were so prominent a feature in the minds of al-Qaeda members, then why travel so far to attack these democratic institutions? Switzerland and Norway, for example, are closer by. There obviously is more to the situation than envy of our way of life, a way of life which from a typical Muslim standpoint includes a fair amount of licentiousness. Presumably the discrepancy in the control and number of military bases, aircraft carriers and so forth in the Middle East between the U.S. on the one hand, and Switzerland/Norway on the other hand, could be an important factor. To tie a few strands together at this point, what Bush essentially argues is there is no purpose, and that purpose is envy. The reader can note both a logical and a factual problem here.

The issue of whether al-Qaeda's goal really is a global goal ("remaking the world—imposing its radical beliefs on people everywhere"), as Bush asserts, was already discussed and called into question, so it need not be taken up again. The evidence suggests the ultimate goals more plausibly deal with the umma, or Islamic community, rather then the world. But the main point here is the fact that this is a political and religious objective, and it conflicts with the view that only pure evil is the motive. Bush may not think al-Qaeda's political-religious objective is a good objective (just as I do not, for its use of illicit terrorism and for its failure, e.g., to separate church and state); but it is an objective or reason nonetheless, and it needs to be acknowledged without inconsistency. Bush quite appropriately and repeatedly distinguishes a perverted al-Qaeda Islamism from the more legitimate moderate Islam, but a perverted religious goal is still a goal.

By my lights, there is a way out of this dilemma for President Bush, Secretary of State Colin Powell and the other proponents of the No Purpose Theory. It is to come clean and acknowledge that the overwhelming evidence, circumstantial and otherwise, indicates that there were/are religious, political and even economic purposes or motives, then admit that evil and a history of terrorism are more ubiquitous among individuals and nations then he (Bush) has let on. Indeed, while President Bush condemns all terrorism, leaders of a close ally, Israel, have openly avowed terrorist tactics under certain circumstances.[38] Mary Wollstonecraft offered good advice when she wrote, "No man chooses evil because it is evil; he only mistakes it for happiness, which is the good he seeks."[39] And Alexander Solzhenitsyn makes a similar point: "If only there were evil people somewhere insidiously committing evil deeds and it were necessary only to separate them from the rest of us and destroy them. But the line dividing good and evil cuts through the heart of every human being."[40] My point here is not to let bin Laden and al-Qaeda off the hook. I trust that was made clear in my earlier remarks about crimes against humanity. Rather, my point is to question the sharpness of the demarcation between an alliance of the purely good and an axis of the purely evil, and suggest how the No Purpose Theory interacts with and reinforces that illicitly sharp demarcation.

Doug Knapp, Inver Hills Community College

Notes

1. See, e.g., Samuel Huntington, *The Clash of Civilizations and the Remaking of the World Order* (New York: Touchstone-Simon & Schuster, 1996). Regarding Huntington's claim that religious motives are primary, consider the counterexample of the current cordial relationship between the U.S. and Azerbaijan, Turkmenistan, Uzbekistan, and Kazakhstan, all with autocratic and Islamist characteristics. It's plausible that the oil and gas reserves in these countries are the driving force, trumping the opposing religious cultures of Judaic-Christian versus Islam.

2. For insightful background reading on this important topic see Jared Diamond, *The Third Chimpanzee: The Evolution and the Future of the Human Animal*, (HarperCollins, 1992). See especially chapter 17, appropriately labeled "The Golden Age That Never Was," in which Middle East examples are provided.

3. See Rome Statute of the International Criminal Court, Article 7, www.un.org/law/icc/statute/romefra.htm; also see Peter Singer, *One World: The Ethics of Globalization* (New Haven: Yale University Press, 2002), especially Chapter 4, "One Law."

4. The extent of the anger toward U.S. policy by Arabs and Muslims is noted by scholars on what I interpret to be both the political left and right. Michael Doran, e.g., writes, "Even a quick glance at the Islamist press in Arabic demonstrates that many Muslims who do not belong to bin Laden's terrorist network consider the United States to be on a moral par with Genghis Khan." ("Understanding the Enemy," Foreign Affairs (Jan./Feb, 2002): 28.) And Daniel Pipes fairly summarizes the polling results completed shortly after 9/11 which show substantial sympathy among Arabs and Muslims for bin Laden and the main grievances. ("Muslims love bin Laden," October 23, 2001, israelinsider.com) While I find Pipes's interpretation of the polling data to be problematic, his summary of the polling data itself is not.

5. "Understanding Terrorism," Harvard Magazine (Jan.–Feb. 2002), www.harvardmagazine.com.

6. Ibid. (Incidentally, a rebuttal similar to mine of the predominate Kennedy School position is given by Richard Rubenstein, "The Psycho-Political Sources of Terrorism," in *The New Global Terrorism: Characteristics, Causes, Controls*, ed. Charles Kegley, Jr. (Upper Saddle River NJ: Prentice Hall 2003).

7. Thomas Friedman, *The Lexus and the Olive Tree* (New York: Anchor Books, 1999; paperback ed. 2000), 402.

8. Frederick Forsyth, author of *The Day of the Jackel*, "What terrorists said to America, and how America replied," Star Tribune (Sept. 7, 2003): AA6.

9. Remarks with Jordanian Foreign Minister Dr. Marwan Mouasher and Jordanian Minister of Planning Mr. Basem Awadallah, 5/13/03; www.state.gove/secretary/rm/2003/20519.htm.

10. See Donald G. Ellis, "Suicide terrorists aren't insane: Westerners should look to factors in larger society," *Star Tribune*, (Sept. 4, 2003): A17. His article was originally published in the *Hartford Courant* in Pennsylvania.

11. "Trail of Tears," *Encyclopedia of American History*, Vol. 4, ed. Malcolm J. Rohrbough, 2003, 344.

12. Henry Steele Commager, "Nations Aren't Innocent," *The New York Times* (June 27, 1985).

13. See, e.g., Ted Honderich, *After the Terror*, (Edinburgh University Press, 2002), or his conversation with Paul de Rooij on Honderich's web site at http://www.homepages.ucl.ac.uk/~uctytho.

14. For example, with regard to U.S. history, slavery surely involved the use of terror tactics to try to stifle revolt, and Noam Chomsky documents the use of terror tactics by the U.S. against "soft" targets (such as rural medical clinics) in Nicaragua in the 1980s, *The Culture of Terrorism* (Boston, South End Press, 1988), Ch. 8.

15. For a moral defense of a conditional surrender in WWII see James Sterba, "Terrorism and International Justice," in *Philosophy: Paradox and Discovery* (5th edition), eds. Thomas Shipka & Arthur Minton, (McGraw Hill, 2004).

16. Friedman, 402. In connection with the numbers of Iraqi children who died, there is this relevant exchange between Lesley Stahl and Secretary of State Madeleine Albright. Stahl: "We have heard that half a million children have died in Iraq. I mean, that's more children than died in Hiroshima. And you know, is the price worth it?" Albright: "I think this is a very hard choice, but the price? We think the price is worth it." CBS News, 1996.

17. Michael Doran, "Understanding the Enemy," *Foreign Affairs*, (Jan/Feb 2002).

18. See, e.g., Osama bin Laden, et al., "Jihad Against Jews and Crusaders: World Islamic Front Statement," 23 February 1998. Available at http://www.library.cornell.edu/colldev/mideast/wif.htm.

19. Dilip Hiro, "Bush and bin Laden," *The Nation* (Oct. 8, 2001). www.thenation.com.

20. Jeremy Rifkin, *The Hydrogen Economy*, (Tarcher/Putnam, 2002), 92. Rifkin in turn draws from Neela Banerjee, "World Oil at a Glance," New York Times (October 14, 2001): C1.

21. Stanley Hart and Alvin Spivak, *The Elephant in the Bedroom: Automobile Dependence and Denial; Impacts on the Economy and Environment* (Pasadena, CA: New Paradigm Books, 1993).

22. See, e.g., Lester R. Brown, *Plan B: Rescuing a Planet under Stress and a Civilization in Trouble*, (New York: Earth Policy Institute, W.W. Norton & Co., 2003).

23. Wirth et al. write, "U.S. dependence on oil leaves the country's economic, security, and environmental destiny to forces beyond America's control. Reducing this exposure—especially in the transportation sector, which is 95 percent dependent on petroleum—must be a primary goal of national energy policy." Timothy E. Wirth, C. Boyden Gray, and John D. Podesta, "The Future of Energy Policy," *Foreign Affairs*, (July/August, 2003): 133–34. Also see, e.g., Andres Duany, Elizabeth Plater-Zyberk, and Jeff Speck, *Suburban Nation: The Rise of Sprawl and the Decline of the American Dream* (New York: North Point Press, 2000).

24. Michael T. Klare, *Resource Wars* (New York: Henry Holt & Co., 2001), footnote #54, 244. Klare points out that the details surrounding the meeting between FDR and the King have not been fully disclosed. But when Dick Cheney was Secretary of Defense under George Bush the elder, Cheney alluded in a speech to the genuineness and importance of the compact. The general consensus by historians is that Roosevelt was looking out for long-range strategic oil interests.

25. "Britain Says U.S. Planned to Seize Oil in '73 Crisis," *New York Times* (Jan. 12, 2004).

26. Jonathan Schell provides quite a long historical list of U.S. alliances with oppressive governments in "The Case Against the War," *The Nation*, (March 3, 2003): 16.

27. The Shah's secret police force, SAVAK, which was trained by the CIA, was particularly brutal. A middle-of-the-road 1982 6th edition textbook on world civilizations makes the point this way: "SAVAK agents, systematically employing terror [emphasis added] and various forms of torture made the Shah's regime one of the most brutal among the many dictatorships afflicting contemporary civilization." Edward McNall Burns et al., *World Civilizations: Their History and Their Culture* (6th edition), (New York: W. W. Norton & Co., 1982), 1262.

28. "Perspective: Iraqi history lesson," *Energy Compass* (February 27, 2003) and Patrick Cockburn; "Revealed: How the West set Saddam on the bloody road to power," *The Independent* (June 29, 1997); Jim Vallette with Steve Kretzmann and Daphne Wysham, "Crude Vision: How Oil Interests Obscured U.S. Government Focus on Chemical Weapons Use By Saddam Hussein," Sustainable Energy & Economy Network/Institute for Policy Studies (IPS), March 2003, version 1.1, 14.

29. Jim Vallette et al.

30. "Rumsfeld: It Would Be a Short War," CBS (November 15, 2002). Com/stories/2002/11/15/world/main529569.html.

31. Jim Vallette et al., 12–13.

32. George Will, "'No Blood for Oil' Is a Dishonest Anti-War Argument," commentary presented on This Week with George Stephanopoulos (March 3, 2003); Thomas Friedman interviewed by Tim Russet (date unknown).

33. Michael Klare, "Bush-Cheney Energy Strategy: Procuring the Rest of the World's Oil," *Foreign Policy In Focus* (January, 2004).

34. Michael Doran, "Understanding the Enemy," *Foreign Affairs* (Jan/Feb 2002).

35. David Johnston, "Report says Bin Laden wanted U.S.-Saudi rift," *New York Times*, as printed in the Saint Paul Pioneer Press (Sept. 9, 2003): 3A.

36. George W. Bush, Address Delivered to a Joint Session of Congress and the American People, Washington D.C. (September 20, 2001), in *Vital Speeches of the Day* (October 1, 2001): 761.

37. More formally, using connecting hyphens to show the close linkage among the relevant ideas, the best interpretation of Bush's intent would go something like this: "These terrorists kill not only merely-to-end-lives, but to disrupt and end a way of life."

38. President George W. Bush: "[T]here is no such thing as a good terrorist." George W. Bush, UN General Assembly Speech (Nov. 10, 2001), in *Vital Speeches of the Day* (Dec. 1, 2001): 103. Yet former Israeli prime minister Yitzhak Shamir, reflecting on the 1930s

and 1940s and the formation of the state of Israel, said "Personal terror is acceptable under certain conditions and by certain movements." Eric Black, *Parallel Realities: A Jewish/Arab History of Israel/Palestine* (Minneapolis: Paradigm Press, 1992) 108–109.

39. Mary Wollstonecraft, *A Vindication of the Rights of Woman*, (London: J. Johnson, 1792), as cited by Edward O. Wilson, *Consilience: The Unity of Knowledge* (Mew York: Vintage Books, 1998), 268.

40. Alexander Solzhenitsyn, *The Gulag Archipelago*.

Weighing Evils:
Political Violence and Democratic Deliberation

MATTHEW R. SILLIMAN

Abstract: Even if war, terrorism, and other acts of political violence are inherently wrong, in so radically imperfect a world as our own there remains a need, as Virginia Held suggests, to evaluate such acts so as to distinguish between degrees of their unjustifiability. This essay proposes a notion of deliberative democracy as one criterion for such a comparative evaluation. Expanding on an analysis of the psychologically terrorizing impact of violence borrowed from Hannah Arendt, I suggest that it is principally this that makes for the special wrongness of terrorism, though that by itself does not show that it is never necessary.

An effort to distinguish clearly the superiority of states over non-state actors (or vice versa) in this regard proves futile, so I conclude that there is no automatic legitimacy to be gained by either sort. It follows that we should weigh an act of political violence on its own demerits irrespective of whether it is done by a state or by a group in opposition to states, and further that we should resist the propagandistic labeling of non-state violence as "evil" or "terroristic," where such terms beg the question of its relative merits, in context, vis-à-vis state violence.

I. Introduction

In this essay, I will seek to understand the wrongness of terrorism as flowing from its "terrorizing" effects on mental and emotional capacities, such as trust and security, that are requisite for democratic deliberation broadly construed, and to illustrate this effect with some recent and contemporary political examples. The peculiar moral awfulness of terrorism as a special sort of violence, I will argue, has something to do not only with its physical and psychological effects on individuals, but also with its larger consequences for relationships, communities, and institutions, and as such. My aim is modest; I attempt to provide neither detailed argumentation for a definition of terrorism nor a point-by-point analysis of any particular historical moment. Rather I offer some suggestions about the concept of terrorism and what might make it such a bad thing, and I chart some possible implications of this for the unjustifiability, for example, of recent U.S. government actions.

II. What Is Wrong with Terrorism?

That terrorism is morally abhorrent would seem uncontroversial, even analytic, but this has evidently not prevented quite a few people from advocating and practicing it. One natural and common way to interpret this fact is to conclude that terrorism's advocates and practitioners, or at least some of them, are simply beyond the moral pale, and thus exterminable without compunction. An equally natural (if at the moment less popular) reading is that although they may wish to be perfectly decent people, terrorists (rightly or wrongly) feel themselves to be driven to such desperately immoral measures by an even greater injustice.[1] On this interpretation, which I will assume for the sake of this essay, terrorists are *weighing evils*, as all of us do in our daily lives on a smaller scale; they are capable of accepting that their actions are very wrong, but have judged (rightly or wrongly) that the evils they oppose render it necessary for them to do those actions nonetheless. In the present political climate it is difficult to state this more charitable interpretation without seeming to defend or encourage terrorism, but it is intellectual cowardice to fear such appearances when they are false, and to do so could leave us with only the xenophobic and exterminationist reading—a very dangerous perspective.

So what *is* wrong with terrorism? I ask the question in this way not to imply that there is nothing wrong with it, but rather to emphasize that what most take to be its self-evident wrongness really does require elucidation. Moreover, I ask this question in preference to the more objective-seeming "What is terrorism?" in deference to the insight that no adequate discussion of the subject can remain above its substantive moral content. Most obviously we might argue that it is morally wrong because it is violent, or an example of violence against innocents, but this does not seem sufficiently to set it off as the unique evil we take it to be. By etymology and logic violence is not mere force; *all* violence invades and transgresses life, honor, dignity, or justice in a way that unfairly injures or diminishes someone who does not deserve such treatment. In this purely formal sense, everyone on the receiving end of violence is innocent. Nor will it help us much to place terrorism's egregious wrongness on its use of violence specifically for *political* purposes, for (as we shall see) that would give us frighteningly little basis for distinguishing it from garden-variety state coercion. The fact that terrorism is indeed morally indistinguishable from far too much state-sanctioned force should not tempt us into a wholesale conflation of the two.

Perhaps the moral evil that accompanies both the intentions and effects of terrorism, and that it may not share with all violence or even all political violence, is its specifically collective psychological impact. Here again etymology may help; terrorism by its name aims to terrify, immobilize, or cow, not so much its victims (who, if all goes according to plan, are mostly dead[2]), but those who witness or hear about it, thereby affecting their state of mind, their relationships with each other and their wider social communities, and especially their relationships with their leaders. This process of undermining the psychological confidence of a group or population, shocking them (for several possible purposes) into a state like what the philosopher Tom Digby calls "radical unsafety," is perhaps what makes terrorism a political act, a darkly vivid demonstration that personal psychological states, perhaps especially fearful and unpleasant ones, have large political effects. But to accept, even provisionally, that this is a key aspect of how terrorism operates and why it is especially violent, we need to know more about the psychological details of terrorization.

III. Terrorization

In a recent paper entitled "Terrorism, Terror, and Coercion, the Uses of a Psychological State," Jeremy Waldron[3] proposes just such a link between terrorism and terrorization, and suggests that we should reserve the term "terror" in this context specifically for a mental state that overrides the faculties of rational deliberation. According to his analysis whereas ordinary, garden-variety fears may function as both data for and measurable influences in our everyday rational decisions, terror proper completely overwhelms such calculations, rendering us panic-stricken, incoherent, and our choices volatile (or not really choices at all). In support of this proposal he cites Hannah Arendt in *The Origins of Totalitarianism*, where describing conditions under the Nazis she writes of "the bestial, desperate terror which, when confronted by real, present horror, inexorably paralyzes everything that is not mere reaction,"[4] and suggests that "under conditions of total terror not even fear can any longer serve as an advisor of how to behave."[5] Waldron observes:

> A man threatened with torture may confess to something that carries an even worse penalty later, because the present prospect of the lash or the electrodes is so awful as to overwhelm any prospect of prudential deliberation about the future. Fear is no longer his guide to action; it is simply the basis of his recoiling from a certain stimulus. The threat that is offered—along with a vivid demonstration of the sanction—so panics those who are confronted with it that they respond immediately to avert it, without consideration of whether even more fearful consequences will accrue thereby.

Waldron dubs this phenomenon "Arendtian terrorization" and contrasts it with more usual instances of coercion in which the options, though fearful and unpleasant, may still be weighed with a certain amount of detachment.[6]

This distinction may be useful for our project of understanding how terrorism is wrong, but it is first worth observing that we experience these effects on a continuum. No rational deliberation, however clear-eyed, is ever entirely free of the influence of (often unacknowledged) fears, doubts, or other unsafe feelings. The other end of the scale is not so attenuated, unfortunately; total terror is a real possibility, but the experience of abject and sustained terror that completely short-circuits calculation is, thankfully, a rarity for most of us. For Waldron's distinction to help us, we would have to identify a threshold, a space on the continuum where the correctable effects on rational deliberation of ordinary fear shift to the ineluctable distortions of Arendtian terror. Although the extremes are not difficult to identify, the boundary is famously difficult to delimit, as witness traditional debates about such issues as the scope of free will and the problem of false consciousness.

IV. Democratic Discourse

Without resolving these puzzles definitively, however, we can certainly identify levels of terrorization that significantly distort clarity of thought, especially as it manifests itself in political, as opposed to purely individual, deliberation. Since terrorism is, as observed earlier, a specifically political form of violence, perhaps the space we must identify is not so much where (game-theoretically idealized) rational deliberation loses viability, but rather where free political discourse becomes so undermined through terrorizing acts and threats that the trust and safety necessary for safe, open communication, and hence effective and respectful democratic exchange, loses its robust, empowering meaning. Difficult as it is to know for certain when and to what extent a person's actions are uncoerced, we may be able to identify with reasonable clarity when a community has lost its ability to function in this way.

Aside, then, from the painfully obvious violence of terrorism toward its victims, and distortions in the rational judgment of the secondary targets that radiate from it, one great (and perhaps the greatest) evil of terroristic means is their tendency to undermine the possibility of democratic relations, whether by intention or merely in their effect.[7] By "democratic relations" I do not principally refer to those periodic ceremonial co-optations of the general will officially known as "free and fair elections." Rather, I have in mind a deeper and somewhat more personal notion of democracy in which human relations on every level are inclusive, respectful and non-bullying, the effect being to promote in all participants a sense of interpersonal safety and empathy that empowers them both to be open to the words of others and to speak freely themselves. Genuinely free elections and other institutional forms of inclusive decision-making would presumably supervene as needed on democratic relations of this sort. Of course, agreement on important issues is far from assured when communication operates on these principles—quite the contrary, for where people feel safe to be heard as well as to listen the results are unpredictable and likely to be diverse and contentious. Thus it is not as an idealized, utopian fantasy that we wish to protect democratic discourse from the effects of terror, but simply as the precondition for everyday decency and respect among people.

Of course, terrorism is not the only force militating against democratic communication as I have described it, so to the extent that this defines the evil of terrorism it will equivalently mark for censure other forms of bullying, intimidation, and silencing, whether perpetrated by common criminals, abusive spouses, rapacious industries, cultural habits, institutional structures, or states. I do not shy away from this consequence, for it helps to put the evil of terrorism in perspective as not only a violator of the human rights of its immediate victims, but of the social rights (so to speak) of its indirect victims or targets, a violation I take to be no less pernicious. That is to say, I aim by this analysis not to downgrade or trivialize the evil of terrorism but rather to upgrade and emphasize the moral importance of democratic communication, and thereby the social conditions that make it possible.

Arendt herself makes a similar point. Speaking specifically of state-perpetrated terrorization—secret laws, secret police, pressure on citizens to inform on each other, apparently random and brutal punishment for unknown offences, and so forth—she notes that such conditions undermine the trust necessary for certain forms of social interaction, specifically discussion among citizens to evaluate or critique what is going on. In Waldron's paraphrase:

> By destroying—through this radical and panic-stricken mistrust—the opportunities for both public deliberation and private conversation, the terrorizing regime effects a radical isolation of individuals from one another, leaving what were once citizens as helpless, terrified, isolated animals.[8]

In Arendt's compelling insight, even the most private of thoughts are parasitic on articulate dialogue among friends and a wider community, so the end result of sustained terrorization is destruction even of an individual capacity for moral deliberation and the exercise of conscience.[9]

I would add to this analysis two suggestions. First, as I have suggested, the destruction of a community's capacity for open deliberation is in itself a great evil over and above its effects on individuals. Second, it is not only state terrorism that functions in this way, as Americans now understand poignantly, but non-state acts of terror as well. Although someone might try to argue that the events of September 11, 2001 have stimulated a salutary focus by (some) United States citizens on certain world injustices, subsequent events suggest that the much larger effect was to launch the nation into a state of permanent warfare—a condition known for fostering neither open and reasonable discussion nor greater justice (though it has tended to generate dangerous illusions of "moral clarity").

V. State and Non-State Terror

If we accept, then, that this terrorizing effect on public discourse is a major component of what makes terrorism particularly evil, it is still worth asking whether there is a sustainable moral distinction between non-state uses of terror and state actions that have comparable social effects. I raise this question in the spirit of Virginia Held's observation that it is important and necessary, in our highly imperfect world, to distinguish degrees of unjustifiability even among acts that are all egregiously wrong.[10] Such a distinction is important, I believe, because it keeps us honest; it is one thing to say an action is necessary though regrettable under evil circumstances, and something rather different to say it is a generally justifiable sort of action. Neglect of the difference may make unnecessary wars more publicly acceptable (as when the Bush administration parlayed an arguably legitimate campaign in Afghanistan into a much more dubious assault on Iraq).

Are there, then, general moral regularities upon which we can rely in evaluating terror? We tend to give states the benefit of the doubt because of their putative role in sustaining the economic, legal, diplomatic, and political context without which social deliberation is next to impossible. States can, and sometimes do, create an environment for human thriving and open communication difficult or impossible to achieve otherwise. Stability in these terms is of tremendous importance to genuine democracy, a value which revolutionaries overlook at everyone's peril, and (at least in the present era) only states can provide it. This sense of inevitability is perhaps why almost everyone rejects anarchism in practice, though it is so appealing in theory, and why we forgive states so quickly for crimes that we would vilify anyone else for contemplating.

In light of this double standard, though, we should observe that it is possible to overrate stability, particularly when it is purchased at the cost of someone else's instability; powerful states are notorious for exporting terror through the support of dictators and repressive regimes deemed economically or strategically useful. Moreover, states have the technological power, which until recently non-state actors generally lacked, to "shock and awe" the people of those terrorizing regimes they have decided are no longer useful—a language and a tactic that makes the distinction increasingly difficult to sustain. The concentration of power in a state, that is, makes it potentially (and often actually) a supremely effective perpetrator of terror, whether against its foreign enemies or at home (as in the case of Hitler's Germany, Stalin's Russia, and perhaps one day soon Ashcroft's America[11]).

This history might incline us to give moral preference to smaller social units, inherently more manageable as deliberative bodies and hence in principle more considerate of individual voices. But no one who has witnessed the political complexities of a corporation, an activist organization, a family, or for that matter a university from the inside will be sanguine about a small group's immunity to micro-terrorization among its members. Nor is such a group necessarily more likely to make a far-sighted or humane choice, in extreme circumstances, when contemplating terrorizing means in an intractably evil context. If states seem marginally more prone to evil choices, perhaps it is only because their position in the world means they trade more frequently, and on a larger scale, in intractable dilemmas.

Again, the question is not who will make the best choice (there being no good options *ex hypothesi*), but what sort of deliberative unit is likely to make choices that in the circumstances are (in Virginia Held's phrase) "least unjustifiable." Though there are of course better and worse states in this regard, and better and worse substate groups, there does not seem to be any general grounds to privilege *a priori* one *type* of deliberative body over the other, where decisions to use or not to use terrorizing violence is concerned.[12] Thus we have no choice but to weigh acts or contemplated acts of political violence in context on their particular demerits, irrespective of the scale of the actor. That such acts are indeed terrorizing is a highly relevant moral datum, but not by itself dispositive.

I began by affirming that terrorism is clearly and egregiously wrong, and have tried to explore what may be wrong with it, specifically as a form of political violence (that is, a violation against open social and political discourse as such, not merely violence with a political end). By thus joining the chorus of condemnation, however, I may risk playing into the hands of propagandists of several sorts, who trade on popular revulsion to this emotionally freighted term to demonize their opponents and justify their own (often terroristic) reactions. Let me conclude, therefore, by repeating my caution against such manipulative uses of strong moral language, which can itself paralyze clear moral thought and conversation. If I have myself offered a "persuasive definition" of terrorism, I hope I have done so in a democratic spirit, and that its upshot is to insist on at least as much nuance in our moral evaluation of non-state terrorism as for warfare and other terroristic acts of states.

Matthew R. Silliman, Massachusetts College of Liberal Arts

Notes

1. An obvious third alternative is that they do not actually describe themselves as "terrorists," but rather as "freedom fighters" or some other benign and heroic-sounding term. However, it is not impossible to describe accurately those who use terrorist tactics as terrorists, regardless of how they wish to describe themselves or what their larger aims might be. Since they are aware of the mayhem their methods wreak, I take this to be a terminological variant of the second reading.

2. This may be too flippant; it is worth distinguishing between the 9/11 terrorists, who apparently sought to maximize casualties, from many earlier non-state terrorist groups, who aimed for maximum publicity while keeping actual deaths and maimings comparatively small. In any case my point here is that the direct *victims* of terrorism, as in war, are not generally its primary *targets*.

3. Jeremy Waldron, "Terrorism, Terror, and Coercion: The Uses of a Psychological State," presented at the University of Arizona conference on Terrorism and Violence (March 7, 2003).

4. Hannah Arendt, *The Origins of Totalitarianism*, new edition (Harcourt Brace Jovanovich, 1973), 441.

5. Ibid., 467.

6. Waldron retells the ancient Jack Benny joke about the man who, confronted by an armed thief who says "your money or your life" makes no answer. Pressed for a reply he protests: "I'm thinking! I'm thinking!" The humor of the joke may turn on the absurdity of the man's treating the threat as a matter for rational deliberation, rather than an effort to terrify him into compliance.

7. Various users of terror might have different aims, and such aims may or may not be rational or coherently considered. My contention is principally, therefore, that terrorism tends to have these *effects*, whatever its express or tacit aims.

8. Waldron, 18.

9. See Hanna Arendt, *The Life of the Mind* (Harcourt Brace Jovanovich, 1978), Vol. 1, 185ff.

10. Virginia Held, "Terrorism and War," presented at the University of Arizona conference on Terrorism and Violence (March 7, 2003).

11. Many people will understandably find this apparently casual comparison offensive, and of course I do not equate these cases exactly. However, numerous domestic initiatives of the Bush Administration, and especially those energetically promoted by Attorney General John Ashcroft, make some comparisons inevitable. I have in mind specifically: 1) several provisions of the USA Patriot act, such as those that enable federal agents to search homes and businesses secretly and obtain a warrant afterward, secretly obtain library records, monitor email, and so forth; 2) the TOPS initiative requiring postal carriers and others to report "suspicious" behavior of their customers; 3) the proposed creation of a "total information center" comprising a massive governmental database on all US residents; 4) several alarming provisions in apparent drafts of the USA Patriot Act II. My contention is that these and other assaults on civil liberties are not fundamentally tools for preventing terrorism (for which purpose they do little), but rather for controlling, intimidating, and repressing democratic dissent.

12. Popular discourse makes much of the distinction between the deliberate targeting of civilians by non-state terrorists, on the one hand, and the "collateral damage" to unlucky civilians in wars on the other, but there is less moral distinction there than meets the eye, since retaliation to terrorism often kills more civilians than the terrorism itself, and since such "unintended" deaths are a known, not a hypothetical consequence of modern warfare.

Rawls's Decent Peoples and the Democratic Peace Thesis

WALTER RIKER

Abstract: In *The Law of Peoples*, Rawls defends the stability of his proposed international order with the democratic peace thesis. But he fails to extend this thesis to decent peoples, which is curious, since they are a non-temporary feature of his law of peoples. This opens Rawls's proposal to certain objections, which I argue can be met once we understand fully the nature of the democratic peace. Nevertheless, there is reason to worry about the stability of Rawls's proposed international order. This worry has little to do with decent peoples, though, and is generated by other features of his law of peoples.

I. Introduction

In *The Law of Peoples* (hereafter *LP*), John Rawls uses the Democratic Peace Thesis to defend the possibility of a realistic utopia, a just and peaceful world.[1] Although Rawls includes decent peoples (non-democratic constitutional republics) in his utopian vision, he discusses the democratic peace as obtaining only between liberal peoples. This is curious, since decent peoples are a non-temporary feature of his proposed world order. By failing to extend the thesis in this way, Rawls undercuts his claim for the stability of his utopian vision and invites the objection that liberal democracies really ought to democratize decent peoples. I argue this objection can be met, once we understand the nature of the democratic peace. Decent peoples are not an inherently destabilizing feature of Rawls's proposed world order, so concern for global stability does not give us reason to democratize them. Nevertheless, there are reasons to worry about the stability of Rawls's society of peoples. His law of peoples allows huge inequalities of wealth to develop between peoples, but denies that international justice requires the development of democratic international or regional institutions. This denies all poorer peoples (liberal and decent) the opportunity to make justice claims for a greater share of the global cooperative surplus. This state of affairs could lead to resentments between peoples that could cause war. Rawls answers that, since the law of peoples treats all peoples as equals, all peoples have been treated as equals and should be satisfied. But this is not a satisfactory response.

Though I discuss this issue from a Rawlsian perspective, this is not a peculiarly Rawlsian problem. Decent peoples are non-democratic constitutional republics, similar to the traditional republics described in Cicero's *On the Commonwealth* (54–51 BC), Machiavelli's *Discourses* (1531), and Rousseau's *Social Contract* (1762). The central issue here is this: would the existence of such republics pose an inherent threat to global peace? Must we democratize all nations in the world in order to secure the possibility of global stability? I argue that we need not go so far, because the most important norms and institutions thought to secure the peace between democratic societies can also be found in decent republics. Global peace could be secured in a world society of liberal democracies and non-democratic constitutional republics. Perhaps the most important implication of this is that a concern for global peace does not give one good reason to democratize non-democratic societies.

II. Rawls's Liberal and Decent (Hierarchical) Peoples

Rawls's "peoples" are not states simpliciter, but artificial corporate moral agents or persons. Peoples possess several features (not necessarily possessed by states) that give them this status.[2] First, they possess some important degree of cultural unity, for instance, in public political culture, that allows them to secure identifiable and determinate ends as peoples. Second, they have the institutional means to act on the global stage to further their ends. Third, they possess a moral character, i.e., the capacity to regulate pursuit of ends according to principles of justice. Rawls maintains too that peoples are well-ordered and self-sufficient schemes of social cooperation among individual human persons.[3] This means that the members of a people constitute and govern themselves as a society through a public and (for the most part) voluntarily affirmed conception of justice, without excessive coercion, manipulation or deception. They recognize that justice is centered on the inviolability of persons and understand their society to be a system of cooperation aimed at and justified by the good of all individual members, and not by some notion of aggregate or corporate good.

Liberal democratic peoples organize the body politic according to one of a family of liberal political conceptions. In these conceptions, individual persons are seen as free and equal citizens who are both rational and reasonable. Liberal conceptions are further characterized by three main features. First, a list of basic rights, liberties and opportunities, such as are found in constitutional societies; second, the assignment of special priority to these rights, liberties and opportunities with respect to claims of general good and perfectionist values; third, measures ensuring all citizens the all-purpose means to make effective use of their freedoms.[4] These features define a generic liberalism that is fleshed out in the cases of particular historical liberal peoples through public political discourse. Rawls's justice as fairness[5] is his preferred conception of liberalism, but he recognizes that it represents only one of a family of such conceptions.[6] The U.S., Canada, and Great Britain, while perhaps not yet thoroughly just, are all generically liberal democracies. None instantiates justice as fairness.

Decent peoples are non-liberal and non-democratic, but they deserve full and good standing in the international community because unlike outlaw states, burdened societies and benevolent absolutisms, they are well-ordered, secure certain conditions of political right and justice for members, and honor the principles of justice that constitute the law of peoples.[7] Most importantly for this paper, they recognize that peoples are free and independent, honor basic human rights, recognize a duty of nonintervention, recognize a right to war only in self-defense, observe restrictions in the conduct of such wars, and observe a duty to assist peoples living under unfavorable conditions that prevent their having minimally decent societies. There may be several types of decent peoples, but Rawls outlines just one, decent hierarchical peoples.

Decent hierarchical peoples are committed to what Rawls's calls a "common good idea of justice."[8] Several things follow. First, decent hierarchical peoples secure human rights for their members, including rights to subsistence and security, to liberty (freedom from slavery and freedom of conscience sufficient for freedom of thought and religion), to property, and to formal equality. Second, a decent people's system of laws fits its common good idea of justice in a way that generates real obligations and duties. The members of decent societies are seen as reasonable, rational, and responsible persons who are cooperating members of their respective groups. They must be able to recognize the relationship between their laws and their common good, in a way that allows them to see their duties and obligations as contributing to the common good. Finally, the officials who administer the legal system must sincerely and not unreasonably believe that the laws are guided by their common good conception of justice.

Decent hierarchical peoples may exhibit several different institutional forms, but all are associationist.[9] Both decent and liberal peoples regard the basic social structure to be a genuine scheme of social cooperation between persons, but they differ in the way each organizes persons into the body politic. In decent societies, group membership mediates between persons and political authority and power, while in liberal societies there is no such mediation. Members of decent societies are seen as individual persons, each of whom is capable of understanding their common good idea of justice. However, from the perspective of public life, these individuals are viewed first and foremost as members of different associations or groups, and not as free and equal citizens. Persons are first associated with groups, the groups are organized into the body politic, and the groups are represented in the legal system in a decent consultation hierarchy. Individual persons have a right to express political dissent at some point in the political process, for instance, by choosing the group's representatives to the government, but there is no commitment to the ideal of "one person, one vote." The representatives express the interests of the group before government officials. The government must listen to representatives, take dissent seriously and offer conscientious replies to complaints, and allow representatives to renew their dissent, so long as such protest is not unreasonable or inconsistent with their common good idea of justice.

As an example of a decent hierarchical people, Rawls describes an idealized Islamic people called "Kazanistan."[10] Kazanistan does not separate church and state. The favored religion is Islam, so only Muslims are allowed to hold the highest government positions. However, other religions are not only tolerated but encouraged. Kazanistan has an enlightened view of non-Islamic religions, believing, among other things, that religious differences are divinely willed, that God alone should hand out punishment for false belief, that different religious communities should respect one another, and so on. Kazanistan is non-aggressive, having rejected military interpretations of jihad in favor of a moral and spiritual one. The Muslim rulers believe that individuals want to be loyal to the country in which they were born, and will stay loyal as long as they are not treated unfairly. To strengthen the loyalty of non-Muslim members, the government allows them to join the military and to hold relatively high positions of command.

Kazanistan has a decent consultation hierarchy, which changes from time to time in a way that responds to their common good idea of justice. Representative bodies of all groups are consulted about political decisions, and each member of society is represented by at least one of these groups. The representative bodies include some members of the groups they represent. The rulers must weigh the views of consulted bodies before making final decisions, and must offer not unreasonable explanations when these are called for by representative bodies. Decisions should be made according to the special priorities of Kazanistan but within the limits set by the overall scheme of cooperation, the common good idea of justice (i.e., individuals cannot be sacrificed for common or aggregate good). These special priorities would include, for instance, the establishing of a decent Muslim people that respects the religious minorities that are part of it.

III. Rawls's Realistic Utopia

In *LP*, Rawls focuses on the possibility of a realistic utopia, a just and peaceful world of liberal and decent peoples.[11] Toward this end, and in line with his commitments to reasonable disagreement and reciprocity, he offers two contractualist original position arguments, one for liberal peoples, one for decent, and shows that a common set of principles would be affirmed by both, from this shared moral point of view. His vision is utopian because it defends the possibility of global peace and justice. It is realistic because it takes peoples as they are and shows how the law of peoples they would affirm, from a shared moral point of view, would produce a peaceful world society, and can be applied to ongoing relationships between peoples.

Rawls's utopia is not the end of human history. It is the realization of certain core moral conditions which, once in place, ensure that the further development of peoples may be regarded as consistent with liberty and justice. Although Rawls argues that all peoples are equal as peoples, and that decent peoples deserve respect, he regards liberal peoples as superior.[12] Thus, in his utopia, liberal peoples may still have reasons to try to liberalize and democratize decent peoples. Due respect means that we cannot coercively demand that all societies be liberal, but it does not mean that we cannot engage in a politics of persuasion, so long as we are careful not to frustrate or otherwise injure the vitality and self-respect of any decent people.[13] If we can extend the democratic peace to decent peoples, then a concern for global peace is not a reason to democratize them.

IV. The Democratic Peace Thesis

The term "democratic peace" refers to two related claims: a) that democracies[14] are not likely to fight wars[15] against each other; and b) that some feature(s) of democratic societies cause(s) this peace. The descriptive claim, that there is a correlation between democracy and peace, is well-supported by empirical evidence[16] and is widely accepted by international relations scholars.[17] The causal claim, that some feature(s) of democratic societies cause(s) this peace, is supported by several different types of accounts.[18] In the following sections I will discuss several common causal accounts: Satisfaction, Constitutional Constraint, Reelection Constraint, Normative, and Interdependence accounts.

Most causal explanations make no essential reference to democracy as such. The mere fact that some society chooses its leaders through popular elections is rarely offered as an explanation of the democratic peace. Rather, they refer to other institutions and norms typically found in liberal democracies. An open question here is whether these, or relevantly similar, institutions and norms are found in decent societies.

In the following sections I discuss these several norms and institutions, but I do not offer them as a list of necessary and sufficient conditions for the democratic peace. In fact, many researchers believe they have found the most important condition of the peace. Rawls thinks the satisfaction account alone is sufficient.[19] However, the criteria are not mutually exclusive either. It is reasonable to think that several factors are at work in any historical instance of democratic peace. In what follows I argue that decent peoples meet enough of the criteria to justify the conclusion that their existence would not threaten the democratic peace. I make particular appeal to the satisfaction and constitutional constraint accounts. This defuses the objection that their existence in Rawls's international order undercuts his claim for the stability of that order. Further, it shows that a concern for global stability is not a reason for democracies to try to democratize decent peoples.

V. Satisfaction Accounts

The main idea behind satisfaction accounts is that democratic societies are satisfied in three key ways, so they have no reason to go to war with each other.[20] First, the basic needs of individual members are met. Second, the members, understood now as whole peoples, are satisfied with and have proper pride in the decency of their shared history and social and political institutions. Third, the interests of democratic societies, again understood as wholes, are compatible with the interests of other democratic societies. Satisfied societies are internally stable and thus peaceful. Further, other societies have no reason to intervene in the domestic affairs of such societies. A world of these societies would also be externally stable, since no society would have reason to attack any other.

The claim that the members of a society are satisfied does not imply that dissenters are nonexistent. To the contrary, every satisfied society will have dissenters. In liberal democracies there are individuals who reject even the most fundamental of institutional arrangements. For instance, some reject winner take all democracy, regarding it as incompatible with genuinely shared political authority. The existence of dissenters, however, does not make a society unstable. In liberal societies individuals are allowed to express dissent, and there is always the possibility of reform. Actual reform is, of course, a remote possibility, but this is enough to give dissenters hope and keep them from despair and violence. Further, it is not clear how dissenters might secure desired reforms through wars. It must be admitted, though, that it is possible that dissenters might seek aid from other states in mounting coups, if they were to lose all hope.

We have good reason to regard the citizens of decent societies as satisfied. The basic human rights of individuals are secured. They understand their society to be consistent with their conception of justice. We can thus believe that the citizens of decent societies may feel a proper pride in what they have accomplished as a people, that is, in the securing of human rights for citizens, in the decency of their institutions, in the vitality of the civic and public life, and so on. This makes them internally stable and makes it unnecessary for any society to intervene in their domestic affairs. Decent peoples respect the law of peoples and see all peoples as equal and free. They are non-aggressive and non-expansionist, and they respect the duties of non-intervention and aid. So the interests of decent peoples are compatible with those of other liberal and decent peoples.

One might object that members of decent societies cannot be satisfied, since they do not all have the rights that we have in liberal societies. For instance, all members of decent societies have a measure of freedom of conscience, but this freedom is not equal.[21] It may be the case in some decent societies that one religion legally controls much of the government, while other tolerated religions are refused access to certain positions. How can we regard the members of these tolerated minority religions as truly satisfied, when they are not all equally free? Here recall that decent peoples are associationist.[22] Members of decent societies view themselves and their fellow citizens in public life first as members of different associations or groups. They do not understand themselves to be free and equal citizens in the way we do. It is reasonable to think they would not need all of the freedoms that we have or expect freedoms to be equally distributed, so we should not regard their unequal distribution as something that would trouble them.

Many critics of Rawls's *LP* have argued that his account of international justice is weak and lacks teeth.[23] This is surely a mistake. In a world society of decent and liberal peoples, massive violations of basic human rights (aggressive wars, genocides, widespread domestic oppression, and so on) would not occur. Both decent and liberal peoples are committed to ridding the world of these problems.[24] This is not to say that all persons would have the full set of rights and liberal aspirations detailed in the various Conventions on Human Rights. The point is that there would be no need for societies to intervene (politically, militarily, or economically) in the domestic affairs of other societies, if all societies were either decent or liberal. Liberal peoples might feel it necessary to engage in a politics of persuasion, in the hope that decent peoples would eventually see the value of liberalism, but there is no compelling justification for intervention.

A world society of satisfied liberal and decent peoples would be stable, according to the satisfaction account. Nevertheless, there is still reason to worry about the satisfaction of peoples (both decent and liberal) in Rawls's international order. Insofar as his law of peoples allows for huge inequalities in wealth to develop, and provides no resources for justice claims that might serve to close the gap, there is a real possibility that poorer peoples will become dissatisfied. I will return to this issue at the end of the paper.

VI. Constitutional Constraint Accounts

Constitutional Constraint accounts are based on constitutional and legal restrictions on executive action typically found in democracies.[25] These restrictions, coupled with public debate, are thought to slow the march to war, providing the states involved with time to find peaceful solutions to disagreements. These restrictions also make it difficult for democracies to launch surprise attacks, which reduces the fear felt by both sides when democracies find themselves at odds.

The term "constitution" has two meanings.[26] It may refer to a text, to some written document that proclaims certain fundamental social rules. The U.S. has a constitution in this sense, while England does not. And there is a prior, deeper meaning, which Samuel Freeman calls its "institutional" sense.[27] In this sense, a constitution is a set of fundamental, shared, publicly recognized and commonly accepted rules for making and applying laws. These fundamental norms define the offices and positions of political authority in a political system, their qualifications, rights, powers, duties, and so on, and the procedures for making, applying and enforcing laws. Written constitutions presuppose the existence of institutional constitutions. Constitutions are written to proclaim the important social norms shared by the writers and those they represent. Both the U.S. and England have institutional constitutions. Institutional constitutions do several things. Most importantly, they restrict the arbitrary rule of leaders.

Decent societies have institutional constitutions. Rulers and the ruled have internalized, to a significant degree, a shared set of fundamental social norms. The members of decent societies have internalized a respect for basic human rights. They also understand their laws to generate genuine obligations and duties. This is because they have internalized their social norms and see their laws as consistent with them, that is, as being grounded by their constitution. Rulers will feel a responsibility to uphold their shared social norms and will feel it necessary to justify departures from them in a way that is not unreasonably inconsistent with the norms. Non-ruling members will similarly feel a responsibility to uphold the rules, and they will want to question any departures and irregularities and ask for reasons not inconsistent with those rules whenever changes are proposed.

Decent societies are committed to fundamental norms that explicitly restrict aggressive behavior, e.g., rules defining *jus ad bellum* and *jus in bello*, and others that implicitly restrict such conduct, e.g., norms regarding basic human rights and the equality of peoples. These commitments bind members to certain political institutions, practices, and procedures, all of which reduce the likelihood of war. Further, these commitments produce in (many) persons a willingness to seek nonlethal remedies to some disputes, i.e., a disposition against unnecessary war.

There is public debate in decent societies. All groups have a voice in the government through the decent consultation hierarchy, and dissent must be taken seriously. While this is not the kind of public debate we are used to in liberal democracies, it is debate nonetheless, and it would slow the march to war.

VII. Reelection Constraint Accounts

Reelection constraint accounts are based on the idea that democratic leaders want to be reelected and hence are especially sensitive to the political consequences of wars.[28] In democratic states there is a high likelihood that leaders will lose their offices after the loss of a war, especially if they are thought to have initiated the war.[29] In liberal democracies the power of rulers is always subject to the will of the citizenry. Individual citizens often have conflicting interests and inclinations, so there is small chance the citizenry will agree about the need for war. Rulers who find war unavoidable will have to develop strong cases, to persuade a substantial majority of citizens, but this is difficult to do. Hence, rulers who pursue war will often have to do so without broad public support. But few rulers wish to proceed against the will of the people, and those who are willing to do so can be removed from office by citizens in elections, so liberal democratic rulers are less likely to initiate wars than leaders of other kinds of societies.

Decent societies are constitutional societies, which implies well-entrenched norms that restrict the use and regulate the transfer of political power. Any society committed to basic human rights and the equality of peoples will have constitutional restrictions on the ability of leaders to engage in war. A commitment to such norms implies a commitment to some means for reining in rogue leaders, for replacing them in office and transferring their power to someone else. Thus we can be confident that decent peoples have the institutional means to replace leaders who lose the confidence of the body politic.

Decent consultation hierarchies ensure that all groups are heard before political decisions are made, and this allows for substantial dissent to be expressed. While it is tempting to think that the members of decent peoples are more similar in inclination and interest than the members of a liberal peoples, this would be a mistake. Decent peoples may be understood as societies based on or instantiating some comprehensive philosophical or religious doctrine. So consider the history of Christianity. This is a shared religious doctrine coupled with a vast number of inclinations and interests. This convoluted, complicated history contains countless alternative interpretations and understandings of a shared history and a common set of ideas. It is not surprising that we rarely find consensus in the Christian population about war. So there is good reason to think consensus will be hard to reach in decent societies too.

But there is still reason to worry about decent societies, since it is not clear that the diversity of opinions likely to be found in them will put much pressure on leaders to conform. Decent leaders are insulated from the citizenry in two ways. First, the consultation hierarchy has a "funneling" effect. In decent societies citizens express themselves to their representatives in the consultation hierarchy. These representatives will not be able to express all of the views of those they represent; they will even likely disagree with some of them, and so will present only certain views to the government. Thus the number of different opinions held by the citizenry will be funneled down to a significantly smaller number of opinions actually presented to the leadership. This may make consensus easier to gain in decent societies than in liberal ones.

Second, it is not clear how much influence the citizenry has on the selection of leaders in decent societies. Decent leaders are not responsible directly to the citizenry, because decisions about the fitness of rulers are made by some favored subset of the population. Imagine a decent society, the majority of whose citizens belong to non-ruling groups. The ruling group cannot ignore the interests of non-ruling groups in selecting rulers, but it is not clear that the members of non-ruling groups have much influence over the eventual selection of leaders. The ruling group may overrule non-ruling groups, as long as this is not unreasonably inconsistent with their shared social norms. In the domestic case for decent societies, reasonable pluralism actually seems to make rulers less responsible to the people generally.

VIII. Normative Accounts

Normative accounts are based on the idea that democracies share cultural or normative features that cause them to perceive each other as peaceful and non-threatening.[30] Democracies tend to see other democracies as peaceful and non-threatening because they perceive them to be committed to liberal ideals and to be reasonable, predictable and trustworthy. Democracies thus believe the intentions of other democracies are always peaceful toward them.

Decent peoples fail on this account of the democratic peace, as they are just not like liberal peoples in several important respects. They are associationist, not liberal. Their view of the relationship between individual persons and political authority and power is very different from our view. Their conception of justice and public life is very different from our own. Their understanding of rights falls well short of the set of rights that characterizes liberal peoples. We may see, in a sense, how they come to the views that they hold, but these views express a very different understanding of the world from our liberal understanding.

It is reasonable to believe Rawls's claim that, through time, as peoples honor the law of peoples, mutual trust and confidence would develop.[31] But this is not the same as saying that liberal and decent peoples would ever come to understand one another. It is easy to believe that this understanding will never develop beyond the mere expectation that each will honor the law of peoples.

IX. Interdependence Accounts

Interdependence accounts are based on the idea that international trade tends to promote peace in several ways.[32] Democracies trade with one another more frequently than they trade with other types of states because democracies are (at least perceived to be) better than these other kinds of states at guaranteeing trade terms and the continual flow of resources and money. International trade increases contacts between states, contributes to mutual understanding, and creates ties better served by peaceful conflict resolution than fighting. Trade also tends to benefit both sides, and since these mutual benefits must often be sacrificed in times of war, they serve to discourage conflicts. Finally, the mutual benefits of trade reduce the potential benefits of conquest. Since war threatens trade, and all that comes with it, each side is less willing to fight over disagreements.

Decent peoples fail on this account of the democratic peace, because there is nothing in Rawls's law of peoples that requires decent and liberal peoples to engage in trade or other cooperative activities. The law of peoples requires that peoples maintain their status as moral agents, as peoples, or else they lose the ability to make justice claims as peoples on the international stage, but Rawls views each people as autarkic with respect to the means necessary for the development and maintenance of its moral status.[33] There are few societies in the world that do not have the resources to become well-ordered. Each people is in principle capable of securing, on its own, the two fundamental interests of peoples, independence and self-respect.[34] This means that any cooperative activity between peoples is, strictly speaking, voluntary. All any people must do is maintain its moral status as a people, which each can do on its own. It is true, though, that in this regard each people depends on others to maintain policies of non-interference, and to refrain from engaging in practices that might threaten the background conditions necessary for the development of peoplehood worldwide. And so while peoples are autarkic with respect to their own moral standing, peoples are perhaps not completely independent, even in this limited sense. Further, taking our world, here and now, as an example, there is every reason to believe that peoples will engage in trade and other cooperative activities. But peoples are not required to do so as a matter of international justice.

All peoples have a duty to assist burdened societies, to help them become well-ordered through the development of decent or liberal institutional frameworks.[35] This duty, however, does not require liberal and decent peoples to work together. Burdened societies often lack political and cultural traditions and the human, material, and technological resources necessary for well-orderedness. It is reasonable to think that decent and liberal societies may, through simple prudential reasoning, come to decide it is best to work together to assist burdened societies. But the law of peoples does not require this cooperative activity. It is entirely up to each decent and liberal people to decide how to assist burdened societies. Rawls claims that the key to assisting burdened societies lies in helping them to develop the right kind of political culture, but he admits that there is no easy recipe for getting this done.[36] Given this, it is reasonable to think that different peoples will disagree about the best way to aid burdened societies. We can also imagine a situation in which liberal peoples band together to aid non-associationist burdened societies, and decent peoples work together to aid associationist burdened societies.

X. Decent Peoples and the Democratic Peace

We can reasonably extend the democratic peace thesis to Rawls's decent peoples, even though they do not meet all of the conditions of the democratic peace set out in the various accounts. Decent societies meet the conditions of the constitutional constraint account. Constitutional societies share a deep commitment to fundamental social norms, which commits them to a variety of institutional practices, all of which slow the march to war. Further, these shared commitments are likely to produce in (many) individuals a willingness to seek non-lethal means of conflict resolution. But these institutions and dispositions may be overcome by, for instance, humiliation, wounded pride, or lack of due respect, so the conditions of the satisfaction account must also be met if we are to regard Rawls's international order as stable. And decent peoples do meet these conditions. So it is reasonable to conclude that a world society of satisfied decent and liberal peoples would be stable, following these two accounts. I am somewhat troubled by the fact that decent and liberal peoples will probably never meet the conditions of the normative account, but this is not a serious worry, as long as peoples remain satisfied. As long as no people feels humiliated, wounded, or disrespected, this lack of shared values should not prove troublesome. The conditions identified by the reelection and interdependence accounts would, in all likelihood, strengthen the democratic peace; however, the fact that decent peoples only partially meet the conditions of the reelection account, and Rawls's utopian vision fails completely to meet the conditions of the interdependence account, does not make peace impossible or even less likely. If either the normative, interdependence, or reelection account were the sole cause of the democratic peace, we might have reason to worry. But I think this unlikely. All-things-considered, we have good reason to extend the democratic peace to decent peoples.

XI. Is Rawls's Utopia Realistic?

I have argued that Rawls's decent peoples meet important conditions for the democratic peace, and thus that their existence in his international order does not undermine his claim for stability. This demonstrates that a concern for global peace is not a reason for democratic peoples to seek to democratize all other peoples. Other features of Rawls's law of peoples do give us reason to worry about the stability of his Society of Peoples. Most important is his treatment of inequalities in wealth between peoples, a destabilizing feature of his theory of global justice.

Rawls's law of peoples generates two broad constraints on economic relations between peoples. First, well-ordered peoples have a duty to aid burdened societies to realize and maintain just or decent institutions.[37] Second, economic relations between peoples must be free, fair, and mutually advantageous for well-ordered peoples in the long-term.[38] Well-ordered peoples must secure, for themselves and burdened societies, an economic and social minimum consistent with the ideal of well-orderedness and the background conditions necessary to continued free and fair trade between peoples. Rawls rejects global distributive principles intended to regulate inequalities between peoples that go beyond this minimum.[39] His broad constraints do not rule out the existence of great economic inequalities between peoples.

Rawls's well-ordered peoples have two fundamental interests.[40] They have an interest in independence: political independence, cultural freedom, security, territory and the well-being of individual members. They also have an interest in proper self-respect as a people, based on their shared history and cultural achievements. Rawls denies that wealth has much to do with how a people fares.[41] It is a healthy political culture that makes a people flourish, and he says there are few societies in the world that do not have the resources for this.[42]

Rawls views well-ordered peoples as corporate moral agents that share a moral point of view, namely, that they see their mutual relations as constrained by justice. He uses this shared point of view to generate the principles of his law of peoples through a contractualist original position argument. Agents representing well-ordered peoples, from behind a veil of ignorance, would agree to the principles he identifies in *LP*. There is an important difference, however, between peoples and individual members of well-ordered peoples. Peoples are independent as moral agents, as they are capable of producing their own moral status. Individual persons exist as moral agents only insofar as they are members of a cooperative system, that is, a people. In the global original position argument, then, peoples need not agree to anything more stringent than those principles that secure the conditions necessary for their continued existence as peoples. Other cooperation between peoples is strictly voluntary, even such cooperation as is recommended by sheer prudential reasoning. Peoples will thus reject global distribution principles that seek to regulate economic inequalities beyond the socially required minimum. Further, peoples will reject democratic international institutions, as these would interfere with their independence.

Here, then, is a situation in which economic inequalities may become enormous, but that presents few options for those poorer peoples who wish to close the gap. Poorer peoples cannot claim, as a matter of justice, that the size of this gap ought to be reduced. Nor do they have any real bargaining power against richer peoples, as richer peoples would seem to control all the advantages in any prospective trade relationships. The enormous wealth of the richer nations would allow them to dictate trade terms, so long as these do not undermine the conditions necessary for well-orderedness, or free and fair trade. Such trading tactics are not, to Rawls, inherently harmful or unfair, since peoples have no fundamental interest in wealth beyond that necessary for the realization and maintenance of their own decent or just social institutions, and thus can safely bow out of any economic interactions they deem unfavorable. Rawls recognizes that this situation might make poorer peoples feel inferior, but claims that any such feelings are unjustified, once a people has sustainable decent or liberal institutions.[43] Rawls also rejects the claim that this situation is inherently unfair. Rawls claims the law of peoples treats peoples fairly because it is generated through his contractualist original position argument, in which peoples are represented as equals. Thus, he says, "larger and smaller peoples will be ready to make larger and smaller contributions and to accept proportionately larger and smaller returns."[44]

Rawls's response to this potential problem is a little too utopian. It is reasonable to worry that poorer peoples will become dissatisfied with this situation, and that resentments will develop between richer and poorer peoples. Dissenters in liberal and decent societies have at least the hope of reform to keep them from the hopelessness and despair that lead to violence. It is not clear that poorer peoples can even hope for reform. So poorer peoples may become inflamed by Rousseau's wounded pride, or by a perceived lack of respect, and this might easily lead to unrest and war between peoples.

This stability problem, however, is not caused by the existence of decent peoples in Rawls's international order. While it may be the case that, here and now, liberal peoples control most of the world's wealth, and (potentially) decent peoples are poorer by far, this is a contingent fact about our world. We can easily imagine a future world of rich and poor *liberal peoples*, or a world where the rich/poor distinction does not track the liberal/decent distinction. There is every reason to think that resentment would develop between peoples in any of these future worlds when inequalities in wealth become great and there is no hope of rectifying the situation. This is important because it shows that a concern for global peace may give us reason to seek to reduce inequalities between peoples. It shows, once again, that a concern for global peace is not a reason for us to seek to democratize decent peoples. And it shows that Rawls's utopia might not be realistic after all.

Walter Riker, University of Tennessee

Notes

1. John Rawls, *The Law of Peoples* (Harvard University Press), 1999.

2. *LP*, 23–30.

3. *LP*, 4, 19, 64–67.

4. John Rawls, *Collected Papers*, ed. Samuel Freeman (Harvard University Press, 1999), 581–582.

5. Rawls develops and defends his conception of justice as fairness in his *A Theory of Justice*, rev. ed. (Harvard University Press, 1999); *Political Liberalism* (Columbia University Press, 1996); and *Justice as Fairness: A Restatement* (Harvard University Press, 2001).

6. Rawls, *Collected Papers*, 581.

7. *LP*, 37.

8. *LP*, 71.

9. *LP*, 64, 68.

10. *LP*, 75–78.

11. For explicit discussion of this theme see *LP*, 3–10, 11–23.

12. *LP*, 62.

13. *LP*, 85.

14. Among the more controversial conceptual problems discussed in the democratic peace literature are the definition of the term "democracy" and the identification of the threshold at which a state becomes democratic enough to avoid wars with other democracies. One fair definition is proposed by James Lee Ray, *Democracy and International Conflict: An Evaluation of the Democratic Peace Proposition* (University of South Carolina Press, 1995, 33), who stipulates that a state is democratic enough to avoid wars if its executive and legislative leaders are selected through fair, competitive elections. Elections are competitive if at least two independent political groups (e.g., political parties) present candidates, and fair if at least 50% of the adult population is allowed to vote and at least one constitutional transfer of power from one political group to a different political group has occurred.

15. Most democratic peace researchers follow the Correlates of War project and define "war" as a "military conflict between independent states leading to at least 1000 battle deaths" (i.e., deaths of soldiers) (Ray, *Democracy and International Conflict*, 31). This definition is somewhat controversial, as, for instance, it rules out the American Civil War, since the South was not an independent state, and also wars between U.S. soldiers and Native American groups. See D. Babst, "A Force for Peace," *Industrial Research* 14 (1972): 55–58, for an alternative definition of war.

16. Empirical research is generally conducted by tracking pairs of states, or "dyads," often on a yearly basis, and comparing rates of warfare in jointly democratic dyads (pairs of democratic states) to rates in other types of dyads (pairs that include at least one non-democratic state). In these studies, it is not uncommon for researchers to statistically analyze over 200,000 "observations" (a dyad tracked through one year is often counted as one observation). One pair of researchers significantly reduced this number by restricting their analysis to "politically relevant" dyads (those dyads that included geographically contiguous states or at least one major power, e.g., China, France, Great Britain, the Soviet Union, or the U.S.) and still analyzed over 29,000 observations (Z. Maoz and B. Russett, "Normative and Structural Causes of Democratic Peace," *American Political Science Review* 87 (1993): 624–638. They found no wars in jointly democratic dyads for the period 1946–1986 and 32 wars in other kinds of dyads. They conclude that non-jointly democratic dyads are 0.1% more likely to

engage in war than are jointly democratic dyads. This difference is statistically significant and, lest one doubt its substantial significance, is comparable to the difference between the proportion of cigarette smokers who develop cancer and the proportion of nonsmokers who develop it (James Lee Ray, "Does Democracy Cause Peace?" *Annual Review of Political Science*, 1 (1998): 35).

Several possible exceptions to the democratic peace thesis are discussed in the literature. For instance, it is often noted that Hitler came to power by democratic means, that the U.S. engaged in brutal imperialistic wars against native Americans, and that the U.S. was almost split in two by its bloody Civil War. However, democratic peace theorists claim that democracies are *less likely to fight other democracies* than they are to fight other kinds of regimes, and that other kinds of regimes are more likely to fight all others than are democracies. Wars between democracies and other kinds of states do not refute the democratic peace thesis. Nor would the existence of a war between democratic states serve as a refutation of the democratic peace thesis, since researchers claim to find a disposition toward peace, and not a natural law.

17. See Ray, "Does Democracy Cause Peace?" 27–46, for a review of recent democratic peace literature. Although the democratic peace thesis has many more proponents than opponents, there is a vocal minority that rejects it. See, e.g., J. S. Farber and J. Gowa, "Polities and Peace," *International Security*, 20 (1995): 123–146; I. Owen, "The Subjectivity of the 'Democratic' Peace: Changing U.S. Perceptions of Imperial Germany," *International Security* 20 (1995): 147–184; D.E. Spiro, "The Insignificance of the Liberal Peace," *International Security* 19 (1994): 50–86; T.S. Szayna, D.L. Byman, S.C. Bankes, D. Eaton, S.G. Jones, R.E. Mullins, I.O. Lesser, and W. Rosenau, "The Democratic Peace Idea," Appendix C in *The Emergence of Peer Competitors: A Framework for Analysis* (Santa Monica, Ca: Rand, 2001).

18. See Ray "Does Democracy Cause Peace"; Szayna et al., "The Democratic Peace Idea."

19. *LP*, 44–54.

20. This is Rawls's favored account of the democratic peace (see *LP*, 44–54). Here he follows Raymond Aron, *Peace and War*, trans. R. Howard and A. B. Fox (Doubleday, 1966).

21. *LP*, 66, footnote 2; 72–75.

22. *LP*, 64; 72–75.

23. See, e.g., Charles Beitz, "Rawls's Law of Peoples," *Ethics* 110 (2000): 669–696; and his "Human Rights as Common Concerns," *American Political Science Review* 95 (2001): 269–282; Allen Buchanan, "Rawls's Law of Peoples: Rules for a Vanishing Westphalian World," *Ethics* 110 (2000): 697–721; Andrew Kuper, "Rawlsian Global Justice: Beyond the Law of Peoples to a Cosmopolitan Law of Persons," *Political Theory* 28 (2000): 640–674; Darrel Moellendorf, "Constructing the Law of Peoples," *Pacific Philosophical Quarterly* 77 (1996): 132–154; Thomas Pogge, "An Egalitarian Law of Peoples," *Philosophy and Public Affairs* 23 (1994): 195–224, and his "The International Significance of Human Rights," *Journal of Ethics* 4 (2000): 45–69; and Kok-Chor Tan, *Toleration, Diversity and Global Justice* (Penn State University Press, 2000), esp. chap. 4.

24. *LP*, 113.

25. See, e.g., J. M. Owen, "How Liberalism Produces Democratic Peace," *International Security* 19 (1994): 87-125.

26. Samuel Freeman, "Original Meaning, Democratic Interpretation, and the Constitution," *Philosophy and Public Affairs* 21 (1992) 3–42.

27. Freeman, "Original Meaning," 6.

28. See, e.g., B. Bueno de Mesquita, J. D. Morrow, R. M. Siverson, and A. Smith, "An Institutional Explanation of the Democratic Peace," *American Political Science Review* 93 (1999): 791–807; Ray, *Democracy and International Conflict*.

29. Ray, "Does Democracy Cause Peace?" 41.

30. See, e.g., S. Chan, "In Search of Democratic Peace," *Mershon International Studies Review* 41 (1997): 59–92; Maoz and Russett, "Normative and Structural Causes."

31. *LP*, 44–45.

32. See, e.g., J. R. Oneal and B. M. Russett, "The Classical Liberals Were Right: Democracy, Interdependence, and Conflict, 1950–1985," *International Studies Quarterly* 41 (1997): 267–294.

33. See, e.g., *LP*, 108.

34. *LP*, 34.

35. *LP*, 105–113.

36. *LP*, 108.

37. *LP*, 105–113.

38. *LP*, 37–38.

39. *LP*, 115–120.

40. *LP*, 34.

41. *LP*, 117.

42. *LP*, 108.

43. *LP*, 114.

44. *LP*, 115.

Terrorism and the Politics of Human Rights

Sharon Anderson-Gold

Abstract: Humanitarian interventions defined as "peace-keeping" missions are becoming an increasingly common occurrence. This paper will consider the relationship between the idea of human rights and the concept of legitimate intervention into the affairs of sovereign nations. I will argue that implicit within the concept of human rights are standards of political legitimacy which render all claims to sovereignty "conditional" upon adherence to these standards. After analyzing how both critics and supporters have viewed human rights interventions, I will consider how the "war on terrorism" may contribute to a further extension of the concept of legitimate intervention. I will conclude with reflections on the implications of these interventions for cosmopolitan democracy and the conditions under which it can be realized.

Humanitarian interventions defined as "peace-keeping" missions are becoming an increasingly common occurrence. This paper will consider the relationship between the idea of human rights and the concept of legitimate intervention into the affairs of sovereign nations. I will argue that implicit within the concept of human rights are standards of political legitimacy which render all claims to sovereignty "conditional" upon adherence to these standards. When sovereignty is regarded as conditioned by human rights, violations are viewed as occasions for interventions which are initially justified by humanitarian goals but which ultimately aim at regime change. While constitutional democratic governments are widely regarded as political ideals, my paper raises questions concerning the use of humanitarian intervention as a legitimate means to further democratic ideals.

After analyzing how both critics and supporters have viewed human rights interventions, I will consider how the American "war on terrorism" may contribute to a further extension of the concept of legitimate intervention. Given the legitimacy of a universal and pre-emptive war on terrorism, the inability of any nation to secure its borders and to provide internal security against the use of its territory by terrorists provides an additional justification for intervention to prevent violations of the rights of innocent victims of potential terrorist attacks. Critics of these new policies of intervention see in human rights a useful ideological instrument that continuously generates new conflicts in order to eliminate disturbing social conditions that stand in the way of securing world peace. Can it be that the cosmopolitan world order that liberals since the time of Kant have set as the supreme moral goal depends upon an ultimate "militarization" of world politics?

In 1948 the United Nations took a rather dramatic step. It criminalized the act of war and empowered the international community to take action against any "aggressor." In the context of the Nuremberg trials, three types of violation of international law were created, all of which presuppose this new view of war as criminal activity: crimes against the peace, war crimes, and crimes against humanity. All of these forms of violence would henceforth be viewed as more than breaches of morality which states may or may not respond to; they would also be viewed as breaches of international law and therefore create obligations on the part of the international community to take corrective action. While the UN Charter also prohibited interference in the internal affairs of states, the classical notion of state sovereignty was clearly transformed by the notion of international crimes. The claim essential to the juridical character of the Nuremberg trials, that officials of state could be held criminally accountable for actions that disturb the peace and security of others, presupposes the legal subordination of national interests to international law.

The UN Charter also took the view that human rights are universal entitlements that are essential to the goal of peaceable association and that these rights should be promoted by all nations both separately and as a whole. Those who had committed crimes against the peace through the initiation of the Second World War had also engaged in genocide. Henceforth, the violation of human rights was connected with a propensity for international aggression in the minds of many statesmen. This sentiment was expressed in the claim of Secretary of State Marshall that, "Governments which systematically disregard the rights of their own people are not likely to respect the rights of other nations and other people and are likely to seek their objectives by coercion and force in the international field."[1] If governments could be internally constrained with respect to the types of violence they could visit upon their own citizens, they might also become less inclined to visit violence on others. Human rights were thus envisioned as an essential part of the scheme of international pacification.

But how was this new doctrine of international human rights to be made legally compatible with the prohibition on interference in the internal affairs of sovereign nations? Initially many international lawyers took the view that human rights covenants were "binding" only in the sense that they represented the intentions and aspirations of the signatories, not that they were "enforceable" by third parties. Under this "idealist" interpretation, international law has been described as "soft law." When states violated these covenants, third parties might alter their own behaviors in such a manner as to impose "sanctions" but direct intervention was deemed to be prohibited by the non interference requirements of the Charter.

In holding to both the principle of noninterference and the criminalization of violations of human rights, the Charter displays a potentially unstable hybrid character, something stretching beyond soft law but without the mechanisms of enforcement characteristic of hard, or positive law.[2] In 1977 international lawyer Louis Henkin prophetically argued that the UN Charter effectively withdraws human rights from matters of domestic jurisdiction for all members of the United Nations.[3] According to Henkin, whatever is covered by international law or agreement is by definition no longer a matter of domestic jurisdiction. While the Declaration also forbids intervention in the internal affairs of another nation, it is not, according to Henkin's insightful interpretation, intervention for one state to respond to violations by another. In fact, one might argue as an inference from the application of the legal doctrine of implied powers that the Charter of the UN authorizes all reasonable action whose purpose is the protection of human rights. Unlawful interference would comprise only those types of interference incompatible with the defense of human rights.[4] Thus the concept of a "humanitarian intervention" whose purpose is to "keep the peace" in order to prevent violations of human rights is implicit in the doctrine of human rights.

Although the UN lacks direct executive-military power to enforce human rights standards, the Security Council, through Chapter VII, Article 2.7, is granted the right to request volunteers to intervene in situations that "threaten international peace and security."[5] Initially reluctant to use military intervention to prevent human rights abuses, the Security Council has during the past decade increasingly interpreted internal conflicts as "threats to international peace and security" because of the violence visited upon civilian populations and the "humanitarian" crises that result.[6] The link between civilian violence and threats to international peace has sometimes been thought to be tenuous, and it is arguable that in this way the Security Council has in effect broadened its mandate to protect human rights directly. To downplay the sense in which such interventions are interferences with national sovereignty, a new language has emerged. Interventions that are responses to perceived threats to human rights are referred to as "humanitarian" and the troops that are sent are designated "peace-keepers." States that are suffering internal conflict are perceived as "failed" states and therefore as possessing insufficient internal sovereignty for intervention to constitute a violation.[7] Humanitarian intervention suggests a "rescue" operation to restore a normal condition and a failed state is something that must be rebuilt. Thus, peace keepers are increasingly vested with the additional task of "state building." But both metaphors are misleading. In neither case is the situation one of simple restoration. Both idioms conceal the normative dimensions of the conflicts that have preceded the intervention and the consequent necessity to impose a new normative order.

While intervention in the affairs of other states is hardly a new development, the use of "humanitarian" to modify "intervention" signals a new form of justification that is characterized as uniquely valid and universal. Previous forms of justification for intervention were various and formulated in terms of the defense of heterogeneous values. What is most striking about the new idiom according to Jovan Babic is that, "As a device to express a new ideology or primary political dogma, it appears to single out a set standard applicable to valid forms of political governance anywhere on the globe."[8] Because international law prohibits war, humanitarian interventions have been conceived as a kind of "police action." However, police action presupposes some form of global law to which all state agents would be continually subjected. But asks Babic, what would international law have to be like to make this possible? He argues that it is not possible to treat the combating of human rights violations as a sort of defense unless there exists a unique point of reference fully authorized to interpret situations without allowance for appeals. Thus a single authority to which all are equally subject is required for the constitution of the global law legitimating interventions.

What then would be the source of this authority? Although the Security Council of the UN is the organ responsible for deciding when interventions are justified, only the most powerful nations have a voice in making these decisions and as things stand in the current international legal order, only the most powerful states are capable of implementing them.[9] This introduces the possibility of selective implementation of human rights interventions that primarily serves the geo-political interests of powerful nations. Given precedents it becomes arguable that even regional interventions such as that undertaken by NATO in Kosovo without UN approval (although illegal in the strict sense) are indeed justified by the principle of human rights. Ultimately Babic fears that states meeting the conditions for intervention may become the subject of attack by any country willing and able to engage in "corrective" activities aimed at "ameliorating" the state of affairs in that country (the "coalition of the willing"). According to Babic, the authorization (from whatever source) of the universal enforcement of human rights would have as its consequence the general militarization of global affairs and "would lead to the practice of an intervention becoming, rather than the exception, quite an ordinary matter . . . this would indicate that the practices of sending American troops around the globe would become a much more common occurrence, unsurprising to anyone."[10] Critics of humanitarian intervention such as Babic question whether even humanitarian interventions, given the current configurations of power, can escape the charge of private justice.

While also sensitive to the charge that the politics of human rights leads to wars disguised as police actions to lend them a moral quality, Jurgen Habermas argues that the current international order can reasonably be viewed as in a state of transition from a form of law of merely provisional validity to genuine cosmopolitan law with positivist juridical credentials.[11] Habermas acknowledges that the world has become stratified and that only the First World has internalized the norms declared by the UN Charter, thereby succeeding to a certain degree in bringing national interest into harmony with the normative claims established by the UN. In order to complete this transition to genuine cosmopolitan law, Habermas argues there would need to be a greater diffusion of these norms as well as a greater equalization of the material and economic status of all nations. Nonetheless, he rejects the claim that human rights interventions are reducible to a "moralization of politics" lacking in juridical character.[12] Human rights according to Habermas have a juridical and "positive" status that is derived from their constitutive role in making a constitutional legal order possible. Thus the ultimate purpose of the juridification of human rights is to bring into existence a cosmopolitan constitution capable of the pacification of the state of nature among states.

In this context Habermas recognizes the strong connection between the criminalization of war and human rights violations and the challenge that these concepts provide to the logic of sovereignty. He states, "The most important consequence of a form of law that is able to puncture the sovereignty of states is the arrest of individual persons for crimes committed in the service of a state and its military."[13] Such a definition of criminal activity contains within it an evaluative conception of war and in effect abolishes the traditional conception of a state of nature between nations in which war is morally neutral. However, unlike some critics of this evaluative conception of war (which defines the aggressor as the one who has failed in the upholding of human rights), Habermas maintains that the return to a morally neutral conception of state behavior (with the fully entailed notion of absolute sovereignty) is no longer possible. The prior conception, he maintains, depended upon defining war as a limited engagement over geographically bounded territory whose justification was determined by the rules of prudence. A defeated aggressor was punishable because he had violated the rules of prudence. Peace as defined under these rules was the temporary cessation of war. Given the current situation of global dangers, with its many forms of "terrorism," war is no longer limited. Therefore according to Habermas our concept of peace has to be expanded to include the claim that war is itself a "crime," a crime against peace. Central to the linking of human rights and peace has been the notion that states must be constrained in the use of violence both internally and externally and that therefore domestic and foreign policies must be symmetrical in their objectives. More recently it has been argued that only democratic constitutional governments can guarantee human rights and that non-democratic governments are therefore implicit threats to international peace. Only on the basis of a global regime of democratically constituted governments could genuine cosmopolitan law emerge.

Thus Habermas's defense of the current state of the "politics of human rights" is linked to historical processes that are considered irreversible and are still in the course of development. Of particular importance to Habermas's defense of the politics of human rights is his notion of a global public sphere which he credits

Immanuel Kant with foreseeing. This is because if the norms of human rights are to become truly internal to the political culture of all states, they must become part of a global communicative structure capable of providing a foundation for the development of cosmopolitan law. Habermas appeals to the force of world opinion in providing for the legitimization of the politics of human rights. In this context he looks to pressures brought by nongovernmental organizations to bring about institutional reforms at both the national and international levels, such as those suggested by cosmopolitan democrats like David Held.[14] It is Habermas's belief that insofar as human rights norms are institutionalized and implemented in a nonarbitrary manner, their juridical character will protect against self-interest parading as 'human rights fundamentalism.' Habermas explains, "Morally justified appeals threaten to take on fundamentalist features when they do not aim at the implementation of a legal procedure for the application and achievement of human rights, but rather seize directly upon the interpretive scheme by which violations of human rights are attributed, or when such moral appeals are the sole source of the demanded sanctions."[15] The justification of human rights, then, depends heavily upon institutional structures that are truly cosmopolitan in purpose.

The problem for many supporters of the politics of human rights is that the one power capable of providing for the enforcement of human rights in the current international environment, the United States, has blocked many of the institutional reforms needed to complete the transition to a cosmopolitan order. In particular, the US has been unwilling to submit itself to any international court. This lack of principled support for international law gives much credence to human rights skeptics who see in the current climate of intervention only the attempt on the part of the powerful to impose their own interests on others and thereby to attain and secure a position of unchallengeable dominance.

The Bush administration appears ready to expand upon prior interventionist precedents by using the war on terrorism as a justification for interventions in countries that are too weak to secure their own borders and territories from possible use by terrorist groups. Since the ability of nations to provide such security is on a continuum, such a principle is potentially quite broad in scope. Terrorism provides a new conceptual challenge in that such actions are not typically attributed to state actors and therefore do not have the characteristics attributed to wars with respect to authoritative originations or terminations. They are neither limited engagements nor are they geographically bounded. It is unclear then what limits could apply to a "war against terrorism."

If the US is justified in taking unilateral actions to defend itself against terrorism, and if weak states are a threat to the type of security necessary to fight terrorism, then the US appears to be committed to an indefinite policing of the globe. Justified threats will include possession of dangerous weapons of "mass destruction," undemocratic governments that are naturally poised to threaten human rights, and weak states that cannot secure their borders and territory. In other words, to systematically pursue a "war on terrorism," as Babic foresees occurring within the logic of humanitarian interventions, the US would have to employ massive peacekeeping operations and engage in major regime change.

Both critics and supporters of the politics of human rights appear to be in agreement about the crucial role of superior power in the transformation of the declaratory force of international law into a constitutive legal order. But there appears to be major disagreement about how what is "the law" (being backed by enforcement) becomes internalized and perceived to be "our law." Babic argues that under the militarization of human rights through interventions, "Liberalism and democracy, hence, no longer have their basis in autonomy. In their places comes one among many possible interpretations of content. . . . This political program becomes the final basis of all legitimization and given its distinct nature, every deviation is defined as 'injustice.'" This circumstance manufactures conflicts that can be "controlled only through securing supremacy over all other sides in this universal conflict."[16]

This depressing diagnosis of recurrent conflict caused by interventions goes to the heart of how to define cosmopolitan democracy and the conditions under which it is possible for it to emerge. I must admit that as one committed to the idea of "cosmopolitan pluralism," I have long put my faith in the possibility of an emergent human rights culture. But a critical assessment of political interventionism reveals the close correspondence between interventions and hegemonic interests. Can then a hegemonic power also provide moral leadership? In "ideal theory" cosmopolitan democracy ought to be the consequence of the internal maturing of civil societies. The unprecedented process of democratization that swept through eastern Europe in the 1990s generated general optimism in the future of democratic governance. But these events had their roots in the prior development of civil organizations that pressed for democratic participation. The regrettable resulting conflicts in some parts of eastern Europe have even been interpreted as the natural consequences of opening up participation in "political will formation" which interventionists in the Bosnian conflict acted to guide toward a "negotiated" settlement.[17] Thus, optimism concerning the future of democracy, while tarnished, has survived in some quarters.

Can this model, which suggests a push/pull process in which external power acts to shape internal democratic forces, be transferred to, say, the Middle East where civil society is either weak or non existent or to Africa where social life is continuously fragmented by civil wars? If we extrapolate from the conflicts which resulted from the opening up of civil society in eastern Europe, contemporary forms of terrorism may be seen to be a consequence of the stirrings of civil society and the processes of liberalization in other areas of the world. The most powerful criticism of the politics of human rights stems from the presumed incompatibility between the externality of intervention and the internalization of norms that is essential to the nature of any law perceived to be "one's own." Autonomy in this context includes the right to be different. But can autonomy include the right to reject human rights as such? Autonomy surely also includes the dimensions of communication and interaction that allows for individuals to create and recreate associations with others in a global context. Thus the argument from autonomy supports the necessity of certain forms of human rights in order that the claim that certain values are "one's own" and deserve to be respected can be founded and distinguished from an authoritarian imposition of order. In this sense international law and its interventions exist to protect persons from the forms of violence and deprivations that are destructive of the exercise of autonomy.

But interventions by their very nature can only be temporary. It is the future condition of democratic flourishing that justifies intervention. Humanitarian interventions then have their ultimate justification in a condition that is yet to be created. The transition to a cosmopolitan order that Habermas envisions and which provides the juridical foundation for the interventions which precede it presupposes global institutional structures that would destratify the material and economic status of the world's states and societies, thus allowing for the pervasive development of civil society. Such a destratification would presumably lead to the internalization of human rights norms and the transformation of the world's political cultures. Those who would intervene then must be held accountable for the creations of such institutions. On this perhaps both critics and supporters can agree.

Sharon Anderson-Gold, Rensselaer Polytechnic Institute

Notes

1.   Quoted by Patrick Flood, *The Effectiveness of UN Human Rights Institutions* (Westport, CT: Praeger, 1998), 32.

2.   The UN Charter calls for the development of an international police force but this was never acted upon.

3.   Louis, Henkin, "Human rights and 'domestic jurisdiction,'" in *Human Rights, International Law and the Helsinki Accord*, ed. Thomas Buergenthal (Montclair, New Jersey: Allanheld, Osmun & Co., 1977).

4.   An intervention that could not be carried out without massive loss of civilian life would violate this principle. Sophisticated technologies, such as smart bombs, that allow for the defeat of military opponents without extensive "collateral damage" might pass this test. Such technologies are in general only available to rich and powerful nations who thus are the only states in a position to become human rights enforcers.

5. Chapter One, Article One of the Charter of the UN stipulates that the purposes of the UN are "To maintain international peace and security, and to that end; to take effective collective measures for the prevention and removal of threats to the peace, and for the suppression of acts of aggression or *other breaches of the peace*" (italics provided by author). The language of this article is broad. It identifies acts of aggression as a subset of "threats to the peace" which apparently can include a wider range of unacceptable actions. Given the repeated references to the protection of human rights as a primary purpose of the UN throughout the Charter, Declaration and International Covenants, it is not difficult to argue that systematic violations of human rights are threats to international security if not the short term peace. *Basic Documents on Human Rights*, ed. Ian Brownie, (Oxford: Clarendon Press, 1971), 94.

6. I have argued that the UN intervention in Somalia was motivated primarily by the desire to prevent civilian massacres from marauding bandits and so did not represent an intervention based upon a generalized threat to international security. If this definition of the purpose of intervention in this instance is accepted, then either human rights become their own purpose for intervention (humanitarian intervention) or their violation is prima facie a threat to international security. Sharon Anderson-Gold, *Cosmopolitanism and Human Rights* (Wales: University of Wales Press, 2001), 124.

7. The "failed state" has both a descriptive and a normative significance. This idiom is increasingly used to characterize underdeveloped nations that lack internal cohesion and suffer from internal conflicts. Such states are said not to be "mature modern nation-states." Yinhong and Zhixiong cite this phenomenon as one of the reasons for the increase in the number and acceptability of humanitarian interventions, "After Kosovo: Moral and Legal Constraints on Humanitarian Intervention" in *Moral Constraints on War*, ed. Bruno Coppieters and Nick Fotion (Oxford: Lexington Books, 2002), 249.

8. Jovan Babic, "Foreign Armed Intervention: Between Justified Aid and Illegal Violence," in *Humanitarian Intervention*, ed. Aleksander Jokic (Toronto: Broadview Press, 2003), 46.

9. Ibid, 56.

10. One could argue that the Security Council stands as the collective will underlying the legitimization of interventions, but critics such as Babic would point out that this body is controlled by the veto powers of a few powerful nations and that states must in the end be willing to contribute their troops. Therefore nations, particularly powerful nations, still control the conditions for intervention. Critics of the current status of international law call for either its abolishment or the reform of the organs of the UN along principles of cosmopolitan democracy.

11. Jovan Babic, "Foreign Armed Intervention: Between Justified Aid and Illegal Violence," 56.

12. Jurgen Habermas, "Kant's Perpetual Peace with the Benefit of 200 Years Hindsight" in *Perpetual Peace: Essays on Kant's Cosmopolitan Ideal*, ed. James Bohman and Matthias Lutz-Bachmann (Cambridge: The MIT Press, 1997).

13. The claim that human rights are moral concepts without juridical foundations is implicit in Babic's argument but was made explicitly by Carl Schmitt as early as 1932, *The Concept of the Political* (New Brunswick, 1976), and more recently by Hans Enzensberger, *Civil Wars: From L.A. to Bosnia* (New Press, 1994).

14. Jurgen Habermas, "Kant's Perpetual Peace with the Benefit of 200 Years Hindsight," 129.

15. David Held, *Democracy and the Global Order* (Stanford, Stanford University Press, 1995).

16. Jurgen Habermas, "Kant's Perpetual Peace with the Benefit of 200 Years Hindsight," 148.

17. Jovan Babic, *Humanitarian Intervention*, 60.

18. Axel Honneth, "Is Universalism a Moral Trap?" *Perpetual Peace: Essays on Kant's Cosmopolitan Ideal*, ed. James Bohman and Matthias Lutz-Bachmann (Cambridge: The MIT Press, 1997). Following a line of interpretation developed by Ernst-Otto Czempiel, Honneth demonstrates how even the "empirical" evidence of increasingly severe conflicts can be interpreted as elements in a democratization process.

Part III:
Social Philosophy

Trotsky's Brilliant Flame and Broken Reed

NELSON P. LANDE

Abstract: Trotsky wrote his *Terrorism and Communism* in 1920, as a response to Karl Kautsky's book of the same title of the previous year. Trotsky's aim was to win over, to the side of the Bolshevik view of socialism, the various European socialist political parties. Trotsky's book is a rare document in the history of political thought. It is a candid and impassioned defense of the Bolshevik view that the period of transition to socialism is incompatible with both individual liberties and democratic institutions as we normally understand them, and requires instead a one-party state with unlimited powers, prepared to use instruments of terror and repression to achieve its goals. In two articles that he wrote in the late 1930s, he elaborated on this view: he sought to provide an explicitly *philosophical* defense of the Bolsheviks' use of terror and repression.

Trotsky's views merit examination for several reasons: first, because they illuminate the ethical underpinnings of the distinctively Bolshevik view of socialism, and second, because they force one to come to terms with the question of how intelligent, reflective, and decent individuals could have advanced policies that strike us today as ghastly. In this paper I try to piece together Trotsky's arguments as they bear upon both the Civil War and the immediate postwar period of reconstruction. (Here I focus on his critique of democracy, his defense of terror, and his defense of compulsory labor service and the militarization of labor. This proves to be an ideal point of entry into the ethical considerations that underlie his conception of party and state.) I also examine criticisms of the policies that Trotsky was defending—criticisms that were advanced by Marxists of such disparate stripes as Kaustky, on the one hand, and Rosa Luxemburg, on the other.

I. Introduction

In 1919, Karl Kautsky[1] published *Terrorism and Communism*, an attack on Bolshevism that was at once detailed, comprehensive, and measured. He argued at length and in detail against both the violent and the undemocratic nature of the Bolshevik state. In 1920, Leon Trotsky[2] published a book with the same title as Kautsky's, *Terrorism and Communism*, and in it he seldom denies Kautsky's charges. Quite the contrary: he argues *against* democracy and *for* the implementation of anti-democratic measures that are to be pursued ruthlessly through various forms of state terrorism by an absolute and avowedly repressive Soviet state. This is a state that in turn is to be presided over by an omnipotent Bolshevik party that rejects the very notion of a loyal opposition and thus bans opposition parties. Trotsky's defense of terror and his attack on democracy—and on such established props of democracy as a multi-party parliament, universal suffrage, freedom of the press, and a free market (of *some* sort) in labor—must constitute, along with Plato's attack on Athenian democracy, the most radical attack on democracy to be advanced by anyone other than a lunatic. I hope to shed some light on the underpinnings of his attack on democracy, his defense of revolutionary terror, and his espousal of deeply illiberal (i.e., repressive) labor policies.

In a 1939 article in which he replies to various left-wing criticisms of the Bolsheviks' putative "amoralism,"[3] Trotsky spells out explicitly the principle that the Bolsheviks use to evaluate a prospective course of action: "Only that which prepares the complete and final overthrow of imperialist bestiality is moral, and nothing else. The welfare of the revolution—that is the supreme law!"[4]

One should not dismiss this as merely rhetorical flourish on Trotsky's part. He articulates this view in greater detail in an article that he wrote the previous year, in which he addresses the general question of how one determines which means of achieving a given end are permissible. One justifies one's conduct by reference to principles that either are relative to a given stage of historical development or else lie "outside of historical society."[5] Only two sorts of principles lie "outside of historical society," those derived from eternal truths (whether Platonic or Kantian) and those derived from divinely sanctioned natural law. The former, however, collapse into the latter, insofar as the "theory of eternal morals can in nowise survive without God,"[6] and insofar as those who start off as Kantians end up as priests or ministers. Given the preposterousness of the very notion of divinely sanctioned natural law, it follows that one cannot justify one's conduct by reference to principles that lie "outside of historical society." Hence one must justify it by reference to principles that are relative to a given stage of historical development. In short, one has to find "earthly roots" for one's morality,[7] and of course different classes find different "earthly roots," i.e., different classes embrace those principles that advance their class interests. Because the welfare of the revolution serves best to advance the interests of the working class, it follows that the welfare of the revolution is the supreme law; hence the attack on democracy, the defense of revolutionary terror, and the espousal of repressive labor policies.

II. The Attack on Democracy

Trotsky rejects democracy for a number of reasons, some of which are independent of the circumstances of the October Revolution and some of which are not.

Arguments that are Independent of the October Revolution

First, Trotsky believes that it was parliamentary democracy that was responsible, in some considerable measure, for the First World War and for the carnage that the War involved. To a Marxist, it was unthinkable that the working class of one country would take up arms against the working class of another country—and it was the various *parliaments* after all (with the support of corrupt Social Democratic parties) that had voted their support of the war, and that had seen to it that "national ideology flamed up . . . at the expense of class ideology."[8]

Second, Trotsky advances the standard Marxist argument that "[i]t is hopeless to think of a peaceful arrival to power [on the part of the working class] while the bourgeoisie retains in its hands all the apparatus of power."[9] Even if a majority within Parliament were to vote for the socialist program, the army, as the decisive instrument of the bourgeoisie, would not permit the implementation of such a program. The upshot would be civil war—in which case those, like Kautsky, who think that one can achieve socialism by means of parliamentary democracy and without civil war are deluding both themselves and the workers.

Third, Trotsky argues for rejecting democracy *of the current bourgeois sort* on the grounds that it is inherently inegalitarian, and that its underlying ideological justification serves to perpetuate a society characterized by political and legal *equality* but economic *inequality*. "The root problem of the party . . . was to create the conditions for real, economic, living equality for mankind as members of a united human commonwealth. It was just for this reason that the theoreticians of the proletariat had to expose the metaphysics of democracy as a philosophic mask for political mystification."[10]

Underlying each of these arguments is an argument that Lenin had advanced two years earlier, in 1918.[11] (1) States come in a variety of forms, and democracy is one such form. (2) Every state exists to further the interests of a particular class. (3) Therefore a democracy—*any* democracy—exists to further the interests of a particular class. (4) Therefore (a) a *bourgeois democracy* exists to further the interests of the bourgeoisie and (b) a *proletarian democracy* exists to further the interests of the proletariat. (5) No democracy is a democracy *simpliciter*: rather, each is a democracy vis-à-vis the dominating class and a dictatorship vis-à-vis the dominated class.[12] (6) A dictatorship of a particular class over other classes is compatible with the existence of a democracy within the class that exercises the dictatorship. (7) A dictatorship of a particular class over other classes is incompatible (obviously) with the existence of a democracy within the classes over which the dictatorship is exercised. (8) Thus (a) a bourgeois democracy preserves democracy for the bourgeoisie but abolishes it for—and as such is a dictatorship with respect to—all other classes, whereas (b) a proletarian democracy preserves democracy for the proletariat but abolishes it for—and as such is a dictatorship with respect to—all other classes.[13]

The upshot of these arguments of Trotsky's and Lenin's is that one is obliged to respect the institutions of the proletarian form of democracy, but not the institutions of the bourgeois form of democracy. I turn now to Trotsky's specific reasons for rejecting the view that the Bolsheviks should introduce bourgeois democracy into their own state.

Arguments that are Dependent on the October Revolution

Throughout the period of Kerensky's Provisional Government, the Bolsheviks, amongst others, had been calling for a legislature: a Constituent Assembly. During the fall of 1917, therefore, the Provisional Government arranged for elections, which, as it turned out, were held following the October Revolution; the Bolsheviks, for a variety of reasons, did not fare well in the elections; and in January 1918, soon after the Constituent Assembly was convened, the Bolsheviks dispersed it. In *The Dictatorship of the Proletariat* of 1918, Kautsky faults the Bolsheviks for having dispersed the Constituent Assembly, and in *The Russian Revolution*,[14] also of 1918, Rosa Luxemburg (1870–1919) faults the Bolsheviks for having failed to call new elections.

Trotsky presents several arguments for the dispersal of the Constituent Assembly.[15] First, the composition of the Constituent Assembly was a reflection of the pre–October alignment of political forces within the country (since the electoral lists were drawn up prior to the Revolution). Within the All-Russian Congress of Soviets (the councils of workers, peasants, and soldiers), the rival to the Constituent Assembly, the percentage of elected delegates who were Bolsheviks had been rising dramatically between June, 1917 and January, 1918. By October they constituted a majority (albeit just barely) and by January, a substantial majority.[16] In Trotsky's view, this indicated that the Soviets were far more representative of the mood of the country than was the Constituent Assembly.

Second, in January, 1918 the Bolsheviks, unlike the parties that constituted the majority within the Constituent Assembly, were prepared to conclude a separate peace with Germany. Trotsky's fear was that if Russia were to remain in the War, with its own troops unwilling and unable to fight, the Germans would soon be occupying Petrograd, the capital. Its fall, he writes, "would at that time have meant a death-blow to the proletariat, for all the best forces of the Revolution were concentrated there."[17]

Third, Trotsky examines Kautsky's charge that "the Soviet Government rules by the will of the minority." The Soviet regime, Trotsky claims, is "more closely, straightly, [and] honestly bound up with the toiling majority of the people" than was the (provisional) parliamentary regime. As such, it is better able to discover and express "the opinion of the country." Unlike the parliamentary regime, it does not simply engage in "*statically reflecting*" a majority but in "*dynamically creating*" it. Consequently, during "the epoch of revolutionary storm," whereas the parliamentary regime "lost its capacity to follow the course of the struggle and the development of revolutionary consciousness," the Soviet regime draws the peasants alongside the proletariat "into the work of ruling the country in the real interests of the laboring masses. Such a democracy," he concludes, "goes a little deeper down than parliamentarism."[18] Soviet (or proletarian) democracy, in other words, is more democratic than parliamentary (or bourgeois) democracy.[19] To be sure, this is not a democracy with universal suffrage: it is, once again, a democracy of those who participate in the Soviets, i.e., the members of the proletariat, the peasantry, and the armed forces—but not the bourgeoisie.

One is inclined to treat Trotsky's view that Soviet democracy is superior to (or more democratic than) bourgeois democracy as wishful thinking (at best) on his part. It might have been quite difficult for workers to participate in the political life of the so-called bourgeois democracies in the early decades of the twentieth century, but it was certainly not impossible. Nor was it impossible for their interests to find political representation. One would say of such democracies that they were seriously, albeit not irredeemably, flawed.

Suppose, though, that Trotsky is correct in holding that it is the *level* of participation of the workers in the political life of the country that matters, and that by *that* standard Soviet democracy surpasses bourgeois democracy. Even so, one wants to question the *meaningfulness* of such participation—and therefore the quality of such a democracy—in the absence of opposition parties, free speech, and a free press. Luxemburg's point is well taken: "[W]ithout a free and untrammelled press, without the unlimited right of association and assemblage, the rule of the broad mass of the people [i.e., proletarian democracy itself] is entirely unthinkable."[20]

Finally, one might think that because of his view that the welfare of revolution is the supreme law, Trotsky does not care much for democracy, and that all of his arguments on behalf of Soviet democracy are just so much window-dressing. His commitment to the Revolution, however, is above all a commitment to the *emancipation* of the workers—emancipation from the exploitation that, in the Marxist view, has always characterized the condition of the workers. In Trotsky's view, furthermore, such emancipation requires the very sort of active political participation on the part of the workers that he, unlike Luxemburg, sees the Soviets as advancing.

Luxemburg faults both Kautsky and the Bolsheviks for having posed a false choice—democracy *or* dictatorship—a false choice that will render the emancipation of the workers impossible. She suggests that there are two sorts of dictatorship: bourgeois dictatorship, i.e., the dictatorship of a party or clique; and socialist dictatorship, i.e., the dictatorship of an entire class—the working class. By the same token she suggests that there are two sorts of democracy: bourgeois democracy (i.e., the democracy of economic unequals, such as Trotsky has just criticized); and socialist democracy, which she sees as identical to the dictatorship of the *entire* working class. She faults Kautsky with suggesting that, having acquired power, the proletariat should opt for bourgeois democracy and reject the socialist revolution. "It cannot follow this advice without betraying thereby itself, the International, and the revolution." At the same time she faults Lenin and Trotsky for opting for the wrong sort of dictatorship, the dictatorship of a clique or party (i.e., *bourgeois* dictatorship).[21] It is clear that in Luxemburg's view, each course—both Kautsky's and the Bolsheviks'—is incompatible with the emancipation of the working class, the former because it preserves the exploitation of the working class, and the latter because it thwarts its political participation.

Lenin and Trotsky would object that even if (contrary to what they proclaim) the Soviets do *not* constitute a dictatorship of the working class as a whole, the sort of workers' participation in political life that they endorse in theory is simply not practicable at present. Nor will it be practicable in Russia for some time, i.e., until the vast majority of the workers attains the level of consciousness that characterizes the most advanced of them. Luxemburg's final reply would be that Lenin and Trotsky are putting the cart before the horse. It is not that heightened consciousness is a precondition for the dictatorship of the working class *as a class*; i.e., it is rather that such a dictatorship—socialist democracy—is a precondition for heightened consciousness. To be meaningful, finally, such a dictatorship requires (*inter alia* and once again) a free press along with the rights of association and assembly.[22]

III. The Defense of Revolutionary Terror

Trotsky is as audacious—and candid—in his defense of the Red terror as he is in his attack on democracy: "The question of the form of repression, or of its degree, of course, is not one of 'principle.' It is a question of expediency."[23] In the course of his life he advanced a number of claims about terrorism. First, he condemned *individual* terrorism in 1911 for two reasons: "In our eyes, individual terror is inadmissible precisely because it *belittles the role of the masses in their own consciousness*, reconciles them to their powerlessness, and turns their eyes and hopes toward a great avenger and liberator who some day will come and accomplish his mission."[24] A terrorist, in other words, sees himself (or herself), and not the class as a whole, as the primary *subject* of, or agent in, the class struggle. Moreover, his primary *object* is not the capitalist system: it is merely a symbol thereof.

Trotsky himself was responsible for a 1919 decree permitting the shooting of enemy commanders captured during the Civil War,[25] and in 1920 he advanced a second claim: during a civil war, the shooting of hostages is a tactic that is necessary to ensure victory. We know that it is necessary because of its occurrence in all civil wars,[26] and moreover, because of its intimidating effect. It is the only deterrent to the taking up of arms on the enemy's part.[27]

These, of course, are hardly compelling arguments. That the shooting of hostages occurs in all civil wars establishes not that it is a necessary tactic, but—at most—that the participants *believe* that it is. That the shooting of hostages has much of an intimidating effect seems implausible; anyone who is prepared to die in battle is unlikely to be deterred by the prospect of being shot, if captured, by a firing squad.

Trotsky's third claim, also of 1920, is that terror is ultimately futile "if it is employed by reaction [i.e., a reactionary class] against a historically rising class."[28] This claim is intelligible, of course, only within the context of a Marxist theory of history.

His fourth claim, again of 1920, is unsurprising. The shooting of hostages is justifiable not simply because, in his view, it is necessary for victory, but because it is necessary for victory of a morally particular sort, namely victory over capitalism. In short, only certain goals justify the use of this tactic: "The gendarmerie of Tsarism throttled the workers who were fighting for the Socialist order. Our Extraordinary Commissions [that constitute the Cheka] shoot landlords, capitalists, and generals who are striving to restore the capitalist order."[29]

Trotsky elaborates on this position in 1939: "Civil war is the supreme expression of the class struggle. To attempt to subordinate it to abstract 'norms' means in fact to disarm the workers in the face of an enemy armed to the teeth." This is akin to the attempt "to 'humanize' warfare by prohibiting the use of poison gases, the bombardment of unfortified cities, etc. Politically, such programs serve only to deflect the thoughts of the people from revolution as the only method of putting an end to war."[30] Trotsky's point here is that the prospective success of the Revolution justifies terrorism insofar as the success of the Revolution is of the highest possible value. It is such because, so he believes, it will bring with it both the emancipation of the working class and—once class societies, international predators that they are, no longer exist anywhere—an end to war.

It is noteworthy in this context that Michael Walzer himself allows for circumstances where it would be morally permissible in wartime to kill innocent people, namely, under conditions of "supreme emergency" such that "the danger [is] of an unusual and horrifying kind."[31] No doubt Trotsky would say of capitalism that although it is not *unusual*, it is *horrifying*. For Walzer, however, the Supreme Emergency Test arises typically (if not only) when genocide threatens a community's very survival.[32] It is obvious that Walzer would deny, and deny vigorously, any suggestion that Trotsky might legitimately invoke the notion of supreme emergency to justify the killing of innocents. Capitalism, after all, unlike Nazism, does not involve the enslavement or massacres of "entire peoples."

Trotsky could make two replies at this point. The first is that capitalist states invariably degenerate into genocidal states, but this, of course, is an historically dubious claim at best. Moreover, Trotsky would have to supplement this claim with another; namely, that socialist states seldom if ever suffer the same degeneration. The second reply that Trotsky could make is that Walzer's criteria for a supreme emergency are too restrictive. Specifically, Trotsky could maintain that the oppressive nature of the life of workers under capitalism is such as to warrant the extension of the Supreme Emergency Test to the killing of innocents as a necessary means of emancipating the workers from the system that oppresses them. Our sympathy with this approach will depend on Trotsky's convincing us (*inter alia*) first, that the workers' condition under capitalism is as grim as he, Trotsky, insists that it is; second, that killing innocent people is actually necessary to remedy the workers' condition; and third, that under socialism, either the workers will not be oppressed at all or else they will be substantially less oppressed.

IV. State Compulsion: The Espousal of Repressive Labor Policies

Trotsky's position on the organization of labor further illustrates the repressive nature of his thinking. Under socialism, Trotsky proclaims, "there will not exist the apparatus of compulsion itself, namely, the State: for it will have melted away entirely into a producing and consuming commune."[33] So far so good; where Marxists are concerned, this is old news. Trotsky, however, continues:

> None the less, the road to Socialism lies through a period of the highest possible intensification of the principle of the State. And you and I are just passing through that period. *Just as a lamp, before going out, shoots up in a brilliant flame, so the State, before disappearing, assumes the form of the dictatorship of the proletariat, i.e., the most ruthless form of State, which embraces the life of the citizens authoritatively in every direction.*[34]

He then spells out the terms of the dilemma that the Soviet state faces. (1) The Bolsheviks seized power in order to inaugurate a socialist society. (2) Consequently, the reconstruction of the economy is to take place under the auspices of an overall *plan* that the Soviet State will formulate. (3) The implementation of the terms of such a plan requires that the State use either market incentives or legal compulsion. (4) But the State is too poor to offer market incentives. (5) Therefore the State must use legal compulsion to implement the terms of the plan.

Trotsky pulls no punches here. "The only way to attract the labor-power necessary for our economic problems is to introduce *compulsory labor service*."[35] The State is to treat the entire population as a "reservoir of the necessary labor power;"[36] it is to introduce what Trotsky calls "the militarization of labor."[37] Compulsory labor service without the militarization of labor is unthinkable. Conscription for military service is the model in terms of which he conceives of compulsory labor service, and the methods that the Red Army uses to deploy troops (i.e., dispatching them where they are most needed) provide the model in terms of which he conceives of the militarization of labor. His experience as Commissar of War obviously played a role in shaping his thinking here.

To the charge that under the militarization of labor the Soviet worker is also a slave, Trotsky replies that oppression *of* the workers and *by* the workers is simply not possible. One is reminded of Rousseau's argument that in the ideal society, oppression on society's part would be impossible. Each individual is to alienate himself "together with all of his rights, to the entire community. . . . [S]ince each person gives himself whole and entire, the condition is equal for everyone; and [therefore] no one has an interest in making it burdensome for the others."[38] Furthermore, "since the sovereign [by which Rousseau means the society as a whole] is formed entirely from the private individuals who make it up, it neither has nor could have an interest contrary to theirs. Hence, the sovereign has no need to offer a guarantee to its subjects, since it is impossible for a body to want to harm all of its members."[39]

Trotsky's thinking is that insofar as the army's role is to ensure the survival of the nation, State, or ruling class, it is common to believe that the State is justified in practicing conscription and that the army is justified in demanding complete submission of its conscript troops. As it so happens, the survival of the Soviet state is at issue, albeit for *economic* rather than *military* reasons. (By 1920 the civil war was drawing to a close.) Survival is survival, however; hence the Soviet state is justified in practicing *labor* conscription and in demanding complete submission of its conscript *labor* troops.

For Trotsky, the productivity of compulsory labor will be the acid test of socialism.

> [I]f these forms of compulsion lead always and everywhere . . . to the lowering of productivity, then you can erect a monument over the grave of Socialism. For we cannot build Socialism on decreased production. Every social organization is in its foundation an organization of labor, and if our new organization of labor leads to a lowering of its productivity, it thereby most fatally leads to the destruction of the Socialist society we are building.[40]

The prospect of "a lowering of productivity" would be catastrophic:

> If it were to turn out that the planned, and consequently compulsory, organization of labor which is arising to replace imperialism led to the lowering of economic life, it would mean the destruction of all our culture, and a retrograde movement of humanity back to barbarism and savagery.[41]

The "imperialism" to which he refers here is what Lenin had cited as the end-stage of capitalism. It found its expression in the First World War, and provided, in Lenin's view, the ultimate cause for the outbreak of that war. Trotsky's point here is that if socialism fails the Productivity Test, then socialism will fail. Capitalism has already failed the Productivity Test; however productive capitalism might once have been, the test came with the First World War and its unprecedented destruction of life and of national economies. There is only capitalism or socialism, however; there is no third possibility. A civilized form of life demands economic productivity, and if neither economic system can provide it, then the outlook for civilization is bleak indeed.

It is crucial to the socialist project—and Trotsky knows that it is crucial—that *most* of the workers attain the perspective, the spirit of self-sacrifice and the devotion to the socialist project itself, that the most advanced workers possess. "The working class," Trotsky writes, "under the leadership of its vanguard, must itself re-educate itself on the foundations of Socialism."[42]

Of all previous thinkers, Plato and Rousseau are the two who come closest to identifying the crux of the problem that confronted the Bolsheviks. How does one transform ordinary human beings, who pursue their own private interests, into the ideal citizens of the ideal community? Plato is seeking to create a *polis* in which the rulers identify their private interests with the interests of the *polis*; Rousseau is seeking to create a society in which the members identify their private interests with the interests of the society; and Trotsky is seeking to galvanize the working class in such a way that the workers identify their private interests with the interests of their class. As he had put it in 1904, in the course of discussing the Party's mission of organizing the workers, the trick is to narrow the gap between "the objective interests of the proletariat and its consciousness"[43] "*by raising* [its] level of consciousness."[44]

The number of approaches that one might take here is limited. Plato, Rousseau, and Trotsky all reject reason as a sufficient instrument for transforming society. No rational argument will convince Hobbesians, after all, that they have failed to grasp their own best interests. Plato relies on myth, the myth of the metals. He is also sufficiently pessimistic to acknowledge, if only implicitly, the impossibility of enlightening the old generation, hence the need to cast out the adult population from the city and to focus on the children and their upbringing. Obviously he is invoking the need for violence here; parents do not normally abandon their children to the city and march off complacently into the wilderness. Rousseau relies on religion, the need for a Moses or a Mohammed, a lawgiver who speaks to the people with divine authority and thereby is able to convince them to accept the very constitution that ultimately will transform them.

In Trotsky's view, the bourgeoisie relied greatly on religion and ideology to motivate the workers. He advocates instead the presentation of an honest account of the obstacles to be faced, along with an appeal to moral incentives. "We say directly and openly to the masses that they can save, rebuild, and bring to a flourishing condition a Socialist country only by means of hard work, unquestioning discipline and exactness in execution on the part of every worker."[45] Trotsky rejects Plato's appeal to myth and Rousseau's appeal to divine authority: "The chief of our resources is moral influence—propaganda not only in word but in deed."[46] By this he means that "publicity and fame" are to be bestowed upon good workers, and shame upon bad workers.[47]

He raises the prospect of the workers' rejecting compulsory labor. "General labor service has an obligatory character; but this does not mean at all that it represents violence done to the working class. If compulsory labor came up against the opposition of the majority of the workers it would turn out a broken reed, and with it the whole of the Soviet order. The militarization of labor, when the workers are opposed to it, is the State slavery of Arakcheyev.[48] The militarization of labor by the will of the workers themselves is the Socialist dictatorship." Trotsky contends that such labor is entirely voluntary. Were it otherwise, the workers would not be contributing "their labor freely to the State in the form of 'Subbotniks' (communist Saturdays)."[49]

The key passages here involves two claims: (1) "General labor service has an obligatory character; but this does not mean at all that it represents violence done to the working class;" and (2) "The militarization of labor by the will of the workers themselves is the Socialist dictatorship." How can Trotsky possibly justify these claims? The answer to this—*the* crucial question—is to be found in Trotsky's view of the relation between the State and the worker. Arguing against the traditional conception of trade unions as instruments whereby workers assert their rights against management, Trotsky argues that the industrial unions that the Soviet State creates are *not* designed to be instruments whereby workers assert their rights against the State: "The worker does not merely bargain with the Soviet State: no, he is subordinated to the Soviet State, under its orders in every direction—for it is *his* State."[50]

What does Trotsky mean by *this* contention, that the Soviet State is *his*—the worker's—State? Trotsky is explicit throughout *Terrorism and Communism* that the Communist Party is to play the decisive role within the State. He replies accordingly to the Menshevik charge that the Bolsheviks have substituted the dictatorship of the Party for the dictatorship of the working class: "In this 'substitution' of the power of the party for the power of the working class there is nothing accidental, and in reality there is no substitution at all. The Communists express the fundamental interests of the working class. It is quite natural that, in the period in which history brings up those interests, in all their magnitude, on to the order of the day, the Communists have become the recognized representatives of the working class as a whole."[51]

Now clearly the Bolsheviks are not "representatives of the working class" in the same way in which members of Parliament are *representatives* of their constituencies. After all, members of Parliament have been *authorized* by their constituencies to engage in the business of making legislation, whereas the Bolsheviks have *not* been so authorized. Trotsky would reply that the Bolsheviks represent *interests* and not *constituencies*—interests that only a minority of the working class currently grasps. The welfare of the revolution, he would remind us, is the supreme law; hence whoever advances the welfare of the revolution thereby advances the interests of the working class and thereby *represents* the working class. The unstated paternalist assumption of Trotsky's is that at some point in the future, the workers will come to acknowledge that yes, the Bolsheviks did indeed grasp those interests of theirs to which they themselves had been blind. History, of course, has not been kind to that assumption.

Nelson P. Lande, University of Massachusetts Boston

Notes

1. 1854–1938.

2. 1879–1940.

3. Leon Trotsky, "Their Morals and Ours," in Leon Trotsky, John Dewey, and George Novack, *Their Morals and Ours: Marxist Versus Liberal Views on Morality* (New York: Merit, 1966), 15.

4. Ibid., 53–54.

5. Ibid., 15.

6. Ibid., 15.

7. Ibid., 16.

8. Trotsky, *Terrorism and Communism*, 35.

9. "The capitalist bourgeoisie calculates: 'while I have in my hands lands, factories, workshops, banks; while I possess newspapers, universities, schools; while—and this most important of all—I retain control of the army: the apparatus of democracy, however you reconstruct it, will remain obedient to my will...'" (Ibid., 36.)

10. Ibid., 40. The idea that "[t]he individual is absolute; all persons have the right of expressing their thoughts in speech and print; every man must enjoy equal electoral rights" may well have been progressive when it was first formulated in the feudal period. The same idea, however, has come "to show its reactionary side" by serving to hinder "the real demands of the laboring masses and the revolutionary parties." (Ibid., 38.)

11. V.I. Lenin, *The Proletarian Revolution and the Renegade Kautsky* (Peking: Foreign Languages Press, 1975). Lenin was replying to Kautsky's *The Dictatorship of the Proletariat*.

12. This premise is implicit in Lenin's argument.

13. Lenin, 9–10.

14. Ibid., 59.

15. Ibid., 43.

16. Ibid., 59. Lenin's figures show that in the elections to the All-Russian Congress of Soviets, the Bolsheviks won 13% of the seats in the election of June 3, 1917; 51% in the election of October 25, 1917; 61% in the election of January 10, 1918; 64% in the election of March 14, 1918; and 66% in the election of July 4, 1918. (All dates are the Old Style Calendar.)

17. Trotsky, *Terrorism and Communism*, 43.

18. Ibid., 45. Italics mine.

19. Trotsky's position is reminiscent of Lenin's. Lenin had contended that "a republic of Soviets [i.e., a proletarian democracy] is a higher form of democracy than the usual bourgeois republic with a Constituent Assembly." (V.I. Lenin, "Theses on the Constituent Assembly," in *The Proletarian Revolution and the Renegade Kautsky*, 123.) This is because "the Soviets . . . by uniting and drawing *the masses of workers and peasants* into political life . . . serve as a most sensitive barometer, the one closest to the 'people' . . . , of the growth and development of the political, class maturity of the masses." (Ibid., 98.) Moreover, a Soviet state serves, by means of the Soviets to draw "scores and scores of millions of new citizens who are kept down under any democratic republic . . . into political life, into *democracy*, into the administration of the state." (Ibid., p. 101.) Finally, "the Soviets, as the organ of struggle of the oppressed masses, reflected and expressed the moods and changes of opinions of these masses ever so much more quickly, fully, and faithfully than any other institution." (Ibid., 58.)

20. Luxemburg, 67.

21. Luxemburg, 76–77. "The basic error of the Lenin-Trotsky theory," she writes, "is that they too, just like Kautsky, oppose dictatorship to democracy. 'Dictatorship *or* democracy' is the way the question is put by Bolsheviks and Kautsky alike. The latter naturally decides in favor of 'democracy,' that is, of bourgeois democracy, precisely because he opposes it to the alternative of the socialist revolution. Lenin and Trotsky, on the other hand, decide in favor of dictatorship in contradistinction to democracy, and thereby, in favor of the dictatorship of a handful of persons, that is, in favor of dictatorship on the bourgeois model. They are two opposite poles, both alike being far removed from a genuine socialist policy. [Kautsky to the contrary, the proletariat] should and must at once undertake socialist measures in the most energetic, unyielding and unhesitant fashion, in other words, exercise a dictatorship, but a dictatorship of the *class*, not of a party or of a clique—dictatorship of the class, that means in the broadest public form on the basis of the most active, unlimited participation of the mass of the people, of unlimited democracy."

22. "But socialist democracy is not something which begins only in the promised land after the foundations of socialist economy are created. . . . Socialist democracy begins simultaneously with the beginnings of the destruction of class rule and of the construction of socialism. It begins at the very moment of the seizure of power by the socialist party. It is the same thing as the dictatorship of the proletariat. . . . But this dictatorship must be the work of the *class* and not of a little leading minority in the name of the class—that is, it must

proceed step by step out of the active participation of the masses; it must be under their direct influence, subjected to the control of complete public activity." (Ibid., 77–78.)

23. Trotsky, *Terrorism and Communism*, 58. (By "repression", in this context, he means terror in general, and the shooting of hostages in particular.)

24. Leon Trotsky, "The Marxist Position on Individual Terrorism," in Leon Trotksy, *Against Individual Terrorism* (New York: Pathfinder Press, 1974), 7.

25. Trotsky claimed in 1938 that "the Decree of 1919 led scarcely to even one execution of relatives of those commanders whose perfidy not only caused the loss of innumerable human lives but threatened the revolution itself with direct annihilation." (Leon Trotsky, "Their Morals and Ours," in *Their Morals and Ours: Marxist versus Liberal Views on Morality* (New York: Pathfinder, 1966), 32.

26. Leon Trotsky, "The Moralists and Sycophants Against Marxism," in *Their Morals and Ours*, 46. Thus Trotsky writes: "The system of hostages . . . has been practiced in all the civil wars of ancient and modern history. It obviously flows from the nature of civil war itself."

27. Trotsky, *Terrorism and Communism*, 58.

28. Ibid., 58.

29. Ibid., 59.

30. Trotsky, "The Moralists and Sycophants Against Marxism," in *Their Morals and Ours: Marxist versus Liberal Views on Morality*, 46–47.

31. Michael Walzer, *Just and Unjust Wars*, (New York: Basic Books Inc., 1977), 253.

32. [I]t is possible to live in a world where individuals are sometimes murdered, but a world where entire peoples are enslaved or massacred is literally unbearable. For the survival and freedom of political communities—whose members share a way of life, developed by their ancestors, to be passed on to their children—are the highest values of international society. Nazism challenged these values on a grand scale, but challenges more narrowly conceived, *if they are of the same kind*, have similar moral consequences. They bring us under the rule of necessity (and necessity knows no rules). (Ibid., 254.)

33. Ibid., 169.

34. Ibid., 169–170. Italics mine.

35. Ibid., 135. Italics Trotsky's.

36. Ibid., 135.

37. Ibid., 137.

38. Jean-Jacques Rousseau, *On the Social Contract* (Indianapolis: Hackett Publishing Company, 1983), 24.

39. Ibid., 26.

40. Ibid., 143.

41. Ibid., 144.

42. Ibid., 146.

43. Leon Trotsky, *Our Political Tasks* (London: New Park Publications, N.D.), 74.

44. Op. Cit., 75.

45. One is reminded here of Churchill's words: "I have nothing to offer but blood, toil, tears, and sweat." Churchill uttered these words while addressing the British House of Commons for the first time in his role as Prime Minister on May 13, 1940.

46. Ibid., 146–147.

47. Ibid., 148–149.

48. Aleksey Andreyevich Arakcheyev (1769–1834) was a general and minister of war under Alexander I.

49. Ibid., 147.

50. Ibid., 168.

51. Ibid., 109.

Transsexualism and "Transracialism"

CHRISTINE OVERALL

Abstract: This paper explores, from a feminist perspective, the justification of major surgical reshaping of the body. I define "transracialism" as the use of surgery to assist individuals to "cross" from being a member of one race to being a member of another. If transsexualism, involving the use of surgery to assist individuals to "cross" from female to male or from male to female, is morally acceptable, and if providing the medical and social resources to enable sex crossing is not morally problematic, then transracialism should be morally acceptable, and providing medical and social resources to facilitate race crossing is not necessarily morally problematic. To explore this idea, I present and evaluate eight possible arguments that might be given against accepting transracialism, and I show that each of them is unsuccessful.

In this paper I wish to propose a deliberately provocative claim, as part of my effort to delineate and understand a set of philosophical problems. I am interested, very broadly, in personal identity transformations via major bodily changes, especially changes produced by means of surgical interventions. Adopting a term from ftm (female to male) C. Jacob Hale, these might called instances of "re-embodiment."[1] I have in mind such phenomena as the following:

- Surgery for transsexual identity changes, intended to assist the subject to "cross" from female to male or from male to female,[2] whether the subject seeks always to pass successfully as the other sex or is sometimes willing to be out as a transsexual;[3]
- The surgical creation of body art, as epitomized by the female artist Orlan;[4]
- Surgery for racial transformation, as exemplified by Michael Jackson, who has deliberately changed the configuration of his face and, possibly, the appearance of his skin,[5] and as also exemplified by some Asian individuals who seek to make their noses narrower and higher and their eyes more rounded;
- Cosmetic surgery, whether to diminish signs of aging or to reduce body size—to become (like) a young person or (like) a thin person;
- Münchhausen syndrome (in cases where it involves surgery), in which the subject seeks the identity of patient or impaired person;

- Voluntary female genital cutting (for example, clitorectomy) on adult women who seek to conform to certain religious norms.

The desires to become or to become like a member of the other sex, or to use one's body as an expression of art, are recognized phenomena whose varied forms of legitimacy feminists now acknowledge, at least some of the time and in some cases, even while remaining critical of the cultural environments in which those desires may be expressed. Feminists no longer see the subjects of such desires as mere victims or unwitting dupes of cultural stereotypes and practices. Yet the desires to become a member of another race, to become significantly younger-looking, more beautiful, or thinner, or to become a sick or disabled person, or to become a woman with surgically altered genitals in conformity with religious or cultural practice, are seldom, if ever, phenomena that feminists—let alone the rest of western culture—are willing to regard as legitimate. Although these processes appear very wide-ranging, all of them have in common the unifying idea of surgically reshaping the body, as a work in progress, a cultural artefact, a religious object, a material performance, or a work of art, in order to generate a new personal and social identity. All of these processes are examples of the literal enactment of what Michel Foucault calls "technologies of the self,"[6] a mode of self-care, self-creation, and self-constitution that redefines identity through the cutting and reconstruction of the body.

In raising this issue I shall focus on just one component, the idea of changing race. However, I am not concerned here with the phenomenon of passing, in which individuals belonging to subordinated races attempt, through altered self-presentation, to be taken as members of dominant races, usually for reasons of safety, self-protection, survival, or personal achievement, without attempting to change race. Nor am I interested in the phenomenon of compulsory assimilation, in which social pressures force individuals, through self-presentation, to appear to become members of another race, whether they want to or not. Rather, I am interested in the possibility of what I shall call "transracialism," a term modelled on "transsexualism." I suspect that the singer Michael Jackson may represent an example of transracialism, that is, the voluntary crossing or attempted crossing from being a member of one race to being a member of another. Jackson has had surgery on his cheekbones, eyes, chin, and nose in order to make his face less "Black"-looking, and more "white." He may or may not also have deliberately changed the colour of his skin. If some individuals can feel that, inside, they are really member of the other sex,[7] perhaps there are people—we can certainly imagine them—who feel, inside, that they are members of another race or ethnic group. If an mtf transsexual such as Deirdre McCloskey can regard transsexualism as "becoming what you are" with respect to sex identity,[8] then perhaps transracialism for some people would be the phenomenon of becoming what you are with respect to race identity. If there is no one who is a transracialist in my sense then my topic is merely hypothetical, but I suggest it's an interesting hypothetical.

I present this hypothetical for purposes of participating in, furthering, and also challenging an ongoing feminist debate (whether by transpeople or by non-transpeople) about the nature of identity and identity change, and about the means by which identity change is sought and obtained. In using terms like "transsexualism" and "transracialism," I am not implicitly claiming an expertise about transpeople or about race that I do not have. I would say that my focus in this paper is not on transsexual people or on racialized people themselves; rather my focus is on what some theorists say or assume about transsexuals and about racialization.

If it is acceptable for a woman to seek to become a man via surgical means, is it also acceptable for an Afro-American or -Canadian to seek to become white? And if it acceptable for a man to seek to become a woman, should it not be all right for a white to seek to become Afro-American? Pat Califia points out that some transpeople "approach sex reassignment with the same mindset that they would obtaining a piercing or a tattoo," and she cites members of the S/M community who demand "the individual's right to own his or her own body, and make whatever temporary or permanent changes to that body the individual pleases either for sexual gratification or for purposes of adornment."[9] Similarly, Hale advocates that feminists and other progressive activists aim for "a world in which the technological and performative means for embodiment of sex, gender, and sexuality would be available on the basis of desire alone."[10] If transsexual surgery is morally acceptable, as these and other feminists argue or assume,[11] and if providing the medical and social resources to enable sex crossing is not morally problematic or even, as Hale suggests, is the response to a right, then transracial surgery should be morally acceptable, and providing medical and social resources to facilitate race crossing is not morally problematic.

Some readers may immediately agree with this hypothetical statement. Others may reject the antecedent. In this paper I am not addressing their views. Instead, I am addressing those who are inclined to accept the antecedent and reject the consequent. I shall call them "rejecters of transracial surgery" or "rejecters," for short. There are at least eight different arguments they might make for rejecting transracial surgery. In what follows I shall try to show that each of these arguments is unsuccessful.

I. First Argument

The rejecter might claim that it is not truly possible to change one's race, that the alleged transracialist is attempting, unsuccessfully, to violate his or her true identity by rejecting natural features of his or her physical being.

But the rejecter can make this claim only if s/he regards race as an inherent, essential, fixed characteristic, while seeing sex as incidental, acquired, or constructed, and hence malleable. Such a stance appears inconsistent. Either both sex and race are inherent fixed characteristics, or, more plausibly, both are socially constructed and socially acquired or ascribed.[12] The latter is more plausible. We have learned to reject the sort of essentialism that says that sex or race is inevitably a fixed identity, equivalent to or founded upon publicly observable physical characteristics. Physical identities are changeable; thus, transsexuals seek to change their public physical identity in crucial ways. (Some regard themselves as "always already" having the identity with which they aspire to make their physical body congruent.) The same would be possible for the transracialist.

The *category* of sex is defined by a social process whereby certain features—e.g., vulva and breasts or penis and testicles—are picked out as being constitutive of the sex one is.[13] One's sex—one's maleness or femaleness—can be reconstructed by such means as shaping the body through exercise and diet and sculpting the body through the use of surgery to alter genitalia and so-called secondary sex characteristics. Similarly, concepts of race—being white, Black, coloured, Asian, mulatto, Métis, Aboriginal, etc.—are defined by the social process of definition whereby certain features—e.g., skin colour, hair texture, facial features—and/or certain ethnic backgrounds (at various times Jews, Italians, Québécois, and Irish have all been examples)—are picked out as being definitive and constitutive of the race one is. One's race can be reconstructed by shaping the body through hair treatments, skin lightening or tanning, and sculpting the body through the use of so-called cosmetic surgery to reshape the eyes, nose, chin, brow, and cheekbones. Therefore, to the extent that it is possible for a woman to become a man, it is also possible for a person of colour to become a white person.

II. Second Argument

The rejecter of transracialism might suggest that it is possible that trans-identified persons have a different hormonal make-up than non-trans-identified individuals with the same genitalia. These individuals would have a biological constitution that impels them to seek sex-reassignment surgery and that for them makes living in a non-reassigned body painful. By contrast, it is unlikely that the supposed "transracialist" would have any such physiological condition that would justify surgery for changing race.

But even if hormones do predispose certain individuals to seek a sex change and that there is no comparable physiological mechanism in the case of transracialism (and the former may not in fact apply to all who seek sex reassignment), this argument assumes that the legitimacy of a desire to change identity is dependent on the nature of the causation of the desire. Making such a connection would commit the rejecter to the necessity of naturalizing desires and beliefs about the self in order to make them acceptable. Moreover, it would require a resort to biological determinism in a way that seems to undermine the agency and self-determination of those who seek to change identity. I suggest that these are consequences that most feminist rejecters would not want to accept. Therefore, regardless of whether there is a physiological cause of or predisposition to the desire to change sex, I don't think such a cause or predisposition can consistently be required by the rejecter in order for transracialism to be legitimate.

III. Third Argument

The rejecter of transracialism might argue that this phenomenon is not acceptable because it is a betrayal of group identity. One has a duty to be a proud member of one's race, to stand up for the idea that it is good to be a member of that race and to bear witness to the errors of racism.

However, it is not at all evident that we always have a duty to stick with our group of origin, or that if we do not, we are inevitably being disloyal to our group of origin. Consider the phenomenon of class mobility, moving from working class to middle class, or vice versa. Or consider the phenomenon of successfully recovering from temporary impairments, so that one is no longer disabled and has therefore ceased to be a member of the group of disabled persons. Such moves do not necessarily or inevitably betray the group of origin or indicate lack of pride in one's past, and they are not inconsistent with solidarity with political struggles against classism and ableism.

In addition, the individual who moves from one identity group to another just may not feel happy in the group of origin, or may strongly feel s/he belongs elsewhere. The rejecter might argue that feelings of inferiority and shame, probably derived from oppression, motivate such identity changes. But even *if* this is sometimes the motivation for racial identity change (and how can the rejecter know that?) then it's the oppression that must be criticized and changed, rather than forbidding the race change itself. People ought not to be excoriated for trying to escape racial oppression, in the case of a possible change from person of colour to white, or for rejecting complicity in racial oppression, as in the possible change from white person to person of colour. Moreover, a person seeking identity change may feel and believe that the identity categories themselves are limited and limiting, obstacles to human flourishing, and so by means of surgery the person seeks to confound the categories and violate their usually rigid boundaries. As socially displaced persons,[14] they are seeking a new means of living in hostile territory.

IV. Fourth Argument

The rejecter might argue that supporting and condoning transracialism simply reinforces oppression. So, even if the transracialist's own motives are untouched by oppression or internalized oppression—which seems unlikely—transracialism as a general practice would reinforce racism, and hence should be rejected.

But this kind of argument is undermined by the existence of persons who seek to move from the oppressor group to the oppressed group. The existence of a white transracialist who seeks to be a person of colour might, if anything, help to undermine racism by showing that membership in the hitherto oppressed group is desirable. Moreover, seeking to be a member of the group to which one is not yet attributed is not, as arguments against Janice Raymond's work have shown,[15] a matter of mocking that group, or acquiescing in or even contributing to its oppression, but rather is an expression of identification and solidarity with and admiration for that group.[16]

Another answer to the worry about reinforcing racism is provided by those transpeople who do not seek to pass as members of the sex to which they are crossing, but rather are out as transsexuals or as transgendered people and are committed to activism on the part of those who do not want or are not able to engage in standard gender conformity. By leaving the sex assigned at birth, the transperson shows the possibilities of "fluidity and transgression" in gender identity, presentation, and behaviour. (Roen 2002, 511). Similarly, in seeking to cross racial boundaries, transracialists might demonstrate the constructed nature of racial categories and thereby contribute to a loosening up of racial boundaries, taboos, and stereotypes.

V. Fifth Argument

The rejecter might argue that transracialism ought to be rejected on grounds of its potential harm to others. For example, if an individual changes his or her race, the transformation could be profoundly wounding to family members, including children and parents, who remain members of the race that the transracialist has discarded. In effect, the transracialist appears to reject his or her race, thus calling into question its value and legitimacy, especially for family members who share that race.[17]

However, there are many significant life changes chosen by some individuals that may seriously disturb other people, including family members, and may appear to undermine their own life choices, yet we do not judge them wrong or unacceptable for that reason. I have in mind such major life events as choosing to have a child or choosing to have an abortion; choosing to marry, especially outside one's religion or ethnic group; coming out as lesbian or gay; choosing to leave a religious group or to enter one that is very different from one's group of origin; or undertaking education in a field that the family may reject. While it is important for individuals not to ignore the wellbeing of their loved ones, potential hurt incurred by loved ones is not necessarily a good reason for failing to remake one's physical being to become the identity that one wants or to create congruence with the identity that one already has.

VI. Sixth Argument

However, the rejecter may say that it is not so much the potential negative effects on individual others that is the problem; instead it is a matter of increased costs incurred by the health care system, and the resulting redirection of resources from other more urgent forms of medical care. Even if the transracialist's surgical change of racial identity is not highly expensive, it could become so, for example if others seek to follow his or her example, or if the medical procedures involved in changing race result in needs for costly long-term health care as a result of radical surgery.

The answer to this counter-argument may vary depending on whether one is talking about a privately funded healthcare system or a publicly funded system. In the former case the principle is user-pay; so a staunch defender of privatized medicine could simply say that if any individual is willing to pay for a transracial identity change—as Michael Jackson has done—then he or she should be able to do so. The issue then might well be one of justice and equity; if someone like Michael Jackson can afford this procedure, and if it is worth having, then is it fair that others cannot?

In a publicly-funded healthcare system such as the one in Canada (a system that I support and advocate) it is necessary to first point out that, just as there is only a tiny minority of transsexual people among all those who are transgendered who opt for full medical intervention to permit a complete surgical crossing from one sex to the other, so also it seems likely that only a tiny minority of transracial individuals (if there are such people) would opt for full medical intervention to permit a crossing from one race to another. Given that public healthcare systems in several jurisdictions already fund transsexual surgery, it would be inconsistent and probably discriminatory not to fund transracial surgery. Transsexual surgery is accessible only after running a gamut of medical and psychological assessments, and access to transracial surgery could similarly be limited. This is not to say that I agree with all of the current ways in which eligibility for transsexual surgery is assessed, and many transpeople themselves are opposed to the medical and mental health gate keeping criteria that currently determine who gets access to the surgery.[18] However, I do believe that, as with any other serious medical procedure with significant costs and risks, it is appropriate for potential patients to be evaluated for medical risks prior to surgery. And the devotion of resources to transracial surgery would have to be evaluated against other serious health care needs.

VII. Seventh Argument

The rejecter might suggest that the real problem of transracialism is that it would harm the individuals themselves who seek to change race, and moreover that physicians who offer such a service could be guilty of medical malpractice. Procedures to change a person's race may be highly risky and could result in real iatrogenic illness, both physical and psychological, as Michael Jackson's own case may show. If these procedures are undertaken, they must have the prospect of being successful or should not be done at all, yet there is no track record of success.

However, people are able to engage in many activities, including risky sports like mountain climbing, hockey, and skiing, that involve potential harm to themselves and that may well incur the need for surgical treatment that may or may not be successful, yet they are not forbidden to participate, prevented from participating, or disapproved of for participating. For the sake of the goal of physical identity change, it is evident that people are willing and able to run very serious risks. Moreover, it is hard to see how the transracial case would be different from transsexual medical interventions, except for the fact that there is a history of "sex change" surgery but not yet for "race change" surgery. Transsexual surgery arguably involves some risks of harm, both short-term and long-term, yet it is permitted. With respect to transracialism, presumably physicians could become better, through research and practice, at performing race change surgery. They would, of course, have to ensure that every individual who undergoes the surgery is fully informed about the likely consequences and is making an autonomous choice. In addition, for some people, even some transsexual surgical change, that is, some reduction of incongruence between gender identity and bodily structure, can be better than no change, and may even suffice for purposes of the individual's identity congruency. (For example, some ftm transsexuals undergo mastectomy but not phalloplasty, and some mtfs seek surgically-created breasts but do not have the penis and testicles removed.) So, even partial or limited surgery for racial change might be not only better than no change but even wholly adequate from the point of view of someone who is seeking it.

VIII. Eighth Argument

Finally, the rejecter of transracialism might suggest that anyone seeking such a form of identity change is confused and psychologically disturbed, and perhaps even lacks full autonomy to choose transracial surgery. Certainly that claim has been made against some prospective transsexuals.[19]

Yet as the history and sociology of sex and gender crossings indicate,[20] there is plenty of evidence that transsexual people are entirely competent and are able to learn effectively, work productively, form strong relationships, and make wise decisions for their own wellbeing. If some individuals seeking identity change suffer from psychological turmoil that turmoil may well be correlated with the discrimination, danger, and oppression they encounter in their current physical form. It is the worst form of paternalism—and circular reasoning—to claim, on an *a priori* basis, that individuals who seek major identity changes are, just for that reason, not autonomous. It is a claim for which evidence is needed; the sheer desire for change cannot, in and of itself, be taken as the sole evidence. We rightly assume that our bodies are our own to change, and therefore there is no good reason to believe that transracialists would not be both sane and autonomous—or as sane and autonomous as it is possible to be in a sexist and racist society—just as are those who seek and receive transsexual surgery.

IX. Conclusion

I wrote this paper because of questions that I have about the nature of identity and identity change, and about the surgical means by which some identity changes are sought and obtained. I started out my discussion by offering the following hypothesis: If transsexualism is morally acceptable and if providing the medical and social resources to enable sex crossing is not morally problematic, then transracialism should be morally acceptable, and providing medical and social resources to enable race crossing is not morally problematic. I then considered eight possible arguments that might be given by someone who rejected my hypothesis, and I argued that none of them succeeds in refuting my hypothesis.

What conclusion should I draw?

One possibility is that my hypothesis is, as far as we can tell now, correct: transsexualism and transracialism should be equally acceptable, *if* they are acceptable at all, to feminists and to others with progressive politics. The only alternatives I can see are that either: a) transsexualism and transracialism are not comparable, for reasons that I have not been able to recognize; or b) one of my rejoinders to the rejecter is unsuccessful; or c) there is another possible argument that the rejecter might bring forward which I have failed to think of and which indicates a valid reason for accepting transsexualism while rejecting transracialism.

I shall close with one final thought. It seems to me that both the real phenomenon of transsexual surgery, and the (perhaps hypothetical) phenomenon of transracial surgery, are predicated upon interestingly contradictory assumptions about identity change. On the one hand, the possibility of surgically changing one's sex and surgically changing one's race presupposes the flexibility of these identities. A man can become a woman; a person of colour can become a white, and vice versa. Yet at the same time, these phenomena also deny the ready malleability and diversity of these identities. They presuppose not that one can simply, through a change in self-identity and self-presentation, choose to be a woman or to be a man, choose to be Black or choose to be white, but rather that these categories are so firm and strong that the individual must be *physically* unmade and remade in order for a true identity crossing or change to occur. It is both this susceptibility to change, and this resistance to change, that sex and race identities have in common.

Christine Overall, Queen's University

Notes

1. C. Jacob Hale, "Tracing a Ghostly Memory in My Throat: Reflections on Ftm Feminist Voice and Agency." In *Men Doing Feminism*, ed. Tom Digby (New York: Routledge, 1998), 124 (n9).

2. Deirdre McCloskey, *Crossing: A Memoir* (Chicago: University of Chicago Press, 1999).

3. Katrina Roen, "'Either/Or' or 'Both/Neither': Discursive Tentions in Transgender Politics," *Signs: Journal of Women in Culture and Society* 27 (2002): 501–522.

4. Orlan, http://www.cicv.fr/creation_artistique/online/orlan/index1.html. Page accessed January 25, 2003; Kathy Davis, "My Body is My Art: Cosmetic Surgery as Feminist Utopia?" in *Feminist Theory and the Body: A Reader*, eds. Janet Price and Margrit Shidrick. (New York: Routledge, 1999).

5. http://anomalies-unlimited.com/Jackson.html

6. Michel Foucault, "Technologies of the Self," in *Technologies of the Self: A Seminar with Michel Foucault*, eds. Luther H. Martin, Huck Gutman, and Patrick H. Hutton (Amherst, Massachusetts: University of Massachusetts Press, 1988), 16–29.

7. I recognize that not all transsexual persons interpret their experiences in this way. As C. Jacob Hale remarks, "Just as some mtfs, such as Kate Bornstein, self-identify as neither man nor woman, some ftms discursively position themselves as neither, or both, or 'all of both and neither of either,' or as members of a third gender, or 'look forward eagerly to the day when there [will] be more genders from which to choose'" (Hale, 103).

8. McCloskey, *Crossing: A Memoir*.

9. Pat Califia, *Sex Changes: The Politics of Transgenderism* (San Francisco: Cleis Press, 1997), 224.

10. Hale, 122.

11. Kate Bornstein, *My Gender Workbook* (New York: Routledge, 1994); McCloskey, *Crossing: A Memoir*.

12. Another possibility is that sex is inherent, essential, and fixed, whereas race is incidental, acquired, or constructed. But presumably by accepting the antecedent of my hypothetical, the rejecter cannot adopt this view.

13. John Stoltenberg, "How Men Have (a) Sex," in his *Refusing to Be a Man: Essays on Sex and Justice* (New York: Penguin, 1989), 25–39.

14. Hale, 114.

15. Janice Raymond, *The Transsexual Empire* (London: The Women's Press, 1979).

16. Califia 1997, 92ff.

17. Similarly, in the case of transsexual surgery, Pat Califia remarks, "The female partners of transsexual men who once identified as lesbians frequently complain that they are negatively affected by the FTM's rejection of his own female morphology. Hormones and cosmetic surgery give the transsexual man a new comfort with his body, but the physical changes he undergoes may negatively impact the female partner's body image." (Califia, 216–217).

18. Califia, 224.

19. Leslie Feinberg, *Transgender Warriors: Making History From Joan of Arc to Dennis Rodman* (Boston: Beacon Press, 1996); McCloskey, *Crossing: A Memoir*.

20. Califia, *Sex Changes: The Politics of Transgenderism*; Feinberg, *Transgender Warriors*.

Part IV:
NASSP Book Award

Church and State: Comments and Questions

JOHANN A. KLAASSEN

This is one of those rare books which is not only fascinating and important, but also accessible and readable. Professor Weithman is certainly to be commended for writing not just the best book in social philosophy in 2002, but one of the finest books I have read in quite some time. I'm sorry that I was unable to be in Boston in person to congratulate Professor Weithman on his wonderful work, which it was my pleasure to read, and I only hope that my comments and questions are not addressed in some portion of the book that I missed or misunderstood.

In fact, after I finished reading this book the first time through, I purchased a copy for my minister—the Unitarian Universalist church to which I belong has a long history of political action and activism, and even though the intended audience for this book is clearly the professional political or social philosopher, its message is clear even to the non-professional. Admittedly, Reverend Ellen hasn't spoken on any particularly political topics since I gave her that copy of this book—but perhaps her reticence is to be expected. The relationship between politics and religion in the US has been an odd one, to be sure, and some of the tensions in this odd relationship form the background of my comments on and questions about Professor Weithman's views.

Weithman's central argument is designed to establish two key principles, a personal political principle (his "5.1") and a public political principle (his "5.2"). In essence, the personal principle says that citizens may base their votes on their religious views, without needing to have other non-religious reasons sufficient to determine their votes; the public principle says that citizens may offer religious reasons for political stances in public debate, without having other non-religious reasons sufficient to justify those stances. There are, of course, some caveats and limitations added to these basic formulations, but I believe that these formulations capture the central points.

The personal principle, interesting and controversial as it is, doesn't pull at me as hard as the public principle. My first (and certainly smaller) question is about an example Weithman offers: "On Sunday, May 24, 1998, John Cardinal O'Connor, the late Roman Catholic archbishop of New York, delivered a homily critical of a domestic partnership act under consideration by the New York City Council" (p. 95). Because of the public media attention given to the Cardinal's homily—attention pretty clearly sought by the Cardinal and his staff—Weithman argues that the homily transcended its "merely" religious context, and effectively became part of the public debate regarding that legislation. Oddly, though, relegated to a footnote is a crucial piece of information: "As *The Times* reported: 'Cardinal O'Connor acknowledged that the church "has no right to impose specifically Catholic teaching on others," and said it had no desire to do so. Instead, he couched his criticism in nonsectarian terms that seemed intended to resonate beyond the Gothic cathedral on Fifth Avenue'" (p. 96, note 3). So we have an important religious figure, making a political statement couched in non-religious terms, within the context of a religious ritual. According to Weithman's discussion of the private principle, it seems clear that the mere fact that the Cardinal expressed his disapproval of the City Council's proposals would be sufficient reason for New York Catholics to vote against the measure, should it come to a vote; but I'm not sure it connects at all to his public principle.

If the point of the public principle is that religious reasons are to count as justifying reasons in public policy debates, then we might have hoped for an example in which a religious figure used explicitly religious reasons in a public political argument. Since the Cardinal, however, apparently intended his arguments "to resonate beyond the Gothic cathedral," and argued therefore in non-religious terms, the principle seems not to apply. This may be a non-issue, since Weithman raises the example in order to talk about why it can be called "a public political argument," rather than "merely" a political argument made to a private (albeit large) audience. I would like some clarification from Professor Weithman as to what the impact of this example really is.

My second question is closely aligned to my first: what of a similarly public political argument which *does* proceed from explicitly religious premises? Here's my concern: Historically speaking, straightforwardly political speech in the United States has enjoyed First Amendment protection; so also has straightforwardly religious speech. But "politics from the pulpit" has often run afoul of the protections that political and religious speech enjoy. That is, we have traditionally drawn a bright line between religious institutions and political organizations. Churches hold special status in our tax codes, for example, which differ from the special status afforded to political parties and other not-for-profit institutions. Those churches which become institutionally active in the political arena can face substantial tax-related consequences. Every election cycle, my minister revises a sermon she has given for quite a while now, decrying the "voter's guides" distributed at the local conservative Christian churches (there are more than a few such churches in Colorado Springs, home to Dr. Dobson's group, "Focus on the Family"). "The principle of the separation of church and state implies that if we want to avoid governmental interference in religious matters, we need to keep our religious institutions out of governmental matters," one common version of Reverend Ellen's argument goes—that is, separation runs both ways, and the political and religious spheres must be kept as distinct as possible. Interestingly, over the last year or so Reverend Ellen has often spoken out against the wars in Afghanistan and Iraq, basing her arguments from the pulpit on the Sixth Principle of the Unitarian Universalist Association: "We covenant to affirm and promote the goal of world community with peace, liberty, and justice for all." She expressed some chagrin when members of the congregation asked her about the tension between these two arguments, and has seemed to stick to less directly political topics recently. But perhaps Professor Weithman would argue that her first argument is simply wrong-headed, that politics from the pulpit is justifiable—it may even be desirable, as it can motivate the participation of otherwise non-participatory citizens, thus contributing to the overall goal of participatory democracy.

My second (and I fear very large) question for Professor Weithman is this: If we want to allow a liberal political voice to speak from the pulpit, we need to allow a conservative voice to speak from the pulpit as well; but does allowing *either* voice to make political statements threaten recent interpretations of the principle of the separation of church and state in a problematic way?

I think that this truly excellent book deserves a great deal of attention from social and political philosophers—and the public at large could probably benefit from the renewed interest and deepened understandings Professor Weithman brings to these issues. I am glad to congratulate him on his excellent book, and now on this award.

Johann A. Klaassen, First Affirmative Financial Network, LLC

American Constitutionalism:
A Formula for Religious Citizenship

SHARON ANDERSON-GOLD

In *Religion and the Obligations of Citizenship*, Paul Weithman appeals to political sociology to enrich the conception that political philosophers have of the proper role of religion in liberal democratic politics, specifically American liberal democratic politics. As one who feels strongly that political philosophy and ethics are applied disciplines, I applaud Weithman's interdisciplinary methodology.

For those of you who may not have yet read the book I will summarize briefly the results of the empirical research that Weithman offers in defense of his claim that religion can contribute to the realization of liberal democratic citizenship. According to Weithman, churches make the following valuable contributions:

1. they contribute to discussions about what it means to be a full participant in a liberal democratic polity;
2. they help realize the "adequate representation" condition by advocating for the needs of the poor and the marginalized;
3. they assist individuals to "realize" their citizenship through greater identification with political issues and through the development of skills, etc.[1]

While point 3 is primarily a contribution to the acquisition of "skills" and arguably is not uniquely characteristic of religious organizations, Weithman reminds us that the poor have less access to social clubs and other civic organizations and that therefore churches frequently provide the only resource for this type of skill-building for the most vulnerable portion of the population. He notes that this is especially true for poor African-Americans.

Points 1 and 2 are more directly relevant to the manner in which individuals form basic moral, social and political "world views" that "motivate political action." The point here is that without adequate world views individuals are not likely to be "motivated" to participate in political decision-making by going out to vote, etc. As economic "consumers" we may "vote" our private preferences with our dollars. But as persons concerned with the good of community we must develop views about the nature of justice, and perhaps even more importantly we must develop "care" and "concern" before we can be motivated to act. This type of care and concern is typically developed in some more or less enduring form of association with others.

Because of the commitment of liberal democracy to the values of freedom and privacy, liberal governments cannot directly create these "cares" and "concerns." The public realm of government and law is distinct from the private realm of liberty. In liberal democracies the development of conceptions of the good and the just depends upon "secondary associations" such as families, civic groups and churches. Liberal democracy needs secondary associations, but does it need churches? Weithman's claims are of course not that liberal democracy "needs" churches but that churches make valuable contributions that do not violate "duties of good citizenship" when citizens rely on the religious reasons for policy preferences that they have developed as a consequence of their church membership. Therefore, Weithman concludes, liberal democrats ought to welcome the contributions that churches make to the "realized citizenship" of their members.

Weithman has two principles which express this positive evaluation of religious citizenship, one that allows for religious reasons to motive personal activities such as "voting" and one that allows for religious reasons to motivate participation in public political debate. In both cases the only "caveat" is the following:

> "provided they sincerely believe that *their government* would be justified in adopting the measures they vote for or that they are publicly advocating be adopted."[2]

I would like to focus my remarks specifically on the question of what it means to maintain that "our government," in this case *the government of the United States of America*, would be justified in adopting a particular policy because I suspect that it is American Constitutionalism that provides for the stable relationship that religion and liberal democracy have enjoyed in this country and that it is from this uniquely stable relationship that these valuable contributions derive.

What distinguishes American liberal democracy from most other liberal democracies is of course American constitutionalism and its Bill of Rights. What apparently has received most attention from what Weithman calls the "standard" approach to the relationship between religion and liberal democracy is the constitutionally required separation of church and state, the infamous "Congress shall pass no law establishing religion" clause. This separation is interpreted under the "standard" approach to mean that only "secular" reasons can be given in support of any political policy whether by public officials or by private citizens. Under the secular reasons interpretation, religious reasons can properly motivate private "charitable" actions but should be "turned off" and checked at the door when one entertains questions of public policy. The conclusion that failure to disengage one's reasons from more comprehensive world views is a failure of civic responsibility is rightly rejected by Weithman. The implication of such a conclusion seems to be that sincerely religious persons ought not to participate in political life.

What receives somewhat less notice in the standard approach is the additional attention given in the Constitution to the prohibition on the restriction of religious liberty. American separation of church and state, I would maintain, has to be understood in the context of the high value that the Constitution places on the exercise of religious liberty. Religious liberty is so highly valued that it is viewed as a natural right and has even made its way with strong American support into the International Covenant on Civil and Political Rights as a Human Right.

Given the high value that religion has in our constitutional system, a value I would term a political value in that the legal prohibitions are directed at the government precisely in order to secure religious liberty to the citizen, how should we understand the "separation" issue? Is it really a two-way separation? Are citizens not to use their religious liberty to engage their political commitments? I think not. If religious liberty is to be meaningful it must mean more than private prayer and charitable action. All major religions contain moral prescriptions concerning the common good and it would be disingenuous to think that their religious significance can be shed when offered for public consideration. I think that Weithman's rejection of secular reasons as a requirement of political participation in American liberal democracy is sound. If we are to respect our fellow citizens we must respect them as "whole persons" whose commitments are shaped by comprehensive world views.

But what role then does separation from the side of the government play? Besides the fact that the government may not establish a "state religion" or prefer one religion over another, I think that what the citizen is to take from the fact that "our government" has this type of restriction is that is inappropriate for "our government" to legislate policies with contents that are specific to particular religious practices and that therefore religious citizens should not seek to use legal means to enforce such practices. Orthodox Jews must not attempt to enforce kosher dietary laws on non-Jews, and Jehova Witnesses must not attempt to deny blood transfusions to others. Of course, it is a different question whether they should be at liberty to refuse for themselves.

American constitutionalism also provides for a separation of powers and invests the Supreme Court, not the people's legislative representatives, with the ultimate authority to decide how this separation is to be effected in law and how particular legal policies including those aimed at the common good are to be made consistent with individual rights including the individual right to religious liberty. American constitutionalism is fairly unique. Some liberal democracies do not strictly separate church and state having either an established or preferred religion (Church of England). Others do not recognize religious liberty in the same sense that we do; for instance, in most Muslim countries it is forbidden by law for a Muslim to change religions and there are serious legal penalties for proselytizing. Israel has legal protections for Judaism. Some countries with significant religious minorities provide proportional political representation based upon minority membership.[3]

So, while I am uncertain as to how much "weight" Weithman intended this phrase to have, if the emphasis is meant to fall not simply on "sincere belief" in the "justification" of a particular policy per se but on the justification for *our government*—*for American constitutional government*, then while citizens must be free to formulate their world views in religious terms and to take from these world views whatever notions of the common good and of justice that these entail, they cannot rightly insist that content specific to their religious practices be entered into public policy, nor may they attempt to gain political privilege for their institutions, nor may they override the individual rights of others as these have been handed down by the courts.[4] To do otherwise would be destructive of the very liberty that their religious commitments depend upon. I believe that the major established religions understand the co-dependence of religious liberty and constitutionally guaranteed rights and that this is why American churches tend to support "responsible" citizenship in Weithman's sense. Constitutional separation is what gives religious liberty life and it is not intended to take it away.[5] Weithman is correct to argue that religious citizenship is compatible with liberal democracy under these conditions and that religious citizens are not in breach of their civic obligations when they do not offer purely secular reasons for their political commitments.[6] However, I suspect that without constitutional separation, religious liberty would not maintain a stable relationship with liberal democracy. But that is for the political sociologist to discover.

Sharon Anderson-Gold, Rensselaer Polytechnic Institute

Notes

1. Paul Weithman, *Religion and the Obligations of Citizenship*, (Cambridge: Cambridge University Press, 2002), chap. 2.

2. Ibid., 3.

3. Vernon Van Dyke, *Human Rights, Ethnicity, and Discrimination* (Westport, CT: Greenwood Press, 1985), Ch. 3. Van Dyke cites numerous instances of republics that base political representation on communal composition that is often primarily organized around religious identity. His examples are dated but he provides a fascinating analysis of the different ways that governments have attempted to deal with religious (and more broadly ethnic) pluralism.

4. Currently the manner in which the Supreme Court has interpreted the implications of the right to privacy (abortion, rights to refuse life-saving medical interventions) are disturbing to some religious citizens. Yet privacy is one of the values that supports religious liberty and most citizens view privacy as an important protection against undesirable governmental intrusions into ethical life.

5. This may have something to do with the fact that Americans are the most religious of the European derived peoples.

6. I am defining civic obligation as the obligation that citizens have to a juridical system that is 'on the whole' just in a Rawlsian sense. Much of Rawls's sense of the justice of a system derives from its basic constitution. Therefore my sense of what constitutes civic obligation is closely derived from the "natural justice" of our constitution which as I have argued restricts government intervention in order to protect religious pluralism and religious liberty. This is a somewhat more strict definition of civic obligation than the notion that Weithman uses that civic duties "depend upon a society's circumstances" (Weithman, 37), but it is less stringent than the recourse to ideal moral or political theory implicit in the "standard approach."

Citizenship and Religion In Liberal Democracies

John R. Rowan

I. Introduction

In *Religion and the Obligations of Citizenship*, Paul J. Weithman has provided a strong defense of two normative principles pertinent to voting and public advocacy in liberal democratic societies. Its receipt of the 2003 NASSP Book Award is deserving for a number of reasons.

First, Weithman offers something of a challenge to existing thinking, which is always appreciated in the field of philosophy. In this context, the existing thinking (dubbed the "standard approach") is that citizens of liberal democracies possess moral obligations to provide, or at least be ready to provide, secular reasons for their votes or for their advocacy of a particular issue in an arena of public political debate. In contrast to this standard approach, Weithman allows for exclusively religious reasons to serve as the bases of both sorts of actions. More specifically, his principles, referenced as (5.1) and (5.2) respectively in keeping with the book, are as follows:

(5.1) Citizens of a liberal democracy may base their votes on reasons drawn from their comprehensive moral views, including their religious views, without having other reasons which are sufficient for their vote—provided they sincerely believe that their government would be justified in adopting the measures they vote for.

(5.2) Citizens of a liberal democracy may offer arguments in public political debate which depend upon reasons drawn from their comprehensive moral views, including their religious views, without making them good by appeal to other arguments—provided they believe that their government would be justified in adopting the measures they favor and are prepared to indicate what they think would justify the adoption of the measures.[1]

The first of these includes one proviso, the second two provisos (the reason being that Weithman, unlike others, sees a morally relevant difference between the practices that warrants the extra proviso in the latter). The contrast to the standard approach provided by these principles is clear.

In addition, this book is written with extraordinary care and precision. Weithman's clarity and thoroughness make his reasoning accessible to a broad audience and contribute to the initial plausibility of his conclusions. His careful handling of both theoretical and empirical considerations is something of an achievement as well, as that balance can be very difficult to achieve.[2] In general, this project is to be applauded for the philosophical rigor with which it was undertaken and carried out. For these reasons, it meets the criterion of being a book that will engender quality discussions of these issues in philosophical circles and beyond for some time to come, and that is the height to which all works in our field ought to aspire.

What follows is some of this discussion. Below, I consider four issues from the book that warrant further examination. The first two issues have their origin in chapter 5, in which Weithman presents his positive arguments in support of the principles. The latter two issues stem from chapter 6, in which Weithman takes on the version of the standard approach offered by Robert Audi.

II. Hostility to Liberal Democracy

First, one might wonder whether the two principles (5.1) and (5.2), and Weithman's reasoning in support of them, allow for consequences that are rather unhappy or perhaps morally problematic. More to the point, such consequences could be in conflict with certain fundamental principles of liberal democracy—the very ground on which the principles ultimately rest. Each principle is a moral permission to rely exclusively on one's comprehensive moral views, including religious views, in the relevant context (voting or advocating positions in public political debate). The concern is that some religions and comprehensive moral views are quite disturbing. Some, for example, do not (contrary to liberal democratic standards) regard women or certain minorities as equals deserving of citizenship. Indeed, we can conjure up hypothetical views that are even worse than any currently in existence. It therefore seems initially plausible to resist the idea of these "bad" religions, on their own and without further justification, to serve as inputs into liberal democratic processes.

Some clarifications will help to convey that this worry is not merely superficial. First, it is indeed the case that Weithman's two principles are about inputs rather than outputs. They are concerned with the motivations on which citizens contribute to the formulation of policies rather than the outcomes of the policies themselves. However, there is certainly a connection between the two, in that enough inputs based on reasons hostile to liberal democracy will generate outcomes that are hostile to liberal democracy. Appeals to fundamental safeguards (such as Constitutional rights in the United States) cannot be made here, since those safeguards are themselves subject to review. Second, this concern is not tantamount to a call for censorship. Rather, it is about the moral obligations of citizens—what citizens owe each other *qua* citizens—which does not entail any governmental permission designed, say, to restrict speech in the form of advocacy based on exclusively religious reasons. (In general, the existence of a moral obligation does not imply that government ought to, or even may, enforce that obligation.) Third, this concern is more than the observation that some views (such as white supremacy or other outlooks hostile to the fundamental equality of persons or to liberal democracy generally) are disturbing. It is, rather, the idea that these views may be offered *only* on the basis of religion. The worry is that Weithman's principles would allow for the support of some abominable social policy just because one believes that policy is called for by the god, or the devil, or whatever entity it is to which one prays. Or perhaps it is called for by a leader whom one takes to be authoritative on moral matters, such as one's priest in church, or one's Klan leader in the local chapter.

Two passages from the book will indicate the real existence of the possibility that Weithman's principles allow for the hazards described above. First, Weithman states explicitly that (5.1) is satisfied by someone who "sincerely but mistakenly believes that there is a justification" for the measure in question, and that (5.2) is satisfied by someone "who is mistaken about what would justify governmental enactment of the measure she favors." (p. 132) Elsewhere, Weithman explains that, "When someone believes government would be justified in adopting a measure, what she believes is that there are good reasons for government to adopt it given what she takes its legitimate ends to be and the moral constraints within which she thinks it must operate." (p.124) Each quotation here makes clear that the satisfaction of the conditions is a subjective function, dependent on the beliefs of the individual engaged in voting or advocacy, and herein lies the core of the concern.

It should be pointed out that Weithman is aware of this possibility. He writes:

> There may, of course, be costs involved in allowing exclusive reliance on religious arguments and religious reasons in politics. Doing so may result in the advocacy of policies which strike us as unjust and which cannot be defended on nonreligious grounds. But the greater cost to liberal democracy would be the political marginalization of those whom churches integrate into political life, most notably the poor and minorities. (p.137)

The reading audience may well request further justification for the claim made in this passage (and in the last sentence specifically). There is a question of balance here involving on the one hand the full realization of citizenship (especially for marginalized populations) and on the other hand the chief concern being described in this section. The claim that the former is overriding will, I believe, generate significant discussion among readers.

III. The Concept of a Liberal Democracy

A second issue pertains to the nature of Weithman's reasoning in chapter 5. It was noted in the introduction above that Weithman deserves praise for his handling of both empirical and theoretical considerations that go toward supporting his two principles. It was also noted that achieving the right balance between these is rather difficult. One might wonder whether, at a crucial juncture in chapter 5, the appropriate balance might have been missed.

Each of the two principles (5.1) and (5.2) concern what citizens "of a liberal democracy" may do. While the overall context of the book makes the scope of these conclusions fairly clear, the language here could raise the possibility of ambiguity. On one hand, the principles could be read as mere existential claims, in which case each would be a conclusion that liberal democracy and the use of exclusively religious reasons (for voting or advocacy) are not incompatible. The idea of this more modest reading, then, would be that there is (or at least can be) a liberal democratic society in which the use of exclusively religious reasons for these actions is morally permissible. On that reading, empirical premises might play a fairly significant role in the process of justification.

However, it seems clear that these are not merely existential claims but are instead universal claims—conclusions pertaining to all liberal democracies. On this stronger reading, empirical considerations may also have a role but must, it seems, share time with theoretical considerations. After all, if the principles are claims about all liberal democracies, then there is presumably something about liberal democracies as such that entails the permissions in (5.1) and (5.2). The curious philosopher would then seek further clarification regarding the salient features of liberal democracies that generate this entailment. Weithman, however, rejects this approach, claiming that it is "far from clear if any description could be given of the conditions common to all and only liberal democratic societies." He follows up by saying that, "Even if such a description could be given, liberal democracies surely change over time so that what was true of all of them at one time may not be true of all of them at another" (p.144).

Those who will be unsatisfied by this approach will point out that a liberal democracy at time t_1 and a liberal democracy at time t_2 are both designated as such because, presumably, they have something essential in common—something essential to liberal democracy. Whatever that component is, it seems that it would have to be closely connected with the permissions in (5.1) and (5.2), assuming again that both are universal claims. Some readers will wish to pursue this theoretical side of the equation a bit further.

IV. Accessibility

The other two issues I will raise stem from Weithman's replies to Audi's defense of the standard approach, discussed in chapter 6.

Audi defends a version of the standard approach along the following lines. Policies that restrict the liberty of others require special justification, meaning that citizens are morally obligated to offer each other "justifying reasons" for their votes or advocacy of such policies. Justifying reasons entail a condition of accessibility, and accessibility in turn entails a condition of secularity. This reasoning leads to Audi's Principle of Secular Rationale, which is at the heart of his version of the standard approach:

> One has a prima facie obligation not to advocate or support any law or public policy that restricts human conduct unless one has, and is willing to offer, adequate secular reason for this advocacy or support (say for one's vote).[3]

Weithman suggests a problem with the use of accessibility here, claiming it is an unclear concept incapable of playing the justificatory role required of it by Audi. The problem identified by Weithman appears to rest on the following premises. First, for the property of accessibility to play the requisite justificatory role, it must be conceived of in the same way by most citizens in the relevant society. There must, in other words, be widespread agreement regarding the precise meaning of accessibility (or, as Weithman puts it, the criteria of accessibility). Second, this widespread agreement is lacking, at least in contemporary American society.

Readers may wish to pursue each of these claims and the critical conclusion they purport to establish. Is it really the case that this sort of agreement in society is necessary for a conceptual case of the sort made by Audi to be made successfully? Is it really the case, empirically, that there is significant disagreement over the conditions of accessibility? Weithman is to be credited for providing reasonable support for his claims, the full details of which cannot be discussed here. While the current discussion must be limited, it can at least be suggested with respect to the second question that there is quite a bit of agreement—enough, perhaps, for the concept to play its role successfully. By way of comparison, the concept of "reasonability" seems to fare no better in terms of any consensus regarding its conditions, yet Weithman does not hesitate to use it frequently throughout the book.[4] A conclusion (one is tempted to say the "reasonable" conclusion) about the use of "reasonability" here and in other philosophical contexts is that despite a certain fuzziness about its precise meaning or criteria, it can play important roles in theoretical analyses. This assumption, or something like it, appears to be operative in Weithman's approach in the book. One might suggest that similar leeway ought to be afforded to Audi.

V. Surrogacy

One of Audi's justifications for his Principle of Secular Rationale—a justification Weithman labels virtue theoretic, though deontological seems suitable as well—is criticized by Weithman on the basis of its reliance on the surrogacy conception of justified coercion. This surrogacy conception provides necessary conditions for justified coercive policies. Two such conditions are as follows:

> (a) Someone else (most often, fellow citizens in the cases that concern us) has a (moral) right, in the circumstances, to have this action performed by this person . . . or at least the person morally ought to perform the action in the circumstances, for example to abstain from stealing from others.
>
> (b) If fully rational (hence willing to imagine a reversal of positions or roles between oneself and others) and adequately informed about the situation, the person would see that (a) holds and would, for the reason in question, say from a sense of how theft creates mistrust and chaos, or for some essentially related reason, perform the action or at least tend to do so. (p. 168)

After taking care to discuss the initial appeal of the surrogacy conception, Weithman criticizes it on various counts, one of which is the plausibility of unanimous agreement among surrogates. His reasoning, in general terms, is that there can be a social problem a solution to which may be found among a set of permissible coercive policies. His example is that of pollution in a local community, the citizens of which are to vote on a referendum supporting either increased antipollution standards for local industries or increased restrictions on auto usage during periods of climactic unfavorability. Each policy restricts liberty, and the adoption of either is assumed to be justified. Weithman's concern is that the observation that either one is justified generates unhappy results for the surrogacy conception. If the former policy is justified, then (according the surrogacy conception) it follows that it would be chosen by our surrogates—those who, in accordance with condition (b) above, are fully rational and adequately informed about the situation. However, it is also the case that if the latter policy is chosen, then (according to the surrogacy conception) it follows that *this* policy would be chosen by our surrogates. In addition to spawning some bizarre results about causal relations (i.e., the decision of the hypothetical surrogates depending on the outcome of the actual vote), it is implausible to think that everyone "would arrive at the same conclusion to these questions if adequately informed and fully rational." (p.174) Weithman contends that this problem with the surrogacy conception of justified coercion, which plays a central role in Audi's version of the standard approach, is thus a problem for Audi's larger project.

A reader might suggest, however, that Weithman's concern rests on the assumption that the surrogates would agree on a single policy of restricted liberty for every social problem calling for a policy of some degree of coercion. It is not clear, though, why a single policy would necessarily be the outcome. Another possibility is that the surrogates, being fully rational and adequately informed, might conclude that there are several permissible policies that would solve the social problem in question. In other words, these surrogates might conclude that one policy must be chosen from among a set of policies each of which, though restrictive, is deemed to be a reasonable solution to the problem. Thus, the surrogates might allow that both restricted auto usage and forced compliance with strict antipollution standards are permissible methods of dealing with a local pollution problem, and a vote among citizens in the community seems a legitimate way to decide the matter. The fact that there is disagreement in the actual world about which specific policy to adopt would not, contrary to Weithman's sense, be a cause for concern. He claims that the existence of disagreement among actual persons but not among surrogates implies that the actual persons are not fully rational and adequately informed—a conclusion that seems to Weithman highly implausible. A two-pronged response may be suggested here. Perhaps this conclusion is not so implausible given the degree to which our own individual interests tend to become inextricably wrapped up in our individual, differing senses of what is just in various cases. On the other hand, perhaps the conclusion is implausible but is not implied in the way Weithman claims, since it is not inconsistent for an actual person to express his own preference for a specific outcome while allowing that the outcome he opposes is, in a larger sense, permissible. (One may, for example, support a particular presidential candidate while allowing that the democratic system allowing for the election of either candidate is permissible.)

Regardless, there are (again) a variety of issues to pursue here, and this is what makes the book praiseworthy. Indeed, even if this opposing view about surrogates is plausible, there are other, related issues raised by Weithman in this part of the book that warrant further discussion. These issues include such matters as the standards for adequate information and rationality.

VI. Conclusion

As the so-called "great conversation," philosophy is (among other things) about generating significant discussion in pursuit of truth. The discussions spawned by *Religion and the Obligations of Citizenship* are certain to be of a very high quality, given the novel and insightful arguments therein, and it will therefore contribute substantially to the principal aim of our discipline. For this, the book is extremely deserving of its award, and Paul Weithman is be congratulated. The four items discussed above represent only a sample of the many covered in the book that may be explored in detail. The philosophical ideas Weithman has prepared are numerous and substantive, it would be a shame for any philosopher or political scientist not to partake of this treat.

John R. Rowan, Purdue University Calumet

Notes

1. *Religion and the Obligations of Citizenship* (Cambridge: Cambridge University Press, 2002), 121. Hereafter, references to this book will be made parenthetically in the text.

2. One example would be the extensive empirical evidence supporting the claim that churches in the United States have contributed quite positively to theoretically plausible conceptions of democratic citizenship.

3. Robert Audi, *Religious Commitment and Secular Reasoning* (Cambridge: Cambridge University Press, 2000), 114.

4. Indeed, part of Weithman's argument against Audi is that there can be "reasonable disagreement" (p.132) about what reasons are accessible.

Response to Klaassen, Anderson-Gold, and Rowan

PAUL J. WEITHMAN

I would like to begin by thanking the North American Society for Social Philosophy for presenting me with its annual book award last July at its annual meeting in Boston. I need only look over the list of past winners to see what select company I have been invited to join. And I need only glance at the shelves of my own office to see some very good books in social and political philosophy that were published the same year as mine. That the North American Society for Social Philosophy judged mine the best of them is an honor indeed, and one for which I am profoundly grateful.

The Society has earned my gratitude a second time by providing me the opportunity to respond briefly to the three generous, thoughtful and penetrating commentators who discussed the book at the session during which the prize was awarded. I have learned a great deal by thinking about how to reply to their essays. I appreciate the inadequacy of much of what I have to say. I shall respond first to the two questions posed by Johann Klaassen. I will then say something about Sharon Anderson-Gold's remarks. Finally, I will take up the questions raised by John Rowan.

Readers of this exchange would no doubt benefit from the provision of some context for it. It is tempting to seize on their need as a pretext to rehearse what I tried to accomplish in the book. But the remarks of my commentators require careful and, as it happens, rather lengthy replies. The length of these replies precludes an overview of the book. I shall therefore restrict myself to just one piece of stage-setting.

In *Religion and the Obligations of Citizenship*, I defend two principles governing citizens' voting and their participation in public political debate. Much of the discussion of the book—especially the remarks by Professors Anderson-Gold and Rowan—was focused on those principles, so I thought it would be useful to repeat them here. They are:

> (5.1) Citizens of a liberal democracy may base their votes on reasons drawn from their comprehensive moral views, including their religious views,

without having other reasons which are sufficient for their vote—provided they sincerely believe that their government would be justified in adopting the measures they vote for.

(5.2) Citizens of a liberal democracy may offer arguments in public political debate which depend upon reasons drawn from their comprehensive moral views, including their religious views, without making them good by appeal to other arguments—provided they believe that their government would be justified in adopting the measures they favor and are prepared to indicate what they think would justify the adoption of the measures.

By defending these principles, I depart from views on religion and the obligations of citizenship that are very attractive, very widely held and very powerfully defended. Even so, I believe that these principles are the best answers to the philosophical questions I took up in the book.

I. Johann Klaassen

In chapter 4, I mention a homily given by the late John Cardinal O'Connor, Catholic archbishop of New York on Memorial Day weekend, 1997. In the homily, Cardinal O'Connor preached against the domestic partnership statute then under consideration by the New York City Council. The Cardinal did not object to the statute on religious considerations. Klaassen understandably asks what the relevance of the example is in a book the announced subject of which is *religion* and the obligations of citizenship.

While it is true that Cardinal O'Connor did not object to the legal recognition of domestic partnerships on religious grounds, I believe he did base his objections on what he thought are precepts of the natural law.[1] According to proponents of natural law theory, precepts of the natural law concern fundamental human inclinations and human goods, including—some say—the goods available in sexual intimacy when it is restricted to marriage. Those who believe that natural law is the basis of morality, such as Cardinal O'Connor, claim that those precepts can be known to everyone and that human law must be consistent with them. It is not always clear what proponents of natural law theory mean by 'can' or under what circumstances they think everyone can know the precepts on which their arguments about human sexuality rely. But whatever they mean by 'can' or whatever circumstances they have in mind, they think that the precepts of natural law are accessible to non-Catholics as well as Catholics. So it is because Cardinal O'Connor based his objections on precepts of the natural law and because he thought those precepts were widely accessible that "his criticism [was] intended to resonate beyond the Gothic cathedral on Fifth Avenue."

My own view is that many of the precepts of natural law strong enough to provide guidance on difficult political questions are at best extremely controversial. Some, particularly those bearing on human sexuality, strike many outside the Catholic tradition—and many within it—as unintelligible. Many citizens will not see those precepts as providing reasons for any political measures at all. If they are to see the point of those measures—if they are to see why someone like Cardinal O'Connor would endorse what he takes to be the political implications of natural law theory—that will only be because those requirements are presented as supported by the larger moral theory from which the precepts of natural law are drawn. Thus various natural law claims about marriage and sexuality may initially strike many people as very difficult to understand. Indeed, they may not seem like reasons for action at all. When those precepts are presented as part of a theory of the human good, they may still be extremely controversial. But they may at least come to be seen as reasons—perhaps not good or compelling ones, but as reasons—for the political requirements in question. If this is the only way the precepts can come to be seen as reasons, then those cannot be credibly presented in public independent of what Rawls calls a "comprehensive view."

Thus by appealing to the precepts of the natural law, Cardinal O'Connor relied on precepts drawn from a view of law and justice that cannot be presented independent of comprehensive doctrine. That view is not religious, but it is a comprehensive view nonetheless. And so Cardinal O'Connor relied on a comprehensive view to criticize domestic partnership legislation even though "he couched his criticism in [non-religious] terms." Being dependent on a comprehensive view, the reasons he adduced were not what Rawls calls "properly public."[2] Moreover, because he thought the terms in which he couched his criticism could be understood by everyone, he did not make good his criticism by appealing to public reasons. He therefore violated Rawls's guidelines of public reason.[3]

Once we see Cardinal O'Connor's criticism this way, its relevance to the principles I defend should be clear. For *contra* Rawls, the principles allow reliance, not just on religious views, but on comprehensive views of all kinds. And so they allow citizens to offer arguments like Cardinal O'Connor's in public. This is an implication which I accept, since I believe that natural law arguments can be introduced into public debate.

But I did not bring up Cardinal O'Connor's homily to argue that it or arguments like it are permissible, though I believe they are. I brought it up to argue that it is public. The debate about political argument to which I tried to contribute is a debate about *public* political argument. Unfortunately, very little is said in this debate about just what makes an argument public. What little is said typically suggests or implies that homilies delivered in churches as part of worship services are not public in the relevant sense.

Cardinal O'Connor's criticism of domestic partnership legislation is of interest to me because, though it took the form of homily delivered at Sunday Mass in St. Patrick's Cathedral, it seems to me to be an example of public political argument. If this is correct, then any account of what makes political argument public must accommodate it. This is something the usual accounts cannot do. I offer an alternative account in the book. According to the account I offer, the public character of an argument does not depend upon where the argument is offered. Indeed, I not only eschew any reference to public spaces, I also eschew the fundamental use of spatial metaphors such as "public forum," "public square" or "public sphere." Instead, I claim, the public character of an argument depends upon the public character of the role adopted by the speaker and the recipient. When each is in the right role, they—as I put it—"instantiate the public forum." I believe my account of what makes public argument public can handle interesting and knotty test cases like that of Cardinal O'Connor's homily.

Klaassen prefaces his second question by noting that if liberal political homilies like those preached by his Unitarian Universalist minister are permissible examples of public political argument, then so too are more conservative homilies. I take Cardinal O'Connor's homily criticizing domestic partnership legislation to be a conservative political homily. I have said that I regard it as permissible. So I concede that Klaassen is correct about the implications of the view I have defended. After noting that conservative and liberal homilies must be permitted by parity of reasoning, Klaassen then asks whether allowing "politics from the pulpits" threatens recent interpretations of the separation of church and state. In particular, he wonders whether it threatens the special status that churches enjoy under U.S. federal tax codes, for example.

Unfortunately I do not know enough law to answer questions about the conditions under which churches can lose their tax-exempt status. The normative question of when a church should lose its status is a difficult one to answer because so much will depend upon circumstances peculiar to a given case. I take it that a number of principles support the public decision to accord churches such status. Some of those principles no doubt appeal to the purposes for which churches are ostensibly organized and to the functions they in fact serve. The judgment that an organization no longer qualifies as a church under those principles is one that must be made with great care and circumspection. I have regrettably little to say about how that judgment should be made, beyond saying that organizations should be given wide latitude, and that such judgments should be made consistently.

II. Sharon Anderson-Gold

I shall not spend long on Professor Anderson-Gold's commentary because I agree with so much of what she has to say. It was especially perceptive of her to seize on an important qualifying phrase in the principles I defended: the phrase that requires citizens to take account of what their liberal democratic government may legitimately do. For I did intend that phrase to bear a great deal of weight, and I intended it to do so for just the reasons Professor Anderson-Gold suggests.

As I hope is clear from the book, I do think that the role of citizen carries with it moral ideals and moral obligations. Some of those ideals and obligations bear on the ways in which citizens may vote and may participate in public debate. Citizens may not say just anything at all. The question that concerns me is not whether citizens are under obligations to regulate their own voting and their own participation in public debate, but what ones they are under.

What arguments the good citizen may offer may well differ from society to society. One of the reasons for this is that societies' basic constitutional and political arrangements usually result from a series of compromises, crucial decisions (including judicial decisions), negotiated political settlements and revolutionary transformations that eventually achieve the status of settled practice. These historical differences make a difference to what arguments citizens may offer.

One need only look at the ways in which the American federal constitution was passed, amended, and interpreted to know what a tortuous path the U.S. has followed to its current—provisional—understanding of fair equality of opportunity, freedom of the press and church-state separation. One need look only briefly at the jurisprudence and the practice of other countries to see that they have followed different paths to different political settlements. I assume that a society's political history is available to its citizens. I also assume that citizens should be in possession of a rough mental map that shows the contours and boundaries of their society's current political settlements. They should have at least some idea what their government may legitimately do given the settlements it has provisionally reached.

Having an idea of what one's government may legitimately do is, I believe, a requirement of responsible citizenship. Thus citizens of the United States should know that that society is committed to the separation of church and state. They should have at least some idea of this commitment's most important implications for legitimate government action. Forming such an idea before engaging in public argument and voting is also a requirement of responsible citizenship. Finally, regulating one's participation in public debate and one's voting by what one thinks about the scope of legitimate government action is a requirement of responsible citizenship. It is, I think, irresponsible publicly to argue for policies that one should know or believe it would be illegitimate for one's government to enforce, and it would be irresponsible to vote for those policies.

I hasten to add that my remarks are not the counsels of conservatism. If citizens wish to advocate measures that are inconsistent with their society's basic political arrangements—if, for example, a country's settled arrangements include arrangements that they think patently unjust—responsible citizenship demands that they have some idea of why those measures would be legitimate. Here they may appeal to ideas that have lost out, to strains of liberal democratic thought that their society neglects or to political ideals that it fails to realize. Citizens in a country which has long had an established church may think that their country should separate church and state. My talk of political settlements does not imply that they may not argue and vote for separation, for I noted that political settlements are provisional. I merely mean that if they are to act responsibly, they should have responsibly held views about why revisiting and revising their settlement would be legitimate.

III. John Rowan

Professor Rowan's comments were particularly detailed and challenging. I cannot hope to do justice to them here. To keep the length of this reply manageable, I will take up just two of the issues he raises: the disturbing character of some religious political arguments and the criticisms I made of Robert Audi's Surrogacy Conception of Justified Coercion.

(1) "Support of Abominable Social Policy"

As I mentioned at the outset, I defend two principles governing citizens' voting and their participation in public political debate. Professor Rowan worries that those principles

> would allow for support of some abominable social policy just because it is called for by the god, or the devil or whatever entity it is to which one prays.

To take just one example, he says, the principles would allow citizens to vote for or advocate white supremacist policies on religious grounds.

I concede that the principles do allow citizens to advocate such policies on religious grounds. And of course I agree that such policies are abominable. The concession that citizens may advocate such policies raises a number of worries. I cannot take them all up here. Instead I shall try to address the worries Professor Rowan raises.

Note first that the principles I defend are principles of citizenship. They are not all-things-considered moral principles. The view that someone may advocate abominable policies without violating duties of citizenship does not imply that he may do so without violating any duties at all. And so the endorsement of abominable policies on religious grounds may violate natural duties. It may also violate religious duties. So the principles do not imply that someone advocating or voting for such policies is blameless. The principles merely remove one among many possible grounds for blame. Furthermore, I think that when others defend policies we regard as abominable, we should organize politically so that abominable policies do not carry the day.

But I do not want my reply to Professor Rowan to depend upon the existence of other duties, including—perhaps—the duty to try to defeat those who advocate and vote for abominable policies. For a reply which depends upon the existence of these other duties does not address Professor Rowan's real worry.

If we are to see exactly what that worry is, we must pay close attention to Professor Rowan's text. In particular, I believe seeing what that worry is requires putting emphasis on the word 'just' in the passage I quoted above. With the emphasis in place, the passage says that the principles I defend "would allow for support of some abominable social policy *just* because it is called for by the god, or the devil or whatever entity it is to which one prays."

The appropriateness of this emphasis is confirmed by Professor Rowan's own emphasis in the sentences that immediately precede the quoted one. There he says his

> concern is more than the observation that some views (such as white supremacy or other outlooks hostile to the fundamental equality of persons or to liberal democracy generally) are disturbing. It is, rather, the idea that these views may be offered *only* on the basis of religion.

These emphases suggest what Professor Rowan is worried about and why. They suggest he thinks that when citizens advocate or vote for an abominable social policy, they should be ready to offer more than religious reasons in its defense. They suggest, that is, that he thinks there is something wrong with or deficient about offering "only" or "just" religious reasons in defense of such a policy. As a first approximation, Professor Rowan is worried that the principles I defend would allow citizens to advocate and vote for such policies without offering anything more.

To pin down the worry more precisely, it is helpful to consider why he raises his worry specifically in connection with *abominable* policies. Why doesn't his worry arise with respect to *all* policies or all *coercive* policies? The parenthetical remark in second quoted passage provides a clue. It suggests that what is abominable about the policies in connection with which Professor Rowan's worry arises is not, say, that they are coercive, demeaning or that they cause physical or emotional suffering, but that they are policies contrary to the demands or commitments of liberal democracy.

Thus I believe Professor Rowan thinks that when citizens advocate a policy contrary to the demands of liberal democracy, they should be ready to offer more than religious reasons in its defense. But I do not believe Professor Rowan's worry is simply that the principles I defend would allow citizens to advocate and vote for policies contrary to liberal democracy while offering only religious reasons. He is also troubled by the fact that the principles which express this permission are defended by appeal to liberal democratic values. So his worry is not exclusively about the permission expressed by the principles. It concerns the way the principles are defended. Perhaps his worry can best be put this way: When citizens advocate and vote for policies which are contrary to the demands of liberal democracy and do not offer anything other than religious reasons, there are costs to liberal democracy; it is not immediately clear that those costs are outweighed by the gains to which I appeal.

An adequate response to Professor Rowan's worry requires more information about the costs liberal democracy incurs when citizens advocate and vote for policies contrary to liberal democracy. I am especially interested to know about the costs incurred when citizens offer only religious reasons for the policies they advocate. Why does their offering only religions reasons make a difference? Is there a cost to civility? If so, how is that to be understood? Or is the problem that there are transaction costs incurred in fighting abominable policies? Professor Rowan's worry seems to depend upon a presumption in favor of supplementing religious reasons with reasons of some other sort. It would be good to know how that presumption is grounded.

Note further that the principles I defend do not allow citizens knowingly or intentionally to defend policies which are contrary to liberal democracy. The policies require that citizens believe their liberal democratic government could legitimately enact the policy. This requires them to have some idea, perhaps a vague one, of whether a policy is or is not contrary to the demands of liberal democracy. It forbids them from defending policies they believe to be contrary to those demands. Without knowing what the costs are which concern Professor Rowan, it is hard to know how far this stipulation goes to mitigating the costs, but I believe it goes some way.

Of course some views about the demands of liberal democracy are closer to the truth than others. Citizens can be wrong—terribly wrong—about what liberal democracy does and does not demand. An interesting question raised by Professor Rowan's worry is how the requirement I imposed on citizens might be tightened. It seems too much to ask that citizens have the right views about the demands of liberal democracy. Perhaps they must be in some way justified or warranted in holding the view that they do. I cannot go through alternatives in detail. Let me just register skepticism about the possibility of defending a requirement stronger than the one I have proposed.

(2) On Audi on Surrogacy

In chapter 6 of my book, I criticized Robert Audi's "Surrogacy Conception of Justified Coercion." The basis of my criticism was what seemed to me to be an unfortunate implication of the Surrogacy Conception. That conception seems to me to imply that, if citizens were all adequately informed and fully rational, they would agree on what policies to adopt. To make this implication vivid, I said it seems to imply that our adequately informed and fully rational surrogate decision-makers would agree on what policies to adopt. This conclusion itself seems to have a number of unreasonable implications. One of these further implications is that political disagreement in the actual world is entirely due to deficiencies of information, rationality or both.

Professor Rowan suggests that I may have been wrong about what the Surrogacy Conception implies. After noting what I took as the damaging implication of the Surrogacy Conception to be, he writes:

> Another possibility is that surrogates, being fully rational and adequately informed, might conclude that there are several permissible policies that would solve the social problem in question. In other words, these surrogates might conclude that one policy must be chosen from among a set of policies each of which, though restrictive, is deemed to be a reasonable solution to the problem. Thus the surrogates might allow that both restricted auto usage and forced compliance with strict antipollution standards are permissible methods of dealing with a local pollution problem, and a vote among citizens in the community seems a legitimate way to decide the matter. The fact that there is disagreement in the actual world about which specific policy to adopt would not, contrary to Weithman's sense, be a cause for concern.

To see whether this suggestion salvages the Surrogacy Conception, it is necessary to return to the conditions that conception imposes on justified coercion. "Coercing a person, for a particular reason, to perform an action in a given set of circumstances, is fully justified," Audi says, only if

(a) Someone else (most often, fellow citizens in the cases that concern us) has a (moral) right, in the circumstances, to have this action performed by this person ... or at least the person morally ought to perform the action in the circumstances, for example to abstain from stealing from others.

(b) If fully rational (hence willing to imagine a reversal of positions or roles between oneself and others) and adequately informed about the situation, the person would see that (a) holds and would, for the reason in question, say from a sense of how theft creates mistrust and chaos, or for some essentially related reason, perform the action or at least tend to do so.

(c) The action in question is both an "important" kind of conduct ... and one that may be reasonably believed to affect someone else[.][4]

Let us suppose, as I did in the book, that some municipality is considering a range of measures to combat air pollution. Public debate shows citizens to be deeply divided. Those in group A favor a law restricting auto usage, while those in group B favor combating pollution by other measures. Suppose further, as Professor Rowan suggests, that if those in both groups were adequately informed and fully rational, they all would see that the measures favored by both groups are "reasonable" and that a majority vote of citizens is the appropriate way to decide which measure to adopt. Finally, suppose that when a referendum is conducted, the citizens are asked to decide among all and only reasonable measures to combat pollution. They pass a measure to restrict auto usage; those who are caught violating the law incur a heavy fine.

Now consider a member of group B—call him Bob—who restricts his auto usage simply because he fears the fine. It seems clear that Bob is coerced. Does that coercion meet the conditions of the Surrogacy Conception?

Condition (a) seems to be satisfied, for under the circumstances, Bob's fellow citizens do seem to be entitled to his compliance. And I shall suppose that (c) is satisfied. What of (b)?

The Surrogacy Conception imposes conditions on coercing people for reasons. And (b) refers to those reasons. So to determine whether (b) is satisfied, we need to identify the reasons R for which Bob is coerced. R presumably includes the reasons for which Bob would grant that restricting auto usage is a reasonable measure were he adequately informed and fully rational. Call those reasons $r_1, \ldots r_n$. Those reasons do not pick out the restriction on auto usage as uniquely reasonable, so they cannot be sufficient to justify coercing Bob. R must also include r_{n+1}: the fact that that measure was preferred by the majority of his fellow citizens.

Since this fact about what the majority has decided is decisive in favor of restricting auto usage, I take it that including this fact in R comports with Professor Rowan's suggestion. Indeed, I take it that including this fact in R is what makes that suggestion so promising. For once we include this consideration in R, it may seem that (b) is satisfied. It may then seem that, if adequately informed and fully rational, Bob would see that his fellow citizens are entitled to his compliance and would be moved by the reasons in R—now understood to include the fact that the majority voted for restrictions on auto usage. In that case, the conditions of the Surrogacy Conception would be satisfied, and satisfied without the implication that everyone would agree on the same measure if adequately informed and fully rational.

But I wonder whether Audi is open to Professor Rowan's suggestion that R include facts about what measure the majority prefers or about how the majority voted.

Note first that when Audi himself gives an example of reasons included in R, considerations of this kind are conspicuously absent. In passing reference to the reasons people may be coerced by laws against theft, he refers to facts about how "theft creates mistrust and chaos." What are we to make of this reference in light of Professor Rowan's suggestion?

Professor Rowan's suggestion requires a distinction between the set of reasons $r_1, \ldots r_n$ which show that a measure is reasonable and the (possibly overlapping) set of reasons—call them $r^*_1, \ldots r^*_n$—those who favor one reasonable measure have for favoring it over other reasonable measures, or would have if they were fully rational and adequately informed. Since Audi himself does not draw this distinction, it is not immediately obvious whether he would put the reasons to which he refers in the first set, the second or both. But Audi clearly means to include those among the reasons for which citizens are coerced under a law against theft. Professor Rowan's suggestion implies that the reasons for which citizens are coerced under a law include reasons showing that the law in question is reasonable. So I shall suppose, somewhat artificially, that the reasons to which Audi refers are reasons which establish that a law against theft is one among a number of reasonable solutions to the problems to which theft gives rise.[5]

The reference Audi makes to facts about mistrust and chaos, the supposition I have made about the set in which they belong, and Audi's omission of the fact that laws against theft are chosen by the majority, are suggestive for the case of Bob—who was, recall, on the losing side of the municipal referendum. They suggest that in Bob's case, R includes $r_1, \ldots r_n$ but excludes facts about majority votes. This suggestion seems to be confirmed by Audi's use of the phrase "some essentially related reason" in (b). We are not told what reasons are essentially related to the fact that theft creates mistrust and chaos, and so it is hard to know what reasons are essentially related to $r_1, \ldots r_n$. But facts about majority preference and majority vote seem different enough from these considerations that I doubt Audi would consider these facts to be essentially related to the considerations to which he refers. So even if Professor Rowan's suggestion salvages the Surrogacy Conception in some form, it is not clear that that suggestion is compatible with Audi's formulation of that conception.

Further doubts about whether Audi can accept Professor Rowan's suggestion arise when we consider the motivation of the Surrogacy Conception. When he introduced the conception, Audi wrote:

> If I am coerced on grounds that cannot motivate me, as a rational informed person, to do the thing in question, I cannot come to identify with the deed and will tend to resent having to do it.
>
> It is part of the underlying rationale of liberal democracy that we not have to feel this kind of resentment—that we give up autonomy only where, no matter what our specific preferences or our particular world view, we can be expected, given adequate rationality and sufficient information, to see that we would have (or would at least tend to have) so acted on our own.[6]

The point of the Surrogacy Conception is to lay down conditions public coercion must meet if it is satisfy liberal democracy's "underlying rationale." And so, according to Audi, the conditions the Surrogacy Conception lays down are conditions coercion must satisfy if someone is to see that the acts he is coerced to perform are acts he would have performed or would have tended to perform on his own, were he adequately rational and sufficiently informed. More specifically, since the Surrogacy Conception imposes conditions on coercion *for reasons*, the conditions the Surrogacy Conception lays down are conditions coercion must satisfy if someone is to see that the acts he is coerced to perform for reasons R are acts he would have performed or would have tended to perform on his own, were he adequately rational and sufficiently informed. Condition (b) is supposed to serve the point of the Surrogacy Conception by requiring that the acts someone is coerced to perform for reasons R be acts he himself would have performed or would have tended to perform for reasons R if he were adequately rational and sufficiently informed.

But condition (b) will serve the point of the Surrogacy Conception only if it is the case that coercion which satisfies that condition can appropriately be described as coercion to perform an act the agent would have performed or tended to perform on her own. It is at this point that questions arise. Let us return to Bob, who complies with a measure restricting auto usage solely because he fears the fine he would have to pay if he were caught in violation. The reasons for coercing Bob are $r_1, \ldots r_n$ plus, we are supposing, r_{n+1}: the fact that the majority voted for the measure. Suppose for the sake of argument that, were Bob fully rational and sufficiently informed, he would restrict his auto usage for these reasons. Is it accurate to say that the act Bob is coerced to perform is one that he would have performed on his own, were he fully rational and sufficiently informed?

I think it far from clear that the answer is 'Yes.' My doubts are due to the inclusion in R of r_{n+1}. For while we are supposing that if Bob were fully rational and sufficiently informed, he would not be moved to comply by fear of the fine, we are also supposing that $r_1, \ldots r_n$ are not sufficient to motivate his compliance. He would comply with the measure restricting auto usage in part because of r_{n+1}—in part, that is, because the majority voted for a measure which, as it happens, he did not. I am supposing that, even if Bob were fully rational and adequately informed, it would remain true that if he had his way, the alternative measure he originally favored would have won. So there is a sense of "on one's own" in which it is not true that an act Bob would perform in part for reason r_{n+1} is an act Bob would perform "on [his] own."

Indeed, I think it is an interesting question whether someone in the position Bob would be in were he fully informed and rational—someone who complies with a law he voted against and complies for reasons $r_1, \ldots r_n$ together with reason r_{n+1}—is coerced. To be sure, such a person would not be coerced by the penalty attached to the law, since aversion to the penalty would not be among his reasons for action. But there may be a legitimate sense of "coerced" in which he can properly be said to be coerced by the majority.

Be that as it may, I have doubts about whether the act Bob would perform for reasons that include r_{n+1} is accurately described as an act Bob would perform "on [his] own." And so I have doubts about whether Audi would or should accept Professor Rowan's defense of the Surrogacy Conception, given what Audi has said about the point of that Conception. It is because of these doubts, and because of Audi's reference to "essentially related reasons" in condition (b), that I explicitly assumed that R did not range over considerations such as "the measure was adopted by a majority" or "the measure is the law."[7]

The doubts to which I just pointed are ultimately due to an unresolved question about the "underlying rationale of liberal democracy" that the Surrogacy Conception is supposed to serve. I did not explore the grounds for that doubt in the book, but would like to do so now.

According to Audi, the underlying rationale of liberal democracy is that liberal democracy is supposed to coerce people only to perform acts which "they can come to identify with." The Surrogacy Conception is then supposed to spell out conditions coercion must satisfy if those who are coerced are to come to identify with the acts they are coerced to perform.

But exactly how does Audi understand the underlying rationale of liberal democracy? Is it that citizens are supposed to come to identify with acts the law coerces them to perform because they come to see that if they were adequately informed and fully rational, they would acknowledge and be moved by $r^*_1, \ldots r^*_n$—the reasons which supporters of the law think show it superior to the alternatives? Or is it, rather, something quite different and more complicated? Is it that they are supposed to come to see that if they were adequately informed and fully rational, they would (i) accept $r_1, \ldots r_n$ and so recognize that that the measure favored by their opponents is reasonable, (ii) recognize that majority rule is a good way to decide among reasonable alternatives, (iii) accept and be moved by r_{n+1}: the fact that the majority favors a law for reasons $r^*_1, \ldots r^*_n$ even though those who are coerced (iv) reject at least some of $r^*_1, \ldots r^*_n$ and so think the measure they favor is superior on its merits?

I assume Professor Rowan thinks that if forced to choose, Audi should pick the latter. For if he were to pick the former, then he would seem to be committed to the claim to which I objected—namely, that everyone would agree on the same measures if fully rational and adequately informed. But there are also a number of problems with picking the latter.

First, the latter lacks a clear merit of the former. The former seems, intuitively, to provide a sufficient condition of identifying with an action we are coerced to perform. For it seems intuitively plausible that if I see that, were I fully rational and adequately informed, I would perform A for reasons R, then I identify with A when I am coerced to perform it for R. It is far less clear that I identify with action A that I am coerced for reasons R when (i) through (iv) are satisfied. Indeed it is not clear that (i) through (iv) have any bearing at all on identification with action as we intuitively understand that notion. To make the connection clear, we would need to know a great deal more about what it is for a coercive policy to be reasonable and about what kind or kinds of reasons can establish that a policy is reasonable. I suspect that we will also need to know a great deal more about why losers are morally bound by the decisions of a majority.

A more serious problem arises when we take into account how much work the "underlying rationale" of liberal democracy is supposed to do. That rationale is supposed to help us pick out features reasons must have if they are to be used as the basis of political decision-making. For Audi thinks that reasons can be used—and here I assume he means "used by the state" or "used by society as a whole"—as the basis of political decision-making about coercive legislation only if citizens coerced for those reasons can come to identify with the actions they are coerced to perform. If we ask ourselves whether reasons that satisfy this condition exhibit any common and significant feature or fall into any significant kind, Audi thinks, it will be clear that such reasons are secular.[8] In the book, I argued that Audi draws a connection between the kinds of reasons that can be used as the basis for political decision-making and the kinds of reasons citizens must be moved by and must be prepared to offer when they advocate and vote for coercive law and public policy.[9] It is because of this connection that the underlying rationale for liberal democracy and the Surrogacy Conception are supposed to support the Principles of Secular Motivation and Secular Rationale.

But if we take the underlying rationale for liberal democracy in the second way, the way Professor Rowan suggests that Audi take it, then the rationale for Audi's Principles of Secular Motivation and Secular Rationale is hard to see. For as Audi states them, those principles bear on the reasons for which citizens think a given policy is to be preferred—reasons such as $r^*_1, \ldots r^*_n$. But once we draw the distinction between those reasons and the reasons that might be available for thinking laws and policies would be reasonable—once we draw the distinction between reasons such as $r^*_1, \ldots r^*_n$ and reasons such as $r_1, \ldots r_n$—it is hard to see why we should be concerned with reasons of the former kind. It is hard to see, that is, why Audi's purposes would not be just as well served by allowing citizens to offer whatever reasons they like for *favoring* policies, provided they satisfy some principle requiring them to be ready to show that those policies are reasonable. If we recognize that any of a range of coercive policies would be reasonable, perhaps all of the interesting moral work can be done by reasons showing that they are. It is hard to see what more work needs to be done by the reasons that Audi's principles bear on, and so it is hard to see why those principles are needed. If I can show my political opponents that a policy prohibiting physician-assisted suicide is reasonable, the reasons I have and offer for favoring the policy may seem far less important.

None of the conclusions of this section may tell against Professor Rowan's suggestion about how to rescue the Surrogacy Conception. Indeed, I think his suggestion has a great deal of interest and promise, though I cannot pursue the matter here. On the other hand, I do believe that the conclusions reached here show Professor Audi cannot take advantage of the suggestion.

IV. Concluding Remarks

Let me conclude by once again thanking the Society for honoring me with its book award, and by thanking Johann Klaassen, Sharon Anderson-Gold, and John Rowan for their careful reading of my book, their generous remarks and their probing comments. I am aware that I have not been able adequately to respond to the many points they raise. I am also aware of how much I have learned by trying to frame responses which repay the time they put into reading the book and writing their comments on it.

The culture of academic publication—and the relative permanence of the media in which we publish—can mislead academics into believing that we are in the business of uttering pronouncements which must stand the test of time. In fact we are in the business of learning. What we write and publish are merely the progress reports we issue when we have had the leisure to collect what thoughts we believe may interest others. Nothing reminds an author that his book is a way-station quite like the opportunity to respond to critics who encourage him to look back or move forward. I am grateful to Johann, Sharon and John for providing just such encouragement.

Paul J. Weithman, University of Notre Dame

Notes

1. The Cardinal said: "It is imperative, in my judgment, that no law be passed contrary to natural moral law and Western tradition by virtually legislating that 'marriage does not matter.'" At this writing, Cardinal O'Connor's homily can be found at: http://cny.org/archive/ch/ch052898.htm.

2. Public reasons are drawn from liberal political conceptions of justice that "can be presented independently from comprehensive doctrines of any kind"; see John Rawls, *Law of Peoples* (Harvard University Press, 1999), 143. In the text I rely on one (undefended) interpretation of the phrase "can be presented."

3. Rawls, *Law of Peoples*, 144.

4. Robert Audi, *Religious Commitment and Secular Reason* (Cambridge University Press, 2000), 66–67.

5. Another acceptable measure might be one abolishing private property, but I shall not pursue thought here.

6. *Religious Commitment and Secular Reason*, 67.

7. Weithman, *Religion and the Obligations of Citizenship*, 173.

8. On p. 67, Audi writes: "If the perspective on liberal democracy I have sketched is correct, then it should be clear to understand why in such a society the use of secular reasons must have a major role in sociopolitical decision-making."

9. Weithman, *Religion and the Obligations of Citizenship*, 166ff.

Contributors

Sharon Anderson-Gold is Professor of Philosophy in the Department of Science and Technology Studies at Rensselaer Polytechnic Institute in Troy, New York. She is the author of *Unnecessary Evil: History and Moral Progress in the Philosophy of Immanuel Kant* (SUNY Press, 2001) and *Cosmopolitanism and Human Rights* (University of Wales Press, 2001) as well as numerous articles in social and political philosophy. Her current interests are in the application of Kantian ethics to issues of international relations.

Richard M. Buck (Ph.D., University of Kansas, 2000) is Assistant Professor, Department of Philosophy, Mount Saint Mary's College. His chief areas of interest are contemporary social and political philosophy, ethical theory, philosophy of law, and contemporary Jewish philosophy (especially the work of Rabbi Joseph Soloveitchik). His current research and writing focuses on political legitimacy and democratic theory.

Todd Calder is on the faculty at the University of Western Ontario. His primary research interests are in ethics, metaethics and social philosophy.

Ovadia Ezra is on the faculty at Tel Aviv University, in the Department of Philosophy. He teaches ethics, political and social philosophy. His book, *The Withdrawal Of Rights: Rights From A Different Perspective* was published in 2002, by Kluwer Academic Publishers. He was incarcerated three times in a military jail for refusing to serve reserve military service in the occupied territories.

Ted Honderich is Grote Professor Emeritus, University College London. He has published articles on a variety of topics and written numerous books, including *After The Terror*, which was prompted by the events of September 11, 2001 but is about much more than that. Among his other books are *Brain and Mind*, *The Consequences of Determinism*, *Conservatism*, and *Philosopher: A Kind of Life*.

Whitley R. P. Kaufman is Assistant Professor, Department of Philosophy, University of Massachusetts Lowell. He received a law degree from Harvard and a Ph.D. in Philosophy from Georgetown University, specializing in ethics and philosophy of law. His publications include articles on the Doctrine of Double Effect, Just War Doctrine, and the ethics of self-defense.

Johann A. Klaassen, Ph.D. (Ethics, Washington University in St. Louis), is Vice President of Managed Account Programs for First Affirmative Financial Network, LLC. Previously, he served on the faculties of the University of Central Arkansas,

Webster University, Millikin University, the University of Idaho and Washington University in St. Louis, teaching courses in environmental ethics and biomedical ethics. His work has appeared in such journals as *Philosophy and Literature*, *The Journal of Social Philosophy*, and *The Journal of Value Inquiry*.

Doug Knapp is Philosophy Instructor, Inver Hills Community College (Inver Grove Heights, Minnesota). He has published articles related to abortion, euthanasia, the new design argument, and environmental ethics.

Nelson P. Lande has been a Lecturer in the Philosophy Department at the University of Massachusetts/Boston for the past twenty-five years. He has published articles on moral philosophy, and he teaches modern philosophy, metaphysics, and formal logic.

Alistair M. Macleod teaches moral and political philosophy at Queen's University. His papers on justice-related issues (rights, economic distribution, the limits of markets, etc.) and on socio-political ideals (freedom, equality, efficiency, etc.) have appeared in a variety of books and in such journals as *The Canadian Journal of Philosophy*, *The Journal of Philosophy*, and *Hume Studies*. His most recent publication is a short book on Social Justice, Progressive Politics, and Taxes (University of Victoria, 2004).

Christine Overall is Professor and Associate Dean, Faculty of Arts and Science, Queen's University, Kingston, Ontario. She is the editor or co-editor of three books, and the author of five, including *Thinking Like a Woman: Personal Life and Political Ideas* (Sumach Press, 2001) and *Aging, Death, and Human Longevity: A Philosophical Inquiry* (University of California Press, 2003). She teaches and researches in the areas of feminist theory, applied ethics, and philosophy of religion. She is an elected Fellow of the Royal Society of Canada, and is the author of a weekly feminist column entitled "In Other Words."

Walter Riker is a doctoral student in philosophy at the University of Tennessee, Knoxville. He is interested in moral and political philosophy. In his dissertation, he attempts to reconcile the idea of democratic political legitimacy with the fact of reasonable disagreement over both comprehensive doctrines and fundamental ideas in democratic theory itself.

John R. Rowan is Associate Professor of Philosophy, Purdue University Calumet. His teaching and research interests include ethical theory, applied ethics, and political and social philosophy.

Matthew R. Silliman is a professor of philosophy at Massachusetts College of Liberal Arts. He teaches social and political philosophy, philosophy of law, and moral theory, among other things. He recently completed a book on moral theory, in dialogue form, entitled *Sentience and Sensibility: a Conversation about Moral Philosophy*.

Paul J. Weithman is Professor of Philosophy and chair of the department at the University of Notre Dame. He is editor of *Religion and Contemporary Liberalism* (1997) and co-editor of the five-volume *Philosophy of Rawls* (with Henry Richardson, 1999). He has also published articles in medieval political thought, religious ethics, moral philosophy, and contemporary political philosophy. His book *Religion and the Obligations of Citizenship* won the North American Society for Social Philosophy's 2002 award for the best book published in social philosophy that year and is the subject of Part IV of this volume.